DEMOCRACY *by* DIPLOMACY

Afro-Saxon Caribbean Diplomats
Challenge the USA
To Improve Its World Leadership
and Expand Regional Freedoms

Ambassador Lionel Hurst
of
ANTIGUA AND BARBUDA

authorHOUSE®

AuthorHouse™
1663 Liberty Drive, Suite 200
Bloomington, IN 47403
www.authorhouse.com
Phone: 1-800-839-8640

First published by AuthorHouse   7/6/2007

ISBN: 978-1-4343-1963-0 (sc)
ISBN: 978-1-4343-1962-3 (hc)

Library of Congress Control Number: 2007904197

Printed in the United States of America
Bloomington, Indiana

This book is printed on acid-free paper.

Acknowledgements

I owe a debt of gratitude to a number of persons who have contributed in no small way to making this publication a reality. Those who read the manuscript or parts of it, including Gloria, Shirley, Edna, Alexis, Lenny and Crystal receive my sincerest thanks for poring over the text and sharing their views with me.

I am especially indebted to Carole Grau, my speech professor from Brooklyn College, who invested her faith in my abilities at an early age; she spent many hours re-reading the text and making many suggestions for improving it. Indebted I am also to Professor Marjorie Thorpe of the UWI who has spent considerable time reviewing my many speeches and this book.

I am unable to mention each and everyone to whom I am indebted. Rest assured that I have forgotten no-one and that my thankfulness is permanently recorded in my heart.

Democracy by Diplomacy:

Afro-Saxon Caribbean Diplomats challenge the US to improve its world leadership and expand regional freedoms

Contents

INTRODUCTION

I

When the author was almost seven years old, an event occurred on the African continent in March 1957 that would permanently alter the history of the continent, change the possibilities of small Caribbean islands, and enlarge the options for the descendants of slaves that now inhabit many independent Caribbean micro-states. In that year, Ghana won its independence from Britain.

Kwame Nkrumah became its first prime minister after having served time in jail, imprisoned by his British colonial master of the Gold Coast for agitating for an end to colonialism. The British were not agents of change or promoters of democracy then, though they appear to be among the main cheerleaders for democracy these days. Fifty years ago when Nkrumah led his West African country to independence, it was not as a consequence of US support and well-wishes, either. The US would subsequently be implicated in a successful plot which ended with the overthrow of Nkrumah in 1966 while he was on a state visit to Communist China, then not a representative state at the UN. The promotion of democracy was not the primary rationale for US foreign policy choices then, though the US is among a handful of states, including the English-speaking Caribbean, that are the main promoters of democracy in these early years of the 21st century. The USA is not now the country it was fifty years ago.

Upon becoming a member of the United Nations in 1957, Ghana set out to end colonialism peacefully. Ghana and other well-meaning states made possible the passage of General Assembly Resolution 1514/XV which, in 1960, declared colonialism unlawful and thereby gave

1

birth to scores of new states by 1970 including many small islands that statesmen wrongfully thought incapable of being independent states.

In 1958, the British forcibly brought the disparate elements of the British West Indies under a single entity which it called *The West Indies Federation.* Antigua, Barbados, Cayman Islands, Dominica, Grenada, Jamaica, St. Kitts-Nevis-Anguilla, St. Lucia, St. Vincent, Trinidad, and Turks and Caicos Islands were to form the new British West Indies Federation. The intent then was eventually to create a single state out of the jumble of islands that had been forcibly acquired by military muscle in the days when territory was secured by might. *The West Indies Federation* failed in 1962 when Jamaica then Trinidad withdrew and became independent states, members of the UN.

West Indian scholars and populist calypsonians condemn the wisdom of these two states' actions; however, this author is convinced that the leaders of these two states, Alexander Bustamante and Eric Williams, made the wisest choice for which history has already rewarded them. Despite the intellectuals' writings and the calypsonians' ragings, Bustamante and Williams created the conditions for the independent English-speaking Caribbean island-states to exercise far more influence globally and opportunities to achieve more good for millions of others, than a single federated West Indian state could have hoped to achieve. I relate those achievements in the text.

Malaysia, Indonesia, Fiji and several other archipelagic states do not and can never hope to exercise the level of influence and weight which the 14 CARICOM islands/territories exert collectively within international institutions. The astute have labeled the CARICOM "*one country, fourteen states*" because of the unity of purpose which the states frequently and jointly exercise. The island-states' ability to become cheerleaders for democracy in multilateral institutions could not have been envisioned and enabled had only one state emerged from the West Indian experiment of 1958.

Development within the smallest of the states would also have been severely handicapped within a federated state arrangement. Antigua was to have been the beef-producing province within the Federation; tourism had not even been considered though it has turned out to be the most reliable source of economic development. Today, the smallest of the island-states, where the economies depend on financial services, tourism, e-commerce and agriculture are the most prosperous and the most appealing places within which to live in the Caribbean. They have fewer criminals and more college graduates per capita, enjoy a higher standard of living than the largest of the Caribbean territories, and are free from many of the pathologies and race conflicts which plague their larger neighbors. Defense and foreign affairs were two factors that weighed most heavily against a vision of independence for the smallest of the island-states of the Caribbean; yet, the institutions spawned by the cleverness of their leaders to address these two presumed inadequacies frequently serve as models for larger regions. Their innovations reflect the genius of the Caribbean people.

II

Independence catches on

Barbados and Guyana followed Jamaica and Trinidad. In 1966, Errol Barrow and Forbes Burnham would lead their respective countries to independence and membership within the United Nations. Lynden Pindling led the Bahamas in 1973 and Grenada was led by Eric Gairy in 1974. Dominica, led by Patrick John, gained independence in 1978 followed by St. Lucia, led by John Compton, in February 1979 and St. Vincent and the Grenadines led by Ebenezer Joshua in October 1979. Belize led by George Price in September 1981, chose independence; followed by Antigua and Barbuda, led by Vere Bird, in November 1981.

In 1983, St. Kitts and Nevis, led by Lee Moore, chose to be an independent state, the very smallest to become a UN member at that time. Two decades and one year following the first entrant, every English-speaking Caribbean island that desired independence had thrown off the colonial yoke and chosen the path of statehood. The role of the trade union movement in achieving this milestone cannot be overstated. Trade unionism metamorphosed into political parties which then secured the privileges that the islands would come to enjoy as states, and ensured their continuation in the democratic mold by the very existence of those unions. Twelve English-speaking states emerged from the ashes of *the West Indian Federation* and none has regretted the experiment. Suriname and Haiti, Dutch and French/

3

Creole speaking states respectively, account for the additional two states -with political histories unlike their English-speaking counterparts- causing the Caribbean Community (CARICOM) number to expand to fourteen.

Significantly, Antigua and Barbuda, the author's country, chose November1, 1981 to declare its independence. That November date coincided with a fateful day in 1736 when the brave leaders of a slave revolt were gibbeted and quartered in Ottos Pasture, St. John's. The proud leaders of *The Legend of the Ravine,* so named by the author of the 1844 publication entitled: *Antigua and the Antiguans,* plotted to eliminate their oppressors and to declare Antigua free, in October 1736, on the birthday of the governor's son. A Barbadian scholar named Barry Gaspar has written of this struggle in *Bondsmen and Rebels.* Like the Nat Turner rebellion in 1831, in Virginia, the Antiguan rebellion, ninety-five years earlier, failed; ironically betrayed by the confessions of a mute. The leaders suffered the consequences then always imposed on the unsuccessful rebellious. Their heroism, however, is now permanently inscribed on the national consciousness.

The people of the Caribbean know that the price of freedom from oppression is not now, and has never been, inconsequential. The Haitian Revolution of 1804 was especially brutal and costly. Napoleon's mighty army was defeated by the scorched earth policy of the Haitian revolutionaries dubbed *"The Black Jacobins"* by another West Indian writer. The French state, having lost, nevertheless exacted a significant price from an independent Haiti, compelling the new state to compensate the French owners of Haitian slaves for the loss of "their property". The US invasion of Haiti in 1915 ensured that the 1804 bill was paid in full.

Though the price of freedom from slavery in the Caribbean was burdensome, violent democratic transformation within states around the globe since 1989 has exacted measurably equal human suffering. Ironically, the 1960 UN Resolution 1514/XV did succeed in making independence virtually cost-free to island-states of the English-speaking Caribbean. Sir Arthur Lewis, the first Nobel Prize winner from the English-speaking Caribbean, asserted that our people did not "earn" our independence; we "negotiated" our independence, he argues, and thus fail to prize it as other populations do theirs. That is faulty logic based on the assumption that shedding blood is a necessary condition for heightening the value of freedom.

The romanticized notion of bloodshed for freedom is precisely the antiquated barbarity that Caribbean leaders and their diplomats reject. Democracy by diplomacy is a major undertaking which the USA now seeks to operationalise globally with Caribbean states providing moral and political support, on their own initiative. Our peoples believe that freedom and democracy can be achieved by pressing leaders from the outside, or top-down, in a manner that engages their conscience and threatens their unjustified hold on power. That is the new experiment. The nascent model of engineering democracy, which the CARICOM states and the USA are undertaking in multilateral institutions, is still in its infancy, but the democracies of the hemisphere and the oppressed peoples of the world yearn for its continued success.

III

Cricketizing Diplomacy

Once the independent English-speaking countries joined the United Nations and the Organization of American States (OAS), their diplomats brought new energy and determination to the yearning for democracy. Caribbean diplomats "cricketized" diplomacy, bringing a sense of innovation and drive to the diplomatic postings in New York, Washington and London similar to the behavior that West Indies cricketers once brought to the game of international cricket. Under Captains Vivian Richards and Richie Richardson, both from Antigua and Barbuda, and Clive Lloyd of Guyana before them, the West Indies Cricket Team, peopled by athletes from all English-speaking Caribbean countries, dominated the sport for almost two continuous decades. England, Australia, India, New Zealand, Bangladesh, Pakistan, post-apartheid South Africa, Zimbabwe, Kenya are the largest states that play the game at the level of the test series. The West Indies team beat them all, convincingly. The team's victories would seem as improbable as having the Toronto Blue Jays baseball team win the World Series each year for twenty consecutive years.

Cricket is deemed a gentleman's game, largely because of the rules which require fairplay and honesty. A batsman who believes that he has been caught out need not wait for the umpire to tell him to leave the batting position. Walcott, Worrel and Weekes, three Barbadian cricketers of legendary cricket fame from the 1950s and 1960s, were among the most gentlemanly of cricketers. While playing aggressively and with grace, they also accepted the fate announced by the umpire without any show of resentment; they would sometimes not await the umpire's decision and begin to walk off the field.

Commentators from the region concluded that the game was played with the object of civilizing the Britons who came to watch them bat and bowl; after all, racism and colonialism were very much in vogue during their time. West Indian cricketers then were behaving not unlike the Caribbean diplomats of today, intent on making the USA follow their lead at times. Unlike the furor generated among America's conservatives by the courageous acts of Tommie Smith and John Carlos, standing with fists raised on the winners' podium during the 1968 Olympics, the West Indian cricketers also made silent civilizing gestures though theirs were well received. Walcott, Worrel and Weekes were very successful and graceful, whether they defeated or were beaten by their opponents.

These small states' cricketizing of diplomacy fuelled an ambition to promote democracy by the only means available to them: **by actively participating in the debates that are the work of the world's multilateral institutions.** Their drive became particularly evident following the demise of the Union of Soviet Socialist Republics (USSR) in 1991.

The determination to be seen as the promoters of freedom and democracy was not simply a policy option which the new states adopted. Rather, it was a visceral reaction to two hundred years of slavery, a hundred years of indentured labor, fifty years of colonial oppression, and filial identification with the blacks of the USA. The African-American struggle for civil rights was forged simultaneously with the anti-colonial struggle for independence in a symbiosis that has not been fully explored.

Nkrumah and Martin Luther King in Ghana, March 1957.

West Indian thinkers and writers living in London, Paris and New York played critical roles in destroying colonialism on the African continent. Nkrumah's biography pays rich tribute to the roles which men like CLR James, George Padmore, Marcus Garvey, Eric Williams, Forbes Burnham, Aimee Cesaire, Frantz Fanon, WEB DuBois, Paul Robeson and a plethora of other writers, scholars and civil-rights activists played in moving African leaders to think about achieving independence from Britain, France, Holland and Portugal. Once achieved, the leaders began to collaborate to secure their countries' new freedom. The collaboration among the anti-colonial leaders in the English-speaking Caribbean caused them to view sovereignty in modern terms, rather than hold the classical, Westphalian view of sovereignty as complete freedom over policy-making. The degree of collaboration and the setting aside of their narrow self-interests led to the creation of the "regional state". I will expand on this idea later in this chapter.

Martin Luther King, in 1966, remarked that the black people of the USA felt as though they were being left behind when they saw how other dark-skinned peoples were winning their freedom while the African-American was still mired in fighting segregationists. Largely un-noticed by the US press, activists of Caribbean descent were attracted to the civil rights movement in the USA and played significant roles in the African-

American struggle for dignity and inclusion in an effort to make the USA a better place for their progeny. Marcus Garvey, Stokely Carmichael, Malcolm X, Harry Belafonte, Sidney Pointier, Shirley Chisholm are among the best known Caribbean descendants who fought to transform the superior material advantages enjoyed by America's black population into a heightened regard and a respectable place for a disenfranchised minority within a majority white country. Bear in mind that the black people of the USA have more wealth than any group of blacks on the planet. American blacks also have more learning institutions and other indicia of well-being than any African or Caribbean state. In an earlier era, despite their relative wealth and learning, the blacks of the USA were robbed of their dignity. The imperfect union that is the USA has addressed those shortcomings, through the Congress and the courts, with more vigor than many conservatives would wish. The African-American people have transformed the USA, in fifty years, making it a more compassionate and demonstrably more just country, capable of a leadership role worldwide, promoting democracy.

Immigrant Caribbean blacks have been a part of this transformation. They have been migrating to the USA since the days of colonialism in British America; they came as servants to many of the British Governors who ruled colonies like North and South Carolina, New Hampshire and New York. Alexander Hamilton, the first Secretary of the Treasury in an independent USA, migrated from Nevis when a young man. It is rumored that he had black blood in his veins but the paintings portray him as unmistakably white. He ascended to a most sought-after post in a new United States, though born in the Caribbean. In the post World War I era, the immigrant blacks came to work in the factories and in the homes of wealthy whites caring for children and households. Jamaica Kincaid, the most well-known Antiguan author, came to the US in the 1970s to work as an *au pair* and transformed her opportunity by sheer talent and drive. The men who came in the early part of the last century worked on the construction of the subways in places like New York and Philadelphia. When the 1920 census was taken, more than 50% of the blacks in New York City were foreign born, from the Caribbean. Marcus Garvey's United Negro Improvement Association had its origins in the black ghettoes of New York where thousands of migrant blacks then lived and worked. These immigrant blacks did their best to improve social conditions for themselves and their offspring.

Caribbean diplomats' ambitions, beginning in the late twentieth century and continuing today, is thus a continuation of this historical drive by black West Indians, carving out a special role for themselves in the promotion of freedom and dignity. Orlando Patterson, a youthful and brilliant West Indian intellectual who taught at Yale but subsequently moved on to Harvard University in the USA, had in fact surmised in *Freedom* that a leadership role was inevitable for those whose ancestors had once been slaves. The nationalist struggles that took root around the globe after World War II were triggered in part by West Indian thinkers and activists, descendants of slaves, who were determined to end the daily insults that colonialism and racism inflicted.

Material support from the USSR in achieving independence was critical in many instances. During the Cold War, the US State Department repeatedly failed to support the nationalist struggles for independence and freedom, though many Americans yearned for the best for those who were colonized by Europeans, as they once had been. The US State Department of that era created opportunities for the USSR to exploit. In the author's view, two factors contributed to the State Department's shortsightedness and failures fifty years ago.

First, the climate of race hostility which permeated life in Washington, D.C. then infected the US State Department and created psychological blocks that made the policymakers think that an independent Africa was unlikely. The duality evidenced in the State Department's racial divide surely contributed to this view. At the heart of the US capital in the State Department, in the 1950s, virtually all the diplomats and policy-makers were white; virtually all the cleaning staff, the waiters, the elevator operators and, more recently, the security personnel were black.

Second, the State Department's recruiting practices virtually assured that only persons within the "old boys" network would become diplomats. The lack of diversity assured a perpetuation of antiquated thinking and old fashioned policies, despite the presence of Ralph Bunche, Andrew Young and tens of black diplomats over the decades dispatched to Haiti, Liberia and Sierra Leone. When US President Bush named Colin Powell as his Secretary of State in 2001, it signaled the death of this duality in the thinking of the US State Department, and it also created a significant place in US diplomatic history of a Caribbean descendant. Bear in mind that Henry Kissinger is an immigrant, as are Madeleine Albright and Zbignew Brezinski; immigrant Europeans have scaled the highest posts in the State Department and National Security, but no immigrant blacks. Colin Powell, the son of Jamaican immigrants, born in Harlem, New York, in 1937, has come closest to matching Alexander Hamilton's rise two hundred years later.

The ancient State Department of yesteryear has another checkered history which helps to explain its anachronistic viewpoint. When the issue of the denial of human rights of the African-American population was first brought to the UN, shortly after its 1945 founding, the US State Department engineered to bury the draft resolution and the report. Almost two decades later, in 1964, when Malcolm X raised the possibility of bringing the USA before the UN on the human rights violations of African-Americans, it seemed like a new idea. Professor Carol Anderson has written on this subject in *Eyes off the Prize: The United Nations and the African American Struggle for Human Rights, 1944–1955*. She has shown how the competition for hearts and minds between the two cold-war giants influenced the behavior of the US State Department.

The treatment meted out to Paul Robeson in the 1950s, one of the greatest voices for freedom of the African-American people before the Civil Rights movement became mainstream, typified the State Department's inability fifty years ago to see beyond race in the anti-colonial struggle for independence and liberation. Robeson's personal history, as told in *Here I Stand* offers a most compelling view of the narrow-minded approach of the US Government then towards its own citizens, and to an outstanding black man who professed a love for Africans and Russians.

The transformation of the USA into a better country, I would argue, has been brought about by courageous African-Americans and their liberal white allies; by the successes of the civil rights movement; by the anti-colonial struggle in Africa and Asia; by the independence of the micro-states of the Caribbean; and by the death of the USSR which gave birth to a new ideology among the US State Department policymakers in a new age. Further improvements in US policy-making and a better appreciation for other peoples have come from the re-birth of a score of East European states and the need for the US to make allies of them. The presence of independent Caribbean states' diplomats, in forums shared by the USA, has been a most significant fillip to an improved USA in the early years of the 21st century.

Stepping back to 1945, the USA had made it clear to its European partners, who had fought wars over colonial empires, that colonialism was at an end and that US taxpayers' money was not intended for the Europeans to reconstruct their destroyed states in order to empower them to return to the old ways. The Marshall Plan was the most magnanimous of US assistance plans to date. Amazingly, the US State Department failed to champion freedom for the colonized in a measurable way, thereby creating the opportunities for the USSR to exploit. That failure is one of the greatest which US diplomacy has recorded in fifty years.

IV

The Non-Aligned Movement

Fearful that they would be deemed puppets of the Soviet bloc, however, the new leaders of the newly independent states created The Non-Aligned Movement. The NAM was a coming-together of the new states as a separate bloc, in the same spirit which drove the historic Bandung Meeting of 1955. The NAM was deemed by the US State Department as hostile to the USA and more embracing of the USSR; yet, the NAM attracted many of the English-speaking Caribbean states, despite their warm relations with the USA and their unrelenting support for the US in the United Nations. The NAM has lost its usefulness with the demise of the USSR and the end of a bipolar world; and, the creation of *The Group of 77 and China* as an alternative to the developed world's *Group of 7* provided an alternative to the NAM. The chairmanship of the NAM falls to Cuba for the period 2006 to 2009; given the hostility between Cuba and the United States, the NAM may instinctively appear hostile to the USA, even today.

After 1991, a new chapter was opened in human affairs. Once the US State Department was deprived of the bogey-man syndrome that marked its knee-jerk, anti-communist reaction to every crisis during the Cold War, a real opportunity emerged to buttress and, at times, to challenge the USA's leadership on democracy promotion. The record reveals that small island-states' diplomats rose to the challenge, promoting democracy within states with greater vigor and commitment on several occasions, pressing the indispensable nation into changing course rather than appear to be led by micro-states.

That is a significant part of the tale which I intend to relate in this publication. Small states, friendly to the USA, chose to snatch leadership when their diplomats believed that the US was straying from its core ideal and endangering its world leadership. By so doing, Caribbean diplomats made the USA an even better champion of global and regional freedom in the process, just as Caribbean immigrants contributed to making the USA a better place in which to live.

The Regional State Shoves

The demise of the USSR undid the cold-war mentality that drove the US State Department's response to legitimate nationalist struggle along right-wing reactionary predilections. The change in US ideology and policy, after 1991, gave greater impetus to democratic ambitions, especially in Latin America, the Caribbean, and further afield. Political scientists surmised that drug trafficking would become the greatest concern of the USA and would thus define its foreign policy in a world where the US dominates. Terrorism has displaced and underlies many other major concerns of the USA following the September 2001 terrorist attacks; and, the spread of democracy is the USA's second greatest ambition in the new uni-polar world. The USA therefore uses the multilateral institutions in which it is a member to promote democracy as a means of reducing the threat of terrorism; and it spends US taxpayers' resources to provide assistance to fledgling democracies as well.

Yet, history recalls that the diplomats from the small Caribbean states, singing as it were from the same hymn sheet, behaved as though they were representatives from one state. They became a "regional state", putting aside differences to pursue a single ambition at all costs. The black Caribbean diplomats have spoken forcibly about democracy in multilateral institutions, advocating positions that would seem to be the domain of the USA, democracy's global cheerleader. The small island-states that form the CARICOM collaborated unceasingly, chorusing a single message that overwhelmed the single voice of the USA, at times.

Small island-states reject the notion that the USA is an "empire", intent on world domination. As diplomats who observed the USA from up close, Caribbean envoys were not fearful of US power or reprisal. Were the USA truly an "empire", interested exclusively in the domination of others, it would have caused the small states to retreat by threats of various sorts. The unwillingness of the elephant to squelch the mouse is largely the result of the importance attributed to public opinion born of the announced democratic creed of the USA, in the post Cold War period. Democracy promotion within states cannot be achieved by suppressing democracy among states; it is this realization that has allowed the small Caribbean states to challenge US leadership in multilateral institutions when the opportunities arose by taking the lead when the US lagged behind.

A culture of US-State-Department lagging is especially evident in the 1960s. When the democratic ambitions of newly liberated states conflicted with the vital interests of the US Government, the State Department was willing to abandon democracy. Noam Chomsky is one among many US scholars who has addressed this proclivity in US foreign-policy design, more widely. His 2006 publication, *Failed States,* examines this penchant of successive US administrations. Whether one is or isn't persuaded to accept Chomsky's hypothesis, I would assert that there were times during my service at the UN and at the OAS in Washington when the US State Department appeared to abandon democracy promotion in support of other interests.

As recently as January 2007, the US Secretary of State, Condoleezza Rice, was back at playing the game of abandoning democratic ideals in exchange for support from a tyrant. She was in Egypt, seeking the support of the Mubarak Administration for the January 2007 US plan for stabilizing Iraq. All pretense of supporting democratic reform in Egypt was shoved aside, prompting the New York Times Newspaper to report that: "It was clear that the United States — facing chaos in Iraq, rising Iranian influence and the destabilizing Israeli-Palestinian conflict — had decided that stability, not democracy, was its priority,

Egyptian political commentators, political aides and human rights advocates said."[1] Egypt subsequently became the first state to send to jail a blogger who used the Internet to criticize the Egyptian president and government.

Many observers may deem these decisions by the US State Department to be simply a commonsense approach to governance. How could the USA alienate Egypt at a time when it requires Egyptian help to mollify a violent insurgency in Iraq? An insurgency that has taken the lives of more than 3200 US soldiers since 2003 when the US invaded Iraq to plant democracy, I might add. The mere acknowledgment that abandonment may at times be necessary negates the assertion that democracy is now the primary objective of US foreign policy. Given the temptation to achieve other objectives and to secure its vital interests by abandoning democratic ideals, the pushing by these tiny states' diplomats in public contributed more to the growth of democracy than the American policy-makers may care to acknowledge.

V

The Crises and the Diplomats

My claim that small island-states, peopled and represented by black diplomats, have been successful at pushing the lone superpower (usually represented by white males) to adopt positions that it preferred not to pursue, may be deemed fantastic. Crises in Haiti, Bolivia, Chile, Ecuador, Paraguay, Peru, Venezuela and other states outside the hemisphere would, however, test the USA's commitment to democratic ideals and principles. Those crises required action by the OAS and sometimes the UN. On those occasions, the leadership of -and articulate defense by- these small states was magnificent. I relate these events in chapter six.

South Africa, Mozambique, and Angola in Africa were caught in the vortex of a war that placed the US policy-makers on the wrong side of history. Under President Reagan, the USA adopted an approach to apartheid South Africa which it labeled "constructive engagement." That was nothing but a subterfuge to continue to invest hundreds of millions of dollars without having to pay attention to South Africa's legal racism. The unremitting commitment of the English-speaking Caribbean to freedom and justice in these African states is not to be discounted. They stood against the USA, especially in their early denunciation of apartheid, despite their material interests and high regard for the USA; and they remained faithful to democratic ideals, despite the probable cost.

Cuba's contribution militarily is also of great significance. Cuba would send its sons to die in Angola and Mozambique, and doctors to relieve the shortage caused by centuries of exclusion and denial practiced by the Portuguese colonials. It was a mistake for the US State Department to cause the USA to lend support to the other side in a knee-jerk anti-communist reaction.

Just as Yugoslavia disintegrated and Bosnia-Herzegovina experienced ethnic war, and other East European states were undergoing crises that would be brought to the attention of the United Nations, the island-states' diplomats would forcefully and repeatedly articulate alternative proposals thereby demonstrating their leadership on democratic transition within states, equal to the USA's.

Global Leadership

Several issues that were global in scope also relied on the diplomats from the Caribbean to lead the way. The global warming phenomenon was championed by the island-states, long before the USA would concede that such a phenomenon existed. The debate to prevent the planned exploitation of Antarctica was also spearheaded by diplomats from Antigua and Barbuda. The rebirth of the International Criminal Court of Justice was pursued with vigor by English-speaking Caribbean States, led by Trinidad and Tobago. The protection of indigenous peoples worldwide energized the diplomats from Antigua and Barbuda, especially. By their assertions, the diplomats frequently pushed the USA to adopt positions that it did not intend to follow. A number of factors account for this courageous bent, or temerity, exhibited by these Caribbean citizens.

First, these small states occupy a superior moral platform handed to them by their history. The Afro-Caribbean people have never colonized or exploited any other people; they have never enslaved another race, although their peoples are the descendants of groups who were themselves enslaved by a mighty race.

Second, since 1951, when universal adult suffrage became the law within the English-speaking (East) Caribbean, the Caribbean peoples have embraced democratic ideals and practiced democracy.' Elections are held at specified periods and governments have abided by the decision of the majority, demitting office when they have lost elections. Other measurements of democracy within states are legitimately employed; but, based on this diplomat's experience, the periodic holding of elections and the voluntary demitting of governments from office offer sound benchmarks of the Caribbean's commitment to democracy. In chapter seven, a further expansion of the subject is undertaken.

Third, the island-states did not have material interests at stake in many of the places where the crises erupted; hence, they could dispassionately view the situation as disinterested judges. There was never any recklessness or lack of sophistication displayed by Caribbean diplomats at those times. Rather, their thoughtfulness and deep consideration won these diplomats applause and earned their countries very high regard. The diplomats brought the determination to lead to these institutions and during these crises, outpacing at times the lone superpower whose material interests and fear of being seen as hegemonic or imperialist frequently colored their policy choices.

Fourth, the nagging question of race, determined by WEB DuBois to be the most consuming issue of the 20th century, drives many island-states' interests. It is not uncommon for many of the Latin American states to be represented (as diplomats) by persons of European descent only. Yet, a visit to their capitals would reveal the presence of large numbers of black persons and indigenous types in their midst. President Lula DaSilva of Brazil frequently reminds global audiences that Brazil's black population is the second largest of any state in the world. What seemed evident to many English-speaking diplomats is that black Latinos are systematically excluded from the ranks of the foreign ministries and diplomatic services of their own countries. We know this because we sit next to them in the multilateral bodies.

The same exclusionary role is found in Latin American air forces and navies, but not their armies. The privileged whites are admitted to the air force and navy, while the blacks readily serve as cannon fodder or foot soldiers in the armies, and then hardly ever among the officer corps. The blacks are also the footballers, the boxers, the musicians, the entertainers but never the diplomats. It is also the case that many whites in Latin America are the inheritors of wealth and can thus afford the schools that nurture pilots, sailors and diplomats. The underprivileged blacks and the indigenous people find themselves left out of the reward system.

In the USA, there is a genuine effort to address centuries of racial discrimination and exclusion which has benefited millions of African-Americans and many black immigrants from the Caribbean, including the author. There is not an identical effort in Latin America to address centuries of exploitation and degradation of their black populations and the Caribbean diplomats know this. The Latinos have little contact with the Caribbean, except in the multilateral organizations, and even less with African countries. In their relations with the USA, the superpower speaks to its material and political interests and does not have the moral authority to lecture on racism. The Afro-Caribbean diplomats are not circumscribed by any compunctions growing out of material interests or historical burdens, and can therefore exercise leadership on this issue. Cuba, by the way, has dispatched many black diplomats abroad, winning the admiration of many English-speaking Caribbean delegations for its fair-mindedness.

While factors other than race influence the policy decisions of the English-speaking Caribbean, race is a determining though not a decisive element. Race is of importance to the nations of Latin America, also; however, they would prefer not to have a conversation about this subject. Interestingly, harmony and peace among the races is one of the island-states' critical concerns because of their reliance on tourism, made up largely of visiting well-to-do whites.

The trade union movement is another of the significant instruments relied upon by the English-speaking Caribbean states in re-ordering their societies. Although trade unions are much weaker in the early years of the 21st century than they were in the mid-20th century period, their lasting impact on the mindset of Caribbean leaders is palpable. Every political party in the English-speaking Caribbean has a trade union as its base support. To the extent that this fact retains currency in Caribbean politics, the trade union will continue to define the interests of the elected officials and the diplomats' pronouncements in multilateral institutions.

Blinding Hubris

The ability to move the lone super-power from its culturally-determined, often calculating reaction is a major achievement which many observers would miss because their prejudices lead them to see the outcome of the debate as US-led and therefore US-determined. There is also a great deal of hubris in the US press. Which US reporter, in the USA, could believe that the US Government is driven to alter its policy choices because micro-states from the Caribbean take the lead on an issue which the USA regards as its domain? It may sound preposterous to those steeped in the notion that the USA and the major powers determine the outcomes of debates in multilateral institutions. Small states, independent for a mere two and one-half decades, in one instance, have several times out-maneuvered and challenged the US, causing it to change its announced position to the benefit of millions in Africa and Latin America.

Other small states challenge the US, as well, on other issues for other reasons. Examine what has happened at the UN since 2003 in relation to its non-nuclear ambition for Iran and North Korea. Both renegade states have decided that they need not bend to the will of the UN despite threats and imposed sanctions. The Caribbean states support the UN, led by the USA, in its drive to halt expansion of the nuclear club; they oppose nuclear weapon possession by India, Israel and Pakistan and yearn for the nuclear states to disarm. When a state challenges the USA on an issue in which the superpower asserts leadership, there is sure to be some consequence. The US press appears to tow the official line, failing to point to the inconsistency of the State Department's position on nuclear arms as it relates to Pakistan and India, relative to North Korea.

The determination to speak out and to push the USA is a clear indication of the island-states' courage, their clever presentations, and their determination to lead on an issue that is vitally important to them. The leadership by the Caribbean states may also be the result of a vacuum created by the inabilities of the USA. Where the USA lacks the moral authority and the courage to assert leadership, smart diplomats from the region have filled the vacuum admirably.

Sitting in the front row of international policy-making, this erstwhile diplomat has seen the effect of visceral democrats on calculated democrats. It is my view that much credit for democracy's survival in Latin America and the Caribbean goes also to tiny black states whose own history of denial, plunder and colonialism at the hands of their colonial masters has led their diplomats and leaders to view democracy in ethical terms rather than as cold, calculated policy designed to further their own material interests. The result has been enormously powerful on the USA and its policymakers, to the extent that they have repeatedly changed course at the OAS and the UN to avoid being perceived as having been pushed by these tiny states' representatives, and to avoid erosion of their leadership roles in the community of nations.

14 States, One Country

What is very evident to an observer is the cohesion that characterizes the CARICOM countries in multilateral institutions. The heads of government and the foreign ministers, the finance ministers and the health ministers, the sports and culture ministers, the heads of the police and militaries, the tourism and economic development ministers of Antigua and Barbuda, Bahamas, Barbados, Belize, Dominica, Grenada, Guyana, Haiti, Jamaica, St. Kitts and Nevis, St. Lucia, St. Vincent and the Grenadines, Suriname, Trinidad and Tobago meet often to decide on a single or coordinated course of action when addressing complex issues.

The agenda of the Council on Foreign and Community Relations (COFCOR) is saturated with issues that each of the sovereign states must examine. However, to do so jointly and to take a joint position on the issues is a sign of their friendship and trust. When the CARICOM states jointly decide on policy, they frequently authorize a single Ambassador to articulate that decision at the UN or the OAS since issues are assigned countries. When there is to be a vote for candidates for election to a body, the CARICOM bloc vote is often decisive.

To many observers, our countries' small size, as measured by geography and population, our similar history, our neighborliness, our cultural oneness, and our collaboration qualify us to be one country. Yet, we are fourteen sovereign states. That is very smart, in a multilateral setting. Bustamante and Williams are responsible for this outcome; they rejected the 1962 attempt to make us a single state, providing thereby the opportunity for our disparate states to emerge empowered from the failed experiment, and to exercise influence and weight globally that exceed expectations.

In 1997, when at an OAS General Assembly in Peru, I spoke about the CARICOM attempt to create a "regional state". By that, it was meant a new phenomenon in international affairs where 14 sovereign states agree to submerge their many disparate interests, to identify several vital issues common to them all, and to seek to maximize the benefits that could flow jointly as a consequence of their collaboration. A regional state can therefore be said to exist when a group of sovereign and independent states agree to subordinate the rights of sovereignty of each in order to achieve a common good which is intended to strengthen the participating membership of all. The end result is that the 14 CARICOM states begin to look more like a single country, given the harmony of their joint chorus.

Adoption of the democratic ideal is one chorus which the CARICOM states pursue with vigor to the benefit of themselves and the states whose challenges come before the multilateral institutions of which they are members. The island-states' interaction with the USA at those times serves as a backdrop against which to measure part of their diplomatic success.

The object here is to tell of the events and moments in recent diplomatic history when island-states were present in multilateral institutions alongside the USA, and made a difference to the benefit of millions in Latin America, Africa and elsewhere. When those moments were triggered by crises that made their way to those multilateral institutions, where the USA and the English-speaking island-states were present, the voices of Caribbean diplomats, then forceful and unapologetic in support of democratic principles, frequently left the USA in these multilateral institutions behind. Unwilling to allow small island-states to appear to be leading as democracy's main advocates, the USA was forced to reconsider its policy options and to bend to the shoving of these tiny micro-states. That is part of the tale which this publication intends to relate.

A cursory examination of the history of the English-speaking Caribbean helps to explain why these diplomats have played such a role and why their policy choices will endure. No other region in the world matches the level of collaboration and cooperation among these tiny states, either, which also accounts for their bravery (or intransigence).

CHAPTER ONE

CARIBBEAN HISTORY IN A NUTSHELL

Renaming Ourselves

The Caribbean was mistaken for India by the navigator Christopher Columbus and labeled *The West Indies* by him, in 1492. Many of us still refer to ourselves as *West Indians* though there is nothing Indian about us, and most of us have our roots in places other than the West. The author prefers the term "*Afro-Saxons*" when referring to the African descendants of British colonial rule from the Caribbean, and thanks the late Lloyd Best for coining it.[2] This group takes great pride in the ability to express itself inordinately well in the English language, despairs of those who cannot employ the English language with the aplomb which their literate classes celebrate, and takes great pride in their Africanness especially since the momentum gathered by the Negritude movement.

Afro-Saxon would be a take-off from the term "Anglo-Saxon" used to describe Britons. The invasion of Germanic Saxons in the 5th century A.D. transformed Britain completely; the "invasion" of the African peoples, after the Europeans' 1492 encounter, transformed the Caribbean irreversibly. According to one priest of the era, Caribbean islands looked like Ethiopia. Rather than perpetuate the misnomer "West Indian", the author prefers to employ a descriptive nomenclature which grasps the complexity of our history and the pride which is justifiably experienced by our overcoming of brutality three hundred and fifty years later.

Many an African scholar in London used to refer to their Caribbean brethren as "deracinated" and "non-tribal". The three-hundred-and-fifty year experience changed behavior and culture permanently. Prime

Minister Lester Bird was attempting to explain to an African head of state at a Commonwealth Heads of Government Meeting that the Cabinet and Parliament of Antigua and Barbuda were peopled by persons born in six different countries. The African head thought about the explanation given about openness and Caribbean brotherhood, practiced by Antigua and Barbuda, in particular, and in several other Caribbean countries. "Ah, I see, you are all of the same tribe!" he exclaimed.

While tribe may explain allegiances in Africa, tribe is irrelevant in the Caribbean. Color, class, language and accent define belonging, in the Caribbean, though people of all races can there be found. So complete was the remake of the new English-speaking Caribbean person that s/he seemed closer in language and customs to the people of England, who oppressed and remade them, than to the people of Ghana or Nigeria from whence they originated. So, though in appearance, the transplanted person looks every inch an African, these modern persons have been re-engineered to behave more like the people who enslaved them. In religion, in pronounced cultural habits, in literary traditions, and in their attraction for the trade union movement, the Afro-Saxon moniker seems apropos, for it combines the two elements that constitute the new person much more so than "West Indian".

The author recognizes that such a descriptive term would apply only to the people of African descent. The East Indian population is not dissatisfied with being labeled East Indian. The Middle Easterners do not appear to take offense at being labeled Arabs; the Chinese and the whites who have been transplanted in the Caribbean also accept their labels. The difficulty with applying a name to the blacks grew out of the successfully cruel attempt to turn their ancestors into beasts of burden, to wipe out any trace of their African past, including language, religion, tribe, history and names.

In the USA, the same difficulty has arisen. American Blacks were once called Negroes, then Afro-Americans, and today the nomenclature is African-American. This has gone on for more than a century. In the case of the Caribbean, rather than perpetuate Columbus' error, the author prefers a more embracing ethnographic term which casts aside the ancient "West Indian". That term still requires an ethnic addition to achieve differentiation, anyway. The intent here is to give a useful name to the people who suffered a particular history.

There are times when "West Indian" must be maintained, and so there will be use of the term hereafter. The cricket team known as "the West Indies" and its players, known as "West Indians", will not disappear from our lexicography. Events that are shaped by the panoply of races in the sub-region will still earn the old-fashioned descriptive term, substituted by "Caribbean" when appropriate. However, the author hopes to cast into history's dustbin this 1492 misnomer and to replace it with Afro-Saxon, a better description given the five hundred year experiment.

I

The Region Begins Its Modern History

To return to the history of the sub-region after 1492, the importance of the chain of Caribbean islands grew after complete colonization of the continental Americas, one hundred years following their revelation to Europeans. The primary purpose of the sailing expedition from Europe had been to find a new trade route to the East that was less dangerous and more efficient than the overland routes across Asia. When the navigator encountered the Caribbean (and then the Americas), he discovered a place that appeared as the paradise described in their religion. The people they encountered were peaceful and friendly; the climate was incredibly perfect; and the beauteousness of the land and sea continues to make the Caribbean a place of wonder even today. Caribbean tourism today lives on these characteristics.

The Europeans determined that there were not many products manufactured in the Caribbean in 1492 by the indigenous Tainos, Arawak, and Carib peoples for export to Europe. However, the plants which they farmed, the dies which they used to adorn their faces, and the tobacco which they smoked seemed to be items that could interest the financiers of future expeditions. The birds were also of great interest as gifts to the monarchs and noblemen who financed the expedition. So were the turtles that became a source of protein for hungry European sailors and, later, millions of their slaves. The leatherback turtles suffered near-extinction by the raiding of their nest eggs which adversely affected their regenerative capacity.

Since the tools of warfare of the indigenous Caribbean people were centuries behind the invading Europeans, it was easy to compel the gentle peoples to submit to the superior brutality of the invaders. After 1493, the Europeans enslaved the indigenous Caribbean peoples and intensified their search for gold and silver, replacing the invaders' thirst for trade in goods; and, when those metals became exhausted, plants exotic to Europe became the new obsession. Tobacco, indigo and maize were deemed to be viable exports from small islands, followed by sugar, molasses and rum. After the possibilities became evident, the importance of the West Indies to Europeans soared. In those days, diplomacy was not the primary tool of interaction among European states; warfare was far more prevalent. Violent confrontation and bloody events became the distinguishing historical marker in the colonizing period following the revelation of the Caribbean to Europe.

Colonization

Britain, France, Holland, Sweden and Denmark were latecomers to colonization after Spain and Portugal had carved up the Americas between themselves, leaving only small specks of land in the Caribbean Sea unoccupied by the invading Europeans by 1600. The Papal Bull had also "granted" Spain the authority to subjugate the infidels and to take their lands after the 1492 encounter. A weakened Spain could not defend every island. Spain was therefore either expelled from her many Caribbean possessions to the benefit of four other European powers intent on sharing the spoils of the New World, or foreclosed from laying claim to the Caribbean by the inordinate spread of the archipelago.

The French thus planted her flag on St. Martin, St. Kitts, Guadeloupe, Dominica, Martinique, St. Lucia, Grenada and Trinidad, as well as French Guyana on the South American coast. The British claimed Tortola and Virgin Gorda in the British Virgin Islands, Nevis, Anguilla, Antigua, Barbuda, St. Vincent and the Grenadines, Tobago and British Guiana on the South American coast. The Bahamas, the Turks and Caicos in the North, Jamaica and the Cayman Islands in the west, Isla de San Andreas y Providenciales off Colombia, and British

Honduras in Central America were also made British territories by force of arms.

The Dutch claimed St. Maarten, Saba, St. Eustatius in the East Caribbean, Aruba, Bonaire and Curacao just off the South American coast, and Dutch Guyana on the South American continent. The Danish claimed St. Thomas, St. Croix, and St. John just off Puerto Rico's south coast. Bear in mind that Puerto Rico, Cuba and two thirds of Hispaniola had been claimed by Spain since 1492, and France had laid claim to the other one-third of Hispaniola which it called Saint Dominique.

The use of force negated the edict of the Papal Bull which had handed Spain the entire New World to subjugate "the infidels", people who did not threaten Europe nor willingly surrender to the invading conquerors. The conquest of the indigenous people was brutal, bloody and wicked. But the Europeans also turned to fighting each other.

Defending against or capitulating to aggression marks the history of Europeans in the Caribbean. Many of the islands switched owners many times as a result of the warring Europeans. Several, like St. Lucia, never became firmly British until after 1800 when Napoleon's navy was badly decimated. Antigua would spend one day as a French colony in 1667. The Treaty of Breda between France and England fixed her ownership in 1767. Trinidad, Grenada and St. Lucia were forcibly taken from the French by the British in 1796. The ships sailed from Nelson's Dockyard on Antigua, equipped to enlarge the colonial holdings of the conquering power by force.

St. Kitts, no larger than the District of Colombia -the capital of the USA- was shared by the French and the British until the French surrendered their portion under the Treaty of Breda that guaranteed her ownership of Guadeloupe and Martinique. Ceding all of French Canada to the British, in exchange for security of ownership of her Caribbean possessions, was based on military (and economic) considerations. Upon reflection, the French and others have learned that it is never wise to depend on military advisers when making long-term national decisions.

The Dutch also shared St. Maarten with the French, dividing another tiny island into a place of two sovereignties, which still lives on today.

When the worth of the Caribbean islands was evidenced, the powers of Europe fought many wars and invested in forts and naval facilities in that theater, in order to gain and maintain control of those possessions. Nelson's Dockyard on Antigua and Brimstone Hill Fortifications on St. Kitts are among the military architectural wonders that still fascinate today. The Fort in Curacao, towering over the harbor, is a marvel of military architecture. So too are the fortifications in Trinidad, Grenada, St. Lucia and St. Vincent.

By 1820, the entire archipelago had fixed European colonizers; then another method of changing ownership would take place. In 1804, Haiti would declare her independence, and the Dominican Republic would declare her independence in 1823. Puerto Rico and Cuba would no longer be Spanish colonies after the 1898 Spanish-American War though many Cubans credit Jose Marti, in 1895, for bringing about the independence that Cuba later attained. The Danish Virgin Islands would be sold to the United States in 1917. There would be no more switching of loyalties or forced acquisitions of any Caribbean islands after the 1917 sale, until independence movements in 1962 ended the rule of the British sovereign. I will share more details on many of these events in other chapters..

There are still islands in the Caribbean chain that remain colonies. Guadeloupe and Martinique remain French, as does French Guiana on the northern coast of South America. The British Virgin Islands, the Cayman Islands, the Turks and Caicos, Montserrat and Anguilla remain British. Aruba, Bonaire, Curacao, Saba, St. Eustatius and St. Maarten remain Dutch. Puerto Rico and the US Virgin Islands remain American territories.

Every two years, the United Nations Committee on Decolonization visits and invites submissions from their leaders. What is evident from these visits is that the populations do not wish for independence. The British, Dutch, French and Americans also prefer to exercise ownership for a variety of reasons, and the populations are pleased to carry the passports and citizenship of the European Union and of the United States.

Frequently, the colonized peoples view with envy the ability of the small English-speaking states to dispatch diplomats to the capitals of the world, to be seated as sovereign states in multilateral institutions, and to forge domestic policy independent of overlords. In many instances, the material advantages which the non-independent Caribbean territories enjoy appear to compensate for this lack of sovereignty, for which they have decided to opt.

Yet, it is also the case that they participate in several UN forums including The Economic Commission for Latin America and the Caribbean (ECLAC) and its Caribbean-specific derivative: The CDCC (Caribbean Development and Coordinating Committee). The CDCC meets for a day or two prior to the biennial ECLAC Meeting, and the representatives all sit at table as though all are equal in sovereignty. The UNDP also includes the non-independent Caribbean in its work programme. During several of the UN global conferences of the 1990s, the non-independent countries have been invited and sat as equals among all the sovereign states. My delegation promoted the resolution that ensured their participation. When the Ambassador of China asked me to withdraw a similar resolution that would have allowed participation of Hong Kong during the period of the handover from the UK, I obliged.

At the CARICOM gatherings, Montserrat and the British Virgin Islands are accorded equal status as the independent Caribbean. Only within the Association of Caribbean States (ACS) are there representatives of the European states sitting in the seats of the non-independent island countries. It is worthy of note that the non-independent Caribbean has many very well-trained and experienced diplomats. Carlisle Corbin of the US Virgin Islands, Joel Mercelina de Jung of the Netherlands Antilles can hold their own as well as any of the independent Commonwealth Caribbean diplomats. The people of the Caribbean are amazingly smart.

II

The Peopling of the Caribbean

It is estimated that more than 2,000,000 indigenous Caribbean people faced genocide or inadvertently died of microbial diseases as a result of their encounter with the Europeans who made the Caribbean their new home, after 1492. There may also have been an urge to destroy the male indigenous population in order to make the females readily available to the European male transplants. Evidence of this urge is now gleaned from DNA studies of the population of Puerto Rico which reveal that 80% of a sample group possesses DNA material that is traceable to the indigenous people. Bartolome de Las Casas, a priest sent on one of the later expeditions, witnessed the degradations, enslavement and murder of the indigenous people and in 1516 asked that Africans be imported to bear the burdens instead.

For centuries, until 1807, untold millions of Africans were kidnapped from their several West African homelands and forcibly transplanted in horrible slave ships to the Europeans' new world. The West Indies and the Americas were their destinations. Just how many persons constituted this human cargo cannot be accurately recalled. Walter Rodney, a Guyanese historian, has written that the robbery of millions of Africa's youth deprived African states of their most precious resource. This decimation of youthfulness led inexorably to the continent's under-development and to Europe's material gain. His book, entitled *How Europe Under-developed Africa,* helps to explain the dynamics of slavery, the importance of the English-speaking Caribbean, and the mastery of the world by Europe.

When the slave trade ended in 1807, two hundred years ago, and slavery was declared at an end in 1838 in English-speaking islands, the need for replacement labor led to India. Millions of indentured Indians were shipped to the Caribbean in the 19th century and form narrow majorities in Trinidad and Guyana today. Portuguese laborers and middle managers were imported into many Caribbean islands to fill positions that the Europeans decided would not be filled by blacks, shortly after slavery ended. So, many traders and small shopkeepers were Portuguese, whose functions were later supplemented by fair-skinned blacks --the progeny of white fathers and black mothers.

In the early 20th century, Arabs from Lebanon and Syria began a migration to the Americas and the Caribbean, and they have remained, peppering the Caribbean with another stock of people. Chinese males were also shipped to the Caribbean after 1850 or at about the same time that Chinese men were being shipped to the USA to build the great trans-continental railway. Only one boatload was dispatched to Antigua, and through miscegenation the Chinese bloodlines have disappeared. But in Trinidad, British Guiana, Jamaica and British

Honduras the Chinese maintained their purity and are still present in small numbers. The migration of Chinese in the past decades and recently has enlarged their gene pool.

The people of the Caribbean are thus from every continent and race imaginable. Except for racial tensions in Guyana and Trinidad, exacerbated by the competition inherent in electoral politics, this potpourri of races is an identifying Caribbean characteristic. It is nevertheless also true that the African bloodline is the most enduring phenotype for reasons found in the overwhelming number of blacks in the population and the secrets of melanin in nature.

Selective Human Breeding

The urge to ensure ever larger profits from the capture, sale and forced labor of humans led a slave-master in Barbuda, the British Virgin Islands and on Antigua to breed extremely tall, strong and strapping slaves for sale and rent. Lord Codrington, who was leased Barbuda by the Crown for "one fat pig per year, if demanded," in 1685 commanded that, on his island and properties, only the tall men and the buxom black women could copulate.

The crown never did demand the pig from its lessee, and his copulation command was obeyed. Codrington grew wealthy from his ownership of Barbuda, his two estates on Antigua, and his subsequent acquisition of more land in Barbados. He became so wealthy that he could endow a school of divinity in Barbados that bears his name even today.

Codrington was also a meticulous record keeper. At some period in the late 19th century, all the records of his enterprise on Barbuda and Antigua were shipped to England and stored in the basement of a church. When the Antiguans and Barbudans learned that the Codrington Papers were to be sold at auction, they raised enough money to make the purchase. A very wealthy businessman contributed a modern archive building to store and display the two-hundred year-old documents, in Antigua. Unfortunately, the centuries-old papers began to deteriorate in the humid Caribbean environment and were promptly shipped back to England for posterity's sake.

The result of Codrington's experiment in eugenics over time has been a population that grew taller on average than any African descendants to be found on any neighboring Caribbean island. A similar experiment in selective human breeding would later be undertaken in Hitler's Germany for reasons entirely unrelated to sale or use. Their descendants today bear no shame, and neither do we in Antigua and Barbuda.

It is interesting to note that all four (successive) Antigua and Barbuda Ambassadors to the UN and three of four of its Ambassadors to the USA and the OAS were men who stood more than six feet tall. Its three Prime Ministers and its living ex-Premier have all been taller than six feet. When the Antigua and Barbuda delegation --to several of the UN General Assemblies-- strolled on to the assembly floor, one remarkable characteristic of the diplomats from the 157th member state was their height.

Hurst, Ashe, Lewis, Challenger and Murdoch at the UN, Oct. '91 (from right). All taller than 6' UN Photo 17636/M. Grant

Then Foreign Minister Lester Bird, Ambassadors Lloydstone Jacobs, Lionel Hurst, Patrick Lewis, John Ashe, Eric Challenger and Colin Murdoch are all taller than six feet. Challenger and Murdoch were permanent secretaries in the Ministry of Foreign Affairs and regularly attended the General Assembly when Antigua and Barbuda took to the podium to participate in the annual debate. An uninformed observer may think that tall men migrate to politics and diplomacy in Antigua and Barbuda; but a better answer is that the average height of this engineered race is such that even a random selection would lead inevitably to the inclusion of these courageous giants. The Dutch are the tallest people among the states of the world, it is claimed; yet, no

Dutch delegation to the UN could ever match the average height of the Antigua and Barbuda UN delegation. The most successful cricketers from Antigua and Barbuda are also six-footers, and they are most aggressive! We have gotten ahead of ourselves.

III

Models of Production and Maturity

When the large-scale planting and reaping of sugarcane, and the manufacture of sugar, was introduced in the Caribbean, a new method of production and organization of labor emerged. All over Western Europe, before 1492, individuals manufactured the necessities that the village, town and cities consumed; there were no factories. Beginning in the early 1600s, the smallest islands of the Caribbean –Hispaniola, Cuba, Puerto Rico and Jamaica, the largest, having been first colonized in 1493- became places for experimentation with mass labor and specialization in production.

The Caribbean islands, places of misery and brutality, played a most important role in providing new models of production and industrialization of commodities; plantation slavery would serve as the underpinning of capital formation in England that would lead to the Industrial Revolution of the 1800s. What emerged from the Caribbean experimentation would later be adapted to modern factories in a Europe that was still agrarian. Just as Henry Ford invented a manufacturing system that accelerated the production of cars in the US which was later adapted to a variety of products, so too did the Caribbean serve as a place from which emerged a new method for accelerating wealth-creation and by specialization in production.

When Caribbean diplomats stroll through the halls of the UN or the Councils of the OAS or of the (British) Commonwealth of Nations, we envision bringing new methods, new systems and inventive ways of addressing old and nagging problems set down by history. This nagging urge to innovate grows out of our history and is reflected in our culture, politics and sports. Although one writer has dubbed us "Mimic Men", the opposite is true. The Caribbean people are very inventive.

It is interesting to note that several small European states, wealthy and highly sophisticated, decided to become members of the United

Nations and to dispatch diplomats to New York only after 1991. These small European states witnessed many small, fairly impoverished Caribbean island-states carving out special leadership roles for themselves at the UN; they came to the conclusion that there was a place for them at the table. Andorra, Liechtenstein, Monaco and San Marino had long chosen to remain on the sidelines during the Cold War. When there was no doubt as to their ability to function effectively within the theatre that other micro-states had, for more than two decades, they stepped in, became UN members, and have never regretted the decision. As the Caribbean diplomats were perceived, so they also perceived themselves.

The Caribbean, the small European, the tiny Pacific and South Asian micro-states, the Indian Ocean island-states, the Mediterranean and the African-Atlantic island-states now participate in an UN-based collaborative organization known as *The Forum of Small States*, led by Singapore and enabled by more than fifty UN small states. At the UN, small is defined as fewer than five million citizens, as well as unspecific geographical limitations. Their primary goal has been limited to the election of candidates to non-paying UN posts; however, an accretion of new issues is sure to cause the ten-year old organization to expand its interests in due course. During the IMF/World Bank Meetings in Singapore in September 2006, *The Forum of Small States* convened to find ways to collaborate in defense of their material interests.

Caribbean diplomats were also instrumental in bringing together the island-states from around the world, whose very existence is threatened by the harmful effects of global warming, to try to save themselves. They have formed *The Alliance of Small Island States (AOSIS)* which promulgated the United Nations Framework Convention on Climate Change and its Protocols, in their effort to reverse a dangerous threat that will surely end civilization as we know it.

Trade Unionism

The single most transformative institution in the English-speaking Caribbean was the trade union. After riots swept through the English-speaking Caribbean in 1938, trade unions began popping up everywhere.

In Trinidad and Tobago, the Oilfield Workers Trade Union led by Tubal Uriah Butler formed the backbone of protestations against the slave-like conditions that kept workers poor and their children hungry. In Guyana, Forbes Burnham became the President of the British Guyana Labor Union, and later the first prime minister of an independent Guyana. In Grenada, the Grenada Workers' Union led by Eric Gairy, a self-taught dock worker who was as colorful as any politician anywhere in the world, won the faith of his people. Archie Singham has written about Gairy in *The Hero and the Crowd* which reveals details not warranted here. In St. Vincent and the Grenadines, Ebenezer Joshua created and led The Federated Industrial and Agricultural Workers Union. Although Milton Cato became the Chief Minister and the Prime Minister, many credit Joshua with creating the conditions for St. Vincent and the Grenadines to mature and to resist the horrible conditions that had imprisoned its people for two centuries.

In Barbados, Grantley Adams formed the Barbados Workers Union in 1938 and the first political party there, The Barbados Labour Party. He would become Barbados' first chief minister though Errol Barrow became its first prime minister. George Charles would repeat the same in St. Lucia forming the St. Lucia Labour Party after establishing the St. Lucia Labour Union, though John Compton became the first prime minister. In Montserrat, W.H. Bramble formed and led the Montserrat Trade Union movement and became the country's first chief minister. In St. Kitts and Nevis, a very articulate trade unionist named Robert Bradshaw emerged to lead that country, becoming its first chief minister.

In Antigua, Vere Bird, a Salvation Army preacher, became one of the founding members of the Antigua Trades and Labour Union and his country's first chief minister, first Premier and first prime minister. In the British Virgin Islands, one Mr. Hamilton Lavity Stoutt was similarly successful, becoming the first chief minister. In Jamaica, Bustamante and Manley duplicated each other's efforts by forming rival unions and political parties that remain alive today, each becoming chief minister at some period. Lynden Pindling would perform the identical leadership role, becoming the first prime minister in 1973.

From the south to the north along the archipelago, trade unions metamorphosed into political parties. Simultaneously, the Caribbean

Congress of Labour served as an ideological underpinning that drew its material support from The Socialist International and even the British Trade Union Congress. The battles within many of the island-countries were epic, much like Rome against Spartacus, but the leaders pressed forward and prevailed.[3]

Christianity and Trade Unionism

Religion played a most important role in every Caribbean island-community during colonization and, later, in the trade union movement. The Africans exported to the West Indies were forbidden to practice their animist religions, and the slave-masters did not actively seek to fill the spiritual hunger of the blacks in British colonies. The African descendants in Hispaniola and Cuba were introduced to Roman Catholicism, and in keeping with the inventiveness of the youthful captives, they combined aspects of their animist beliefs with the monotheism of Christianity; the product is called Santeria and it has been legitimized in Cuba.

In the English-speaking Caribbean, the Church of England reigned. By mid-18th century, the Anglican Church had built countless houses of worship in virtually every village in every island. In the tourism of today, visiting quaint churches is one of the "must do" items on the visitors' list. The head of the Church was the monarch of England to whom fealty had to be pledged. It was after the revolution led by Cromwell that disestablishment laws were passed in the colonies, and the end of an official religion became law.

Other Christian sects, like the Moravians and the Methodists, who opposed slavery and saw no merit in illiteracy, were active in helping to overcome the social conditions that existed among the blacks in the British Caribbean colonies.

Overleaf is a photo of the St, John's Cathedral, the most imposing building in all of St. John's, the capital city of Antigua and Barbuda. Rebuilt in 1848 for the third time and thus 159 years old at the time of writing, the Cathedral is still the most dominant building in the city, attesting to the importance of religion in the life of the colony and of the independent state. Sitting majestically atop a hill, only a nine-storied hotel on the west coast is taller. The photo of the Cathedral is taken from the archives of the author.

The St. John's Cathedral.

By mid-19th century, the churches built schools and trained black teachers. In fact, Arthur Lewis, the first Nobel Prize winner (1979) from the English-speaking Caribbean, a St. Lucian economist, is the product of Antiguan parents who graduated from the Moravian Leeward Islands Teacher Training College on Antigua. They migrated to St. Lucia before Arthur was born, in order to reduce a teacher shortage that Moravian Schools there were suffering.

St. Lucia produced a second Nobel Prize winner in 1992, Trinidad and Tobago has produced one; Guadeloupe has given birth to one. Many countries in Latin America have not produced any. The blacks became Christianized and literate, and they have largely so remained. Indians would bring Hinduism and Islam to the West Indies which survive today. The Chinese did not appear to bring their native religions, but there are Jews in Suriname and Guyana.

Although Christianity speaks of delivery after death, many trade unionists saw in its message eternal hope while alive. The trade union leaders all embraced Christianity and flirted with socialism or Marxism. The search for an ideological platform upon which the justness of their cause could stand, drew many trade union leaders to the ideals of a socialist/Christian world. Marxism is very similar in its promises to Christianity, promising a world wherein each person will have sufficient to meet needs after contributing talents: *To each according to his needs; from each according to his ability* is the underlying dogma. Alsdair MacIntyre has addressed this baffling subject in *Marxism and Christianity*.

In 1938, the year of the riots throughout the region, the trade union leaders could not count on the Church of England to support their efforts to bargain for better wages and improved working conditions; though, in Antigua, the Anglican Church was very accommodating to the new trade union leaders before its 1939 establishment and after. That was not the experience throughout the English-speaking Caribbean where churches tend to be very conservative, working most times to preserve the social order.

It is likewise of interest to note that the African-American people and their leaders saw the same hope in Christianity. The doctrine of forgiveness and brotherly love which underpinned the US Civil Rights movement is a tenet of Christianity. The civil rights leaders, mostly priests, deliberately intertwined Christian aspirations with American capitalist-democratic ideals. Contrastingly, Malcolm X and the Black Muslim Movement and the Black Panther Party, served as scary alternatives to moderate reform, and as an indispensable fillip to white American generosity.

Additionally, the strong appeal to Christian values in a nation overwhelmingly Christian, made the Civil Rights movement appear centrist and expressive of the American ideal of inclusion. It is also not co-incidental that the civil rights movement gained momentum in the 1960s, just as colonialism was being brought to an end. The competition between the Soviet communist-control system and the American democratic-capitalist alternative changed the global political climate and compelled the USA to seek to end the pervasive racism that alienated its black population. The decisions of the (Warren) Supreme Court, after 1954 beginning with *Brown versus Board of Education*, reflected the changing world that was emerging, following the horrors of racist theories carried to their logical conclusions by the Nazis. The Cuban experiment, after 1961, also lent urgency to the US domestic reform.

Immigration and War

The large scale movement of immigrants from the West Indies to England following World War II, the award of scholarships --no matter how few-- also lent opportunities for Caribbean writers, thinkers and activists in London, Paris, Amsterdam to tell their own stories to a reading public in Europe. The writers and activists, at home and abroad, created the intellectual underpinning for the nascent nationalist/ independence movements in the English-speaking Caribbean. The idea of self-determination, though given great importance by US President Roosevelt, was being promoted by the West Indian intellectuals in their hope for Africa and India.

Many Britons also began to understand the price of empire; the degradation, the exploitation and the misery that empire requires did not appear so attractive to working-class Britons, centuries following Britain's ascendancy. After the threat posed by Hitler and his attempt to subjugate them, and the decimation of British cities by German blitzkrieg, the British working class felt revulsion at colonialism and elected a government that would indeed help to dismantle his Britannic majesty's empire. Winston Churchill lost the election after World War II to a Labor Party on the rebound. World War II was a great evil that brought about a movement of people and an upliftment of the downtrodden. It weakened many European powers and thus enabled their colonies to fight more vigorously for independence.

It is very evident that a confluence of forces gave rise to freedom from servitude and colonialism in the Caribbean. Many of those forces gave birth to trade unionism later on, and lit the fire that created Caribbean independence, that in turn led to the creation of states and the possibilities for diplomacy of an experimental variety. Caribbean history informs and shapes Caribbean diplomacy, giving her diplomats extraordinary fortitude and a desire to find creative new solutions to ancient and vexing challenges. To grow democracy within states is one of history's most enduring challenges and one which the English-speaking Caribbean diplomats, the Afro-Saxons, assiduously pursue.

CHAPTER TWO

WAR, DIPLOMACY AND DEVELOPMENT

War is politics with violence, and politics is war without violence. Diplomacy is politics hoping to prevent violence, and multilateral diplomacy is the surest way to prevent war from occurring among states and to hurry along tectonic shifts among states. Multilateral diplomacy is proving to be a method by which development and democracy within states can be enhanced. The admission of new states to the UN after 1960, especially the African and Asian countries, helped to propel US civil rights advances more swiftly. The US could not afford to be embarrassed by racism at home while preaching democracy and anti-communism abroad. The US civil rights movement also drew some of its strength from the anti-colonial struggle; and, the anti-colonial struggle was in turn inspired by the moral uprightness and the challenge to power which the movement witnessed.

It may seem unlikely to a casual observer that tiny states can prevent war among large neighbors or enable democracy within states far removed geographically from the small states. Yet, the history of the English-speaking Caribbean in war and in diplomacy, since independence, has demonstrated an ability to alter outcomes in war and diplomacy. Their primary foreign policy drive has been to secure their sovereignty and to promote development by nurturing democracy within and among states, including their own. Their leaders believe that by improving the relations among states, they contribute to global peace; a world without war leads to an enhanced material well-being of the Caribbean people, especially those dependent upon tourism.

The level of success in promoting good relations among states has varied within regions over the past twenty-five years, or since Antigua and Barbuda has joined the effort. I have compared our region's success to our West Indies cricket team and have thus written about the diplomats as one would about players on any successful sporting team, I have relied on my own country's timeline as a means of applying this hypothesis, and invoked my own knowledge and participation as a diplomat in multilateral settings to provide context and meaning.

A brief look at each of the states and territories that make up the archipelago is undertaken in this chapter. I begin with the region's oldest, sovereign states; proceed next to those countries that help to define the region; then the author examines seriatim the fourteen CARICOM states and their diplomats. People make history, especially the lowliest; that is an underlying assumption of this text which I employed throughout.

Despite her poverty, the oldest independent Caribbean state has had a defining effect on the character of the diplomacy of her neighbors. First, the method used by Haiti to achieve her sovereignty, and the brutal treatment meted out to her as a consequence of her success, resulted in material conditions from which it has been extremely difficult for her to escape. That and many other lessons have not been lost on the leaders of a modern and independent English-speaking Caribbean.

Second, by becoming Haiti's primary advocate for peace and development, the diplomats from the English-speaking Caribbean learned that they could play a meaningful part in multilateral diplomacy that need not be confined only to their region and their material interests.

Third, by being active and expressing their perspective on issues outside of their region, the CARICOM learned that they served as a model; this view of the group enhanced its standing and caused it to seek even more roles that helped to further define its place in multilateral organizations.

Despite the relatively small population size –St. Kitts and Nevis is 50,000 souls, Antigua and Barbuda is 80,000 -the CARICOM states have learned that size is not the determining factor. Sovereignty, and the use to which it is put, ultimately determines the place a state will win on the international stage. Haiti's courage and Cuba's daring have proven central to developing CARICOM's unvarnished view of their diplomatic capabilities.

I

Haiti and Diplomacy

The Haitian Revolution of 1804 came twenty-eight years following the culmination of the successful 1776 revolution which gave birth to the new country known as the United States of America. It is important to recall that France was an important military ally of the revolting Americans and, more than two decades later, the two powers wished to see Britain weakened further so that its two competitors could be strengthened. Power among states, in an era where warfare is prevalent, is a zero sum game. France was still enjoying the fruits of its West Indian colonies at the time of the Haitian revolution. Saint Dominique, in 1803, soon to become Haiti, was its most important source of overseas trade and mercantilist profits.

The successful 1804 Haitian declaration of independence dealt a serious blow to France's prestige, severely undermined France's military might, even compelled France to sell Louisiana, its North American colony, to its ally, the USA, in order to finance its expeditionary force against Spain and Britain. Napoleon Bonaparte was so severely humiliated by the defeat at the hands of slaves --one of whose leaders came from Grenada-- that he kidnapped the Haitian leader, Toussaint L'Ouveture, in 1802, and locked him in a dungeon in the mountains of France until he died of pneumonia from exposure to cold. It was unmitigated treachery.

Toussaint L'Ouveture was invited on board a French Navy ship anchored in the Haitian harbor after hostilities had ceased. He had not anticipated that France would have acted criminally. The French also knew that the Haitians were not capable of invading France to rescue their leader. When the Americans invaded Panama and took its president back to the USA for trial, in 1989, it was also because the US knew that Panama could not mount an invasion of the USA to rescue its president.

This enormous power to change regimes at will has led mighty states to act out of self-interest. The US policy makers have even coined a term for this illegal action; they call it "regime change." The invasion of Iraq in 2003 is a case of the USA defying international law and acting entirely out of self-interest. The acquisition of nuclear power by less powerful states that feel threatened by this unlawful use of greater power (like North Korea, Iran, and earlier Cuba) is undoubtedly one of the warped results. The world is better off with fewer nuclear states, and fewer nuclear arms. The North Korean Six-Party Talks that persuaded that state to de-activate its nuclear weapons in exchange for assistance and diplomatic recognition, in February 2007, has proven the value of diplomacy over violence. But that history is not yet complete and so all peoples must hope for a peaceful outcome, eventually. At any rate, this ability of the very powerful to disregard rules and international law, to change regimes at will, is opposed by tiny states from the English-speaking Caribbean. They are dutifully attempting to contain the exercise of this unlawful power by promoting democracy among states.

The 1804 Haitian Revolution was a most inconvenient threat to all the slave-holding colonizers in the New World. Word of the successful revolution spread quickly throughout the West Indies, North- Central- and South-American colonies of Spain, Portugal and Holland. The possibility of independence now infected the leaders of the New World colonies. "If the enslaved blacks could declare themselves independent, then surely the free whites can do the same," the Latin Americans were thinking. The 1789 revolution in France and the 1776 US revolution also inspired many Latin Americans. Over a period of two decades, after Haiti's revolution, the Spanish colonies of Central and South America and Brazil --Portugal's only colony in the new world-- successfully declared themselves independent republics. Brazil actually declared itself an empire, ruled by a king; the others mimicked the newly independent republic of the USA.

In 1826, when the first meeting of the presidents of the newly independent states of the Americas took place in Panama, then a province of Colombia, the US President refused to attend if the Haitian president was to be seated as an equal. Colombia therefore sent a letter of dis-invitation to Haiti's President Boyer, who was already on his way, withdrawing the earlier invitation. The US President's delegation arrived late to the meeting because of the need for approval of the US

Congress to travel abroad. In the interim, the Haitian President who arrived in the city on-time was not allowed to take his seat at the table of Presidents gathered in Panama City.

The Haitian President had planned to speak forcibly about the need to end slavery in the countries of the New World and to fix the trading system that kept Haiti from selling its produce on the world market. That he was not allowed to take his seat is a moment of shame in history which the USA and Colombia, and the other new-world states, will live down forever. Haitian diplomacy was defeated by bigotry. The building where that meeting took place still stands in Panama today, though the neighborhood is now run-down. In 1996, during the OAS General Assembly, the delegations sat in the chairs occupied by the presidents.

Insistence on the continued denial of human rights to a significant number of black persons born or imported into the countries of the Americas would characterize the culture of the new-world countries. Exclusion continues to deny equality to the African descendants in many of the states of the New World, and the independent Caribbean states are pledged to defeat that kind of bigotry by using multilateral platforms as a pulpit.

The USA did not recognize Haiti until 1862, a year before it declared slavery unlawful, and a year after it commenced a civil war to end the brutal practice in its southern states. There were no multilateral regional institutions before 1915, certainly none which Haiti and her Caribbean neighbors could wield in order to foster development and to tackle the bigotry that would lock them in underdevelopment for a very long time.

Haiti as Refuge and Liberator

Haiti, like the USA before it, provided the fillip to the new-world colonies to declare themselves independent of their European masters. Haiti went one step further. The newly-created Haitian state declared that any person of African descent who set foot on Haitian soil would immediately have Haitian citizenship conferred, and would no longer be a slave. This declaration was very much ahead of its time in international law. It surpassed the benefits of refugee status conferred on persons fleeing persecution which would become accepted law in the 20th century.

Haiti would become a refuge for many runaway slaves from the USA, the Caribbean and South America. The Haitians hated slavery and wished to end it in the New World. Haiti, among all the countries in the world, can be credited with being the first state to use diplomacy to promote freedom and democracy within states. But the Haitians also used military might to free thousands of new-world slaves.

The Haitian army invaded the other two-thirds of Hispaniola, liberated the slaves there in Santo Domingo, and remained the rulers of an enlarged Haiti until 1823. In that year, with help from Simon Bolivar of Venezuela, who ironically had been provided with arms and men from Haiti in his struggle for independence, the Dominicanos were able to mount a successful offence, drove the Haitians back across to the one-third of the island previously acknowledged as theirs, re-instated slavery and declared themselves an independent state. Accordingly, the Dominican Republic in 1823 declared itself independent of Haiti, not Spain.

Haiti was invaded in 1915 by the USA under a very shallow pretext about German collaboration. The USA put into action the Monroe Doctrine which declared the countries of the Americas to be within its backyard, and pledged to defeat any power that sought to extend its influence there. German friendship with Haiti was considered harmful to US interests and so the relatively tiny state felt the weight of its giant neighbor.

The USA remained in Haiti until 1934 and a succession of Haitian presidents followed, marked by a period of instability. In 1957, Dr. Francois Duvalier was elected President in an election that was suspect for excluding many eligible voters. Curiously, Dr. Duvalier embraced and advanced the Negritude Movement that had its genesis in France and England among West Indian and African intellectuals, spread to the Caribbean and to the English-speaking Americas. Duvalier's diplomats were leaders in fighting apartheid at the United Nations and he was a champion of the anti-colonial movement in Africa. He wrote poetry and essays, invigorated the University of Haiti that was the envy of many for its high scholarship, and legitimized the Haitian religion that the invading Americans found so objectionable. Duvalier has always been portrayed as a buffoon in the US media. Far from being stupid, Duvalier contributed meaningfully to diplomacy and the fight for freedom in Africa. His greatest sin is attempting to hold on to power at any cost rather than ruling through democratic means. Robert Mugabe of Zimbabwe, once a freedom fighter, is replicating this sin in 2007.

The Duvalier rule came to an end in 1986 when the younger Duvalier was exiled to France. Haiti began a painful transition to a democracy which culminated in 1990 with the election to the Presidency of Father John Bertrand Aristede, a Catholic priest. The English-speaking Caribbean countries played a significant role in this transition, at the UN and at the OAS. Caribbean leaders and diplomats repeatedly remarked, following the end of Duvalier's rule, that the end of the slave trade in 1807 and the subsequent death of slavery in 1838 throughout the English-speaking Caribbean were a direct consequence of the successful 1804 Haitian Revolution. The 20th century descendants of those who benefited from the emanating insecurities generated by the 1804 Haitian Revolution owed the people of Haiti a historical debt. That debt could only be repaid by doing all in their power to bring freedom and prosperity to an impoverished Haiti now that they were positioned to deliver.

At the OAS and at the UN, Caribbean diplomats joined with Canada, France and the USA, taking a lead role in helping to transform Haiti into a working democracy. The Haitians also discovered that independent Caribbean countries existed and that these small island-states could be relied upon as allies in multilateral institutions to promote democracy and development within. Prior to Aristede, Haiti looked to its large traditional benefactors only; there was little contact between Haitian diplomats and her neighbors'. After 1986, Haiti and the English-speaking Caribbean both learned that their sovereignties, and their membership at the UN and the OAS, could enhance freedom and development more swiftly. Haiti thus became a member of the CARICOM in 1994.

The Haitian crisis served as an epiphany from which the English-speaking island-states have drawn many lessons and forged diplomatic leadership. Aristede's election and subsequent overthrow taught the newly independent English-speaking Caribbean countries lessons in diplomacy and the possibilities flowing from active participation in multilateral institutions.

In 1994, the US sent a force to Haiti with the express permission of President Aristede and the collaboration of his English-speaking Caribbean neighbors. It restored Aristede to power. Like the 1983 force sent to Grenada, the USA was welcomed by the people and their legitimate governments. In 2004, when Aristede was threatened by an advancing rebel force, the US would only offer him an airplane to escape first to Jamaica and then to Africa. The Haitian story is not yet over, and neither is the role of the English-speaking Caribbean in catalyzing democracy and development in Haiti.

II

Dominican Republic and Diplomacy

In 1965, the USA invaded the Dominican Republic following the assassination of President Trujillo. Again, the USA acted in its best interests, not necessarily in the interest of the small state. The Antiguans and other English-speaking sugarcane workers who returned to their homelands during Trujillo's leadership would remark how brutal he was. The 1965 invasion was triggered by reports of a massacre of more than 10,000 Haitian men, women and children at the Haitian-Dominicano border. Intrigue, conspiracies and military coups marked the history of the Dominican Republic before the US invasion.

After 1965, a changing world, including freedom of tiny island-states, irreversibly altered the tradition of coups and military intervention in that Caribbean country. It was not until the Dominicanos discovered the benefits of tourism --a staple of the English-speaking Caribbean countries' economies long before 1985-- that economic growth, fuelled by political stability, began to outpace the population explosion and economic stagnation that had kept the people of the Dominican Republic so poor. Like other West Indians, the Dominicanos also discovered immigration to New York City as an alternative to grinding poverty. "Which is the largest city in the Dominican Republic? New York," goes the response. It is said that more Dominicanos live in that city in the USA than in Santo Domingo, their capital.

The Dominican Republic never did rely on its independence in 180 years to promote freedom anywhere, especially since it was not a crucible of freedom for its own black citizens. In fact, within the Dominican psyche lies a hatred of its African heritage. The dark-skinned Dominicanos will frequently boast of their European ancestry as one stares irrefutably at the rich Africanoid features and biological traits that evidence their ancestry. The author has seen (female) Dominicano household-help, in other Caribbean countries, hoist umbrellas while placing laundry to dry on the clothes-line in the backyard in the blazing sun; the women fear becoming dark-skinned and suffering the decrease in aesthetic magnetism that is deemed to flow from fair skin.

The Negritude movement did not appear to infiltrate the Dominican Republic, and the contempt for Haitian people is so deeply ingrained that the Dominican Republic saw no special need to promote freedom using its diplomatic weight. The author believes that CARICOM leaders are wary of the Dominicanos, know their history and their prejudices, and know that the Dominican Republic offered no assistance in securing its neighbors' freedom. The leaders have thus, the author believes, foreclosed membership of the Dominican Republic in the CARICOM despite its repeated attempts to become the 15th member. These may be determining factors rather than decisive factors for Haiti has been accorded membership in the CARICOM.

Despite the relative poverty of the Dominican Republic, large numbers of Haitian workers migrate across the border to the sugarcane fields of its neighbor. Reports of horrific exploitation at the hands of Dominicano overseers has not deterred the Haitian migrants. The Dominican Republic correctly perceives a breakdown of law and order in Haiti as a threat to its own stability, since thousands of Haitians flee across the border to the Dominican Republic whenever repression increases in Haiti. Geography has thus placed the Dominican Republic in a position to want to ensure that Haitian democracy succeeds for it has a measurable stake in the outcome. For this reason, Dominicano diplomats at the OAS and the UN have also been active in helping to bring democracy and development to Haiti, since 1991.

The Dominican Republic assigns two ambassadors to Washington, unlike all other Caribbean countries that assign a single ambassador with dual responsibility. The Dominican Republic assigns one to the White House and, more recently, the second to the OAS. With regularity, the OAS Ambassador is rotated every three years. The author has known only two OAS Ambassadors from the Dominican Republic; Flavio Dario Espinal has been the better-known envoy though both have all been very friendly to their English-speaking counterparts and have begun collaborating on many issues. However, it is important to note that the Dominican Republic refused to pay its annual obligations to the OAS for three decades, and did not assign an Ambassador there, until after 1995.

III

Cuba and Diplomacy

Cuba was the third country in the Caribbean to become an independent state. Not surprisingly, there were interests in the US who sought to annex Cuba to the USA as early as 1848. In fact, US President Polk is said to have offered to purchase Cuba from Spain for quite a tidy sum. Cuba's nationalists, however, fought for independence. In 1895, Jose Marti led an armed struggle in which he was killed. Then, the destruction of the US warship in the Havana harbor led to an invasion by US forces and triggered what has become known as the Spanish-American War. When the USA invaded Cuba in 1898, the defeat of Spain was not very difficult. The US imposed a twenty-year trusteeship rule but the nationalists resisted, albeit far more peacefully than in the Philippines. In 1902, Cuba became an independent country, though the US retained the right to intervene in its defense and in foreign affairs.

Cuba was very reliant upon the sale of commodities in order to earn hard currency; sugar and tobacco were Cuba's main agricultural exports. Cuba, like its neighbor the Dominican Republic, was a place where the wealthiest persons were the descendants of Spanish colonialists who had settled on the island, enslaved and decimated the indigenous population, and imported millions of African peoples who were made slaves upon arrival. Its history mirrors that of the East Caribbean in these significant ways.

Cuba's independence and sovereignty were conceived as benefits to be further enjoyed by the people of European stock, and its darker skinned citizens were not deemed a significant element in this new dispensation, despite the fact that many of Cuba's elites had African blood flowing in their veins. When US interests began to seek profits from the presence of the US military on Cuban soil, after 1898, the racism that defined domestic politics in the USA became cultural practices which were easily adapted in Cuba. Blacks were not allowed in the hotels which the Americans built; black Cubans were not welcomed in the University of Havana, and what obtained in the southern states of the USA was transferred to Havana. Cuba never sought freedom for other Caribbean countries; in fact, Cuba needed to protect its own freedom from the crushing presence of as powerful a neighbor as the USA. The author hastens to point out that the USA and the English-speaking Caribbean island-states are the best of friends in 2007, as are the island-states and Cuba, despite the twisted racial history. In Bosnia, Burundi and Iraq, ethnic grievances that go back 800 years still generate hostilities and civil war. The modern Caribbean rejects hatred and strife, opting for democracy and material well-being.

When the 1959 Cuban Revolution took place, the English-speaking Caribbean had been for one year experimenting with a Federation. The Cuban Missile Crisis, as the 1962 event is known, caused great consternation and fear among Caribbean leaders who listened to the events unfurling without any ability to affect an outcome. The English-speaking Caribbean was a hapless observer of events, though our sympathies lay with the USA. A calypsonian of note would sing in a paean to US President Kennedy:

You better turn those ships in the opposite direction
Kennedy is the man for them
Any retaliation will be met with explosion
Kennedy is the man for them.[4]

Eric Williams, the first Prime Minister of Trinidad and Tobago, would later write a scholarly work entitled: *From Columbus to Castro* in an effort to explain the forces that influenced the making of the Caribbean. He viewed the Cuban Revolution in very sympathetic terms, especially the socialist ideal of providing education to all, free health care, and an end to racism.

Cuba, however, even up until 1991, did not care that the other Caribbean existed. During the author's first trip to Cuba, to attend a 1991 UN Congress on Crime, he met with Fidel Castro. When Castro was told that VC Bird had been the head of Government in Antigua and Barbuda since 1956, except for a five-year hiatus, he declared that impossible. "I am the longest serving head of government in the Caribbean," he jokingly asserted.

Castro enquired about Antigua and Barbuda, asked about the manner in which we solved our recurring water-shortage problem, and listened with interest to the benefits garnered by reliance upon tourism. Fidel Castro asked many more questions than he answered though he did arrange for the author to visit a Cuban water-works project and sought to establish friendly relations with us. The author was instrumental in signing the declaration establishing formal diplomatic relations between Cuba and Antigua and Barbuda at the Cuban Mission to the UN on April 6, 1994, less than one month after Lester Bird became Antigua's second prime minister.

Cuba distinguished itself from the other states in Latin America not only by its economic and social systems, but also by its deliberate efforts to make friends with the English-speaking Caribbean, after 1991. When support from Russia came to an end, Cuba had to find the means to support itself and to establish a new basis for regional friendship. Cuba's role in support of Mozambique and Angola against Portuguese colonialism –sending its soldiers to die on battlefields there- had warmed Cuba to many of the CARICOM states and their leaders. It seemed so unlikely that a relatively small Caribbean country of 14 million people could be so pivotal in the fight against European colonialism and South African apartheid.

The debate which took place within the Ministry of Foreign Affairs of Antigua and Barbuda prior to April 1994 was primarily about the retaliatory policies which the USA might impose for befriending a state hostile to her. By 1994, almost all of the CARICOM countries had established diplomatic relations with our largest Caribbean neighbor. In fact, in 1972, Barbados, Guyana, Jamaica and Trinidad and Tobago established diplomatic relations with Cuba simultaneously. Antigua and Barbuda's turn would come only after VC Bird was no longer the Prime Minister. During VC Bird's rule, he remained adamantly opposed to Cuba for its hostility towards the USA. Like E.H. Lake, Antigua and Barbuda's first Ambassador to the OAS and the USA, VC Bird believed that only free and fair elections could determine which leader and systems a people wanted. He saw Castro as a dictator.

The younger generation of Antiguans and Barbudans saw great courage in Castro, and experienced the generosity of the Cuban people. They would nevertheless find revolting the absence of the freedoms which are enjoyed in Antigua and Barbuda but denied the Cuban people. Our elections are boisterous and Carnival-like affairs that heap insults aplenty on the heads of the Prime Minister and the cabinet members. There can be no criticism of Fidel Castro and his ministers by the Cuban people in public. In my visit to Cuban homes, Cubans have expressed their disdain for a system that keeps them impoverished; they blame the USA and its embargo rather than the Cuban government.

Today, every English-speaking Caribbean country has scores of students studying at various Cuban universities on scholarship, and their governments have established embassies in Havana.

The Antigua and Barbuda Embassy in Cuba, September 2006.
(Photo by Millet)

It is of interest to note that during the Non-Aligned Meeting in Cuba, in September 2006, the new Prime Minister of Antigua and Barbuda met with the President of Iran and proposed to establish diplomatic relations with that state. This occurred at a time when the USA and Iran are locked in a battle over the development of nuclear arms in Iran. Former Prime Minister Lester Bird, upon learning of the intent of the Antigua and Barbuda Government, wrote to the new Prime Minister Spencer hoping to dissuade the latter from such a course. "The Iranian Government has shown a penchant for disregarding international law and for proceeding as an outlaw nation that need not abide by the rules governing inter-state relations. It is unwise for Antigua and Barbuda to seek to befriend Iran at a time when that state is challenging the legitimacy of the UN Security Council and is openly hostile to the USA –our main ally and trading partner." So that two reasons are proffered by the former prime minister for not proceeding with the establishment of diplomatic relations; the author is of the view that the latter is the weightier reason. The new Prime Minister recoiled from the proposed befriending of Iran and so Antigua and Barbuda awaits the outcome of the disagreement before proceeding, despite its freedom to move forward as its head sees fit.

Caribbean leaders in Jamaica (2005); Cuba now seeks friends in the region. (Photo by Millett).

Cuba has dispatched many capable diplomats to the UN and to its Interest Section in Washington. They have done their very best to befriend the Caribbean states and their diplomats. The Cuban diplomats are the best prepared, the most vocal, and the most challenged. Thankfully, the USA does not sit with the Group of Latin American and Caribbean States (GRULAC) at the UN; Cuba does. Canada does not sit with the GRULAC either; they sit with the Western Europe and Other Group (WEOG); all the majority white states sit in this group, including Australia and New Zealand. Hence the 33 states of the hemisphere frequently get an opportunity to decide on many issues free from the "burdensome" presence of the USA in our midst.

Cuba exercises influence far above its weight, primarily because its diplomats are very articulate and informed. The Cubans invest a lot of talent and resources in their UN Mission since it is one body from which the USA cannot exclude it –like the OAS- or marginalize its voice. All nations sit as sovereign equals in the UN General Assembly, each exercising one vote no matter how large or small. That is the miracle at the UN, the savior of mankind.

IV

Puerto Rico and Diplomacy

On April 25, 1898, the US Congress declared war against Spain. The Spanish-American War saw Spain deprived of its two remaining island-colonies in the Caribbean. Cuba was in limbo until 1902, and Puerto Rico was transformed permanently into an appendage of the USA. The Puerto Ricans have benefited materially from this arrangement and never seriously pursued independence. Even in the heady days of the anti-colonial movements in the 1950s, only a small and determined group of Puerto Ricans acted to move their island to becoming an independent country. One Puerto Rican nationalist attempted to assassinate President Truman in 1950, and several even discharged firearms in the US House of Representatives in Washington, but failed to generate sufficient support in Puerto Rico to sustain a viable independence movement.

The Puerto Ricans see themselves as the most fortunate of the Spanish-speaking countries in the New World, today. Their standard of living is superior to most, though many families rely on US Federal anti-poverty programs to succeed and though they have a murder rate which makes San Juan one of the most dangerous places in the

Americas. Their adherence to periodic election schedules and the free functioning of unions give the Puerto Ricans a sense of control over their destiny. Yet, the automatic conferring of US citizenship on every Puerto Rican and the use of the US dollar as the currency of exchange, convey appendage status that also remind other Caribbean states of Puerto Rico's dependency. The United Nations has also reviewed Puerto Rico's status from as early as 1952 and every two years thereafter to the present. The Puerto Ricans embrace the arrangement with the US which they call "commonwealth status."

The absence of independence or statehood yields measurable material advantages. Many US pharmaceutical companies have established a presence there as a result of a tax incentive causing many jobs to materialize on Puerto Rico. The incentive expired in 2004 and the academics are still measuring the economic outcome of loss of this benefit. Infrastructure in Puerto Rico is superb and the University of Puerto Rico is quite an asset. Schooling is universal as is healthcare, and the per capita income is impressive, by Caribbean standards.

Those features have not stopped millions of Puerto Ricans from migrating to New York and other cities in the USA. Once on the US mainland, many Puerto Rican immigrants have found the language differences as a barrier to upward mobility resulting in poor performance, high crime, and other maladies within several of their immigrant communities. Like all immigrant groups, Puerto Ricans have their successes. Herman Badillo, a Puerto-Rican-descendant politician in New York has fought alongside African-Americans in New York City to enhance opportunities for his country folk. Puerto Rico's musicians, actors and models have also fascinated the larger population in New York City. Tito Fuentes is probably the best known Puerto Rican musician within the USA.

Puerto Rico has simultaneously become a magnet for undocumented immigrants, from the Dominican Republic especially, who make the treacherous crossing by sea in un-seaworthy craft, take many jobs which the Puerto Ricans scorn, and remain an underclass in Puerto Rico. When the Puerto Ricans look out into the Caribbean Sea, they see poorer states, peopled with African descendants, with more severe challenges than they face and hence they look, not to the Caribbean for joint solutions but rather, to the USA.

Puerto Rico has thus shown little sustained interest in furthering friendship between itself and the states of the region. When US President Clinton visited Barbados in 1997 to meet with CARICOM leaders, the governors of Puerto Rico and of the US Virgin Islands were invited to attend the Summit. In the lead-up to the Summit, the CARICOM leaders insisted on having Montserrat's chief minister present, to which the US objected. As a compromise, the English-speaking Caribbean negotiators suggested that the US Caribbean territories send their own heads of government. The US agreed and the Governor of Puerto Rico was invited; he sent his deputy.

Puerto Rico does not see itself as linked to the Caribbean except as a hub for air traffic and as a transit point for cruise tourists. The six countries of the East Caribbean, in October 2006, opened a joint office in San Juan to promote tourism and trade from Puerto Rico, at the invitation of the current governor. Only two Puerto Rican Governors in recent times have extended a hand of friendship to the neighboring Caribbean. Whenever the mood swings, the Puerto Ricans are quick to abandon their dark-skinned cousins that populate the independent Caribbean in favor of richer pastures elsewhere. That has not been the case of the US Virgin Islands, geographic neighbors of Puerto Rico but culturally coupled to the English-speaking Eastern Caribbean.

V

The US Virgin Islands and Diplomacy
The way a Caribbean writer tells the story, the USA was actually swindled out of a bundle of money by Denmark in the sale of the Danish Virgin Islands, in 1917. The Danish Government had tried to sell their only West Indian colonies before the turn of the century when the colonies proved more costly than their worth. The Americans, who had purchased Alaska from Russia in 1867 to peals of laughter from many who thought the Russians had sold ice to Eskimos, made the USA very reluctant to spend tax-payers money for no apparently good reasons. When the Danes reported that a substantial offer had been made by the Germans, following German hostility in the Caribbean, the Americans stepped forward and made the purchase of the US

Virgin Islands for a tidy sum of $25 millions. It is understood that the US military saw wisdom in this 1917 purchase.

One hundred and fifty years earlier, under the 1767 Treaty of Paris, the French Government was persuaded by its military to yield its Canadian dominion to the British in exchange for security of ownership over Guadeloupe and Martinique, two Caribbean islands. The military defeat of France also helped to persuade France to sue for peace. The continued hostility of French Quebec to inclusion in the English-speaking Canadian state is the result today. But the US Virgin Islanders have not regretted their islands' purchase by the US Government.

In the early part of the last century, the Virgin Islands' acquisition resulted in the creation of stateless persons. Quite a number of male Virgin Islanders had gone to the Dominican Republic to cut sugarcane during the 1916/17 cutting season and had remained there. When the US purchased the Virgin Islands, it set a time limit for those born there (before the purchase) to claim US citizenship. Those who failed to act on time, as did many of the male Virgin Islanders in the Dominican Republic, forfeited the opportunity forever. Since the Dominican Republic did not grant them citizenship --they were seasonal workers who had remained illegally, as far as the Dominicano Government was concerned— they became stateless persons. There was always residual resentment towards the English- and Danish-speaking immigrant men in the Dominican Republic; these men played cricket, read the King James Bible, and were Protestants in an overwhelmingly Catholic state. The men died stateless.

The US Virgin Islands played a most significant role in projecting the possibilities of a tourism-based economy to its East Caribbean neighbors. The Virgin Islands were the first to exploit their sunny winters and white sand beaches as a place for mainlanders to frolic, following the end of World War II and the arrival of Pan American Airways to the region. The model of economic success which the Virgin Islands conveyed in that post-war period also drew many male and female immigrants from the English-speaking East Caribbean, where sugar and bananas still dominated their economies.

By 1970, when an economic recession reduced employment opportunities in the Virgin Islands, thousands of English-speaking

Caribbean immigrants were forcibly repatriated. Many had never regularized their status in this US territory and were thus vulnerable. Antigua and Barbuda's newly-elected premier, George Walter, nevertheless understood the threat which hundreds of unemployed returning males posed for the stability of his country. He dispatched his Minister of Home Affairs, Donald Halstead, to the US Virgin Islands to discuss with the US-appointed Governor a slowing of the deportations. The US Virgin Islands authorities were in no mood to listen, and so the deportations continued unabated. Hundreds of the affected Antiguan males skipped to Puerto Rico and then to New York, Boston and other cities on the mainland where it was far more likely that they would escape detection.

A few hundred English-speaking Caribbean males, escaping from the Virgin Islands, also enlisted in the US military. In 1970, the Viet Nam War was still raging and the US law compelled forced conscription of young male citizens. Any source of canon fodder was helpful to the cause; so, many English-speaking Caribbean young men, escaping deportation from the Virgin Islands, became casualties of the Southeast Asian hostilities with which they had no connection. They became US citizens after basic training, allowing them to file residency immigration petitions for parents and siblings. In one of the most altruistic moments in their lives, many of these Caribbean males chose risk of death for the benefit of their families. Everyone holds them in high regard in their countries.

The US Virgin Islands have become culturally linked to the East Caribbean by way of calypso, carnival and cricket. The Caribbean people have exported their frolic and sport to the countries and cities that welcomed them worldwide, but especially to the US Virgin Islands. The availability of inexpensive air transport and now the Internet has made travel and communications readily affordable. The University of the Virgin Islands, now a considerable source of training for youth from St. Kitts and Nevis, Antigua and Barbuda, and Dominica, ensures that a steady flow of youngsters renew the aging bonds of a previous generation. Family ties extend the boundaries and create interlocking building blocs that irrevocably bind the destinies of the Virgin Islands to the states and territories in the Caribbean archipelago for the foreseeable future.

VI

Jamaica and Its Diplomats

On September 30, 1962 Jamaica achieved its independence and set off on a course, full of high ambitions that have not yet been fully realized. During its forty-four years as an independent country, Jamaica has had to struggle with many of the challenges faced by the states that came of age after the anti-colonial struggles of the last century. Despite her shortcomings, this small island-state has nurtured a university that is outstanding, producing intellectuals and scholars that are remarkably talented. Her statesmen and diplomats have been hailed as visionaries, possessing as they did the Jamaican fighting spirit. Jamaica has repeatedly won medals in the once-every-four-years World Olympics. Her athletes have been outstanding. Jamaica's musicians have also given to the world a music form that is globally recognized and appreciated. Bob Marley is acknowledged as the progenitor of reggae. He is clearly one of her most creative sons, as are several musicians of more recent vintage.

Jamaica continues to produce an abundance of talented people. In business, Butch Stewart of the Sandals Hotels Resort chain and Air Jamaica fame has also been compared to astute wealth creators in the USA, despite talk of downsizing the airline. In international and regional politics, former Prime Minister Michael Manley was the embodiment of the finest West Indian orator and statesman. He occupied a global stage from which he challenged the USA, Western Europe and the USSR to live up to their promises and their potential to relieve human suffering and poverty by spreading their wealth. He was a principal spokesperson for the Third World and "The New International Economic Order," which was intended to address a challenge that has not diminished since the 1960s. Michael Manley was vilified in the US press for seeking to establish ties with Fidel Castro's Cuba, and for borrowing Cuban models in agriculture, water conservation and state ownership of their bauxite deposits. On his death, he was hailed as an outstanding figure in the century just ended. But many Jamaicans fled to Miami during his rule. His political defeat came after much support by operatives from anti-Castro elements in the USA; again, the anti-communist bogey was invoked to weaken his regime and end his rule.

Manley's successor, Edward Seaga, was the first head of government to be invited to the US capital to meet the newly inaugurated US President Reagan in 1982. Following the defeat of Prime Minister Edward Seaga, the Jamaican electorate has been consistently disapproving of the Jamaica Labor Party's stewardship. For three consecutive terms, the Jamaican people have returned the People's National Party of P.J. Patterson to power, and on March 30 2006 placed the second female in the history of the English-speaking Caribbean at the helm of an independent state. Jamaica is a land of stark contrasts and surprises.

Jamaica has a history of talent, courage and failings that is also reflected in its diplomacy. During the author's seven-year posting in New York, four UN Ambassadors from Jamaica were assigned to New York. The first left shortly after the author's arrival. He was a poet who regularly impressed his colleagues with his knowledge of the writings of Cuban and Dominicano writers; he spoke Spanish fluently, and German since his wife was of that nationality. The second was Lucille Mair, who brought her long history of struggle for women's rights to her job as the Jamaican permanent representative. She had also been an employee of the UN, ascending to a very high post of Assistant Secretary General. Ambassador Mair was very articulate though she appeared often fearful of offending the USA. The author has learned that she suffers from Alzheimer's disease. The third was a former central banker who was called "fog horn" (unknowingly) by his colleagues. He was often in the habit of beginning his statements by making believe that he had much to contribute, then, he would say little that mattered and therefore earned that aptly applied sobriquet. The fourth was another female, Pat Durant, who was charming, smart and courageous. During her tenure, Jamaica ascended to a non-permanent seat on the UN Security Council and distinguished itself as a leader among the CARICOM countries. She was instrumental in forcing settlement of the Haitian issue at the UN.

In Washington, Richard Bernal served continuously and for a period that matched the author's. He is bright and articulate, very self-assured to the point of being cocky, and studious. He would grasp the most complicated issues, especially in trade, and be able to share a point of view with great clarity and conviction. Ambassador Bernal relished the posting to the White House but despised the OAS; he seldom graced the place with his presence. Yet, he had very able deputies who took their assignments very seriously. The Jamaican seat was seldom without representation in the various committees, and the diplomats would frequently have meaningful statements to make, contributing to the outcomes.

Ambassador Hurst is introduced by Ambassador Bernal to the Jamaican Governor General 1997 (Photo by Edwards)

The author often felt that Jamaican diplomats reluctantly followed the lead of a smaller Caribbean country diplomat, a dictate of the prejudice of size. Gail Mathurin was one of the exceptions. She was raised in St. Lucia, I was told, and did not imbibe fully the penchant to be "in charge." Jamaica is the largest of the English-speaking countries, in terms of population, and assumed that it must also have the very brightest of diplomats. The penchant to lead may also have been the intense competition that marks life in Jamaica, each having to prove his/her worth in order to succeed, never relenting in that quest. The competition is less intense in smaller states though the candidates for posts are intellectual equals.

During the final two years of the author's posting in Washington, a new ambassador was dispatched there. He used to be the Deputy Prime Minister of Jamaica. A very capable and likeable man, he would leave much of the fighting to his more youthful staff members while he performed many of the ceremonial duties of protocol.

It seems to me that after the Manley era and the punishing response that the US Government (and some say the Central Intelligence Agency) inflicted, Jamaica's foreign policy was thereafter guided by an indistinguishable CARICOM-determined path, and avoidance of conflict with the USA. There was therefore a very cautious and non-threatening diplomacy practiced by Jamaica. It pursued vigorously issues related to trade and aid; but, at the OAS, Jamaica did not appear to be interested in larger questions of democracy and human rights, unlike its 1962 fellow traveler on the early independence road, Trinidad and Tobago.

VII

Trinidad and Tobago and its Diplomats

The cultural and intellectual capital of the Eastern Caribbean had been firmly planted in Trinidad by an abundance of calypsonians, steel-pan musicians, thinkers, writers, academics, politicians, trade unionists and activists who exported their craft to the region. The St. Augustine Campus of the University of the West Indies (UWI) was an important ingredient in achieving this "capital" status. The UWI Graduate Institute of International Relations contributed in no small way. Forty-one years old in 2007, it has served as a training ground for many of the civil servants who subsequently joined their Ministries of Foreign Affairs.

Eric Williams, Trinidad and Tobago's first black head of government, was among its most prolific writers and thinkers. In 1944, he had published his classic review of slavery in the Caribbean entitled *Capitalism and Slavery* that placed him among the most revered of thinkers from the English-speaking sub-region. He argued in his doctoral thesis that industrial development in Britain was made possible by enormous quantities of capital generated by the West Indian slave trade and slavery, for more than 200 years. It was such a fresh perspective of an ancient puzzle that he was able to sell his novel interpretation of history to a publisher. Williams also conducted a series of lectures around Trinidad at the behest of The Political Education Movement after 1948, upon his return there from Howard University. By the time he entered politics, in 1956, he was already very well-known.

Williams seized upon the issue of a US naval base, located at Chaguaramas on the western tip of Trinidad, and insisted that it must go. The British had granted permission in 1941 to the USA to build bases on several of its West Indian colonies, in exchange for destroyers. The war having ended in 1945, Williams saw an opportunity to galvanize support for a nationalist ambition. One of the famous calypsos of the era tells of the exit of the US sailors from Port of Spain, the capital, and the resultant decline in the cost of pleasure when its major purveyors had disappeared:

> ....*If you catch them broken*
> *You can get them all for nothing*
> *Don't make a row*
> *For the Yankees gone and Sparrow take over now.*[5]

Williams had become a professor at Howard University in Washington, in 1939, and was exposed to the daily insults that racial prejudice in the US capital inflicted on all African peoples. He left Washington in 1948. Though Williams never expressly wrote that his assaults on US interests in Trinidad were related to his lingering resentment of the white Americans' racial prejudices, it was evident that he did not want to appear to be doing the bidding of the USA. He was a proud man who was certain of his own worth and would brook no reduction of it, or of his country's. He succeeded in driving the US military out of Port of Spain. He would later succeed in nationalizing the petroleum industry of Trinidad owned by the British, so that many of his admirers could claim that his was an anti-imperialist bent rather than a purely anti-US predilection. He became the head of government in 1956 following constitutional advancement, and would remain the head of an independent Trinidad and Tobago until his death in 1981, a total of twenty-five years.

Williams offered Trinidad as the capital of the West Indies Federation in 1958. Four years later, he would lead Trinidad and Tobago into independence with the famous quip that "10 take away 1 equals 0". He refused to join the Organization of American States until 1966, seeing it as a tool of the USA and not wanting to be directed by the US Secretary of State.

During the year of Trinidad's independence, the world was brought to the brink of nuclear war by the "Cuban Missile Crisis". In 1962, the US was easily able to compel the OAS members to suspend Cuba from OAS membership; only Mexico would not vote in favor. Williams also knew well the history of the USA's gunboat diplomacy in the Caribbean and Latin America, witnessed the operationalizing of the Monroe doctrine, and did not wish to be seen as a lackey of the USA. He preached a defiance of the USA which would subsequently be transformed into out-maneuvering the USA in the OAS and the UN on democracy issues. In 1970, when faced with the possibility of a military coup, a US destroyer appeared off the coast of Trinidad, apparently sufficiently intimidating of the coup plotters to cause them to return to their barracks, some believe. Williams may also have been taken aback by the black power militancy of the coup plotters. He made several speeches during the crisis indicating that he too was in favor of black power. Williams must be credited for successfully rescuing democracy in the English-speaking Caribbean; successful coups in Africa destroyed democracy for succeeding generations.

The story is told that when Williams' first Ambassador to the UN requested instructions on a vote at the General Assembly, he was told to use his best judgment. Trinidad's diplomacy has matured significantly since that time, four decades ago. Trinidad and Tobago led the United Nations, during the regime of Prime Minister ANR Robinson, to reviving the International Criminal Court of Justice which is today a reality. Prime Minister's ambassador to the UN was a very competent UWI Professor named Marjorie Thorpe. She brought an intellectual finesse and an innovative style to her appointment. Her impact on the UN is memorable and significant. Annette Desilles followed as her country's representative at the UN. She was fluent in Spanish and intellectually sound. Her leadership of the Alliance of Small Island States, and her membership on the UNDP Governing Board, are lasting legacies which set her apart. Her husband, an outstanding jurist, was invited to serve on a UN panel on Haiti; he declined a second term.

In Washington, Desilles' counterpart, whom I came to know after 1995, was Corrine McKnight, a fierce and caustic speaker who would insult her Latin colleagues if the moment required it. She was feared by a few for her sharp wit; in a setting that required the soft touch, she was pugnacious. Its next Ambassador to the USA and the OAS was Michael Arnaud. He was a very garrulous and pleasant executive from a large Trinidad firm called Neal and Massey. He would make Trinidad's large home in Washington available to his CARICOM colleagues, and he showed great impatience with the slow pace of business at the OAS. His wife was a great diplomat.

At the World Bank, one of Trinidad's smartest daughters, Jeanette Sutherland, has served as a consultant. She speaks French and Spanish, has a working knowledge of Portuguese, and writes analytical papers with the precision for which Trinidad's Nobel Prize winner is known. Trinidad and Tobago produces very intelligent and gifted diplomats, just as it has produced a plethora of writers and thinkers.

During President Clinton's eight-year administration, he initiated summits of the American presidents. A series of topics would be included on the presidents' agenda. Narcotic trafficking was one such topic. Trinidad and Tobago took the leadership on this issue.

VIII

Guyana and Its Diplomats

If any country in the English-speaking Caribbean has turned out to be a disappointment, in economic terms, it has been Guyana. Endowed with relatively large useable land, large rivers, known deposits of minerals and other natural assets, Guyana could be a showcase for the achievements of liberated Africans and Indians equal in scale to Singapore. Forty-one years following its 1966 independence, Guyana is a woefully underdeveloped country, its population dispersed throughout the Caribbean, North America and Europe, its towns and cities beset by crime and other maladies that have trapped it in underdevelopment.

Guyana also has a problem of race that is hampering its climb out of the morass into which the immediate past has imprisoned it. Guyana's history is very much like every other Caribbean country's despite its location on South America's coast; however, shortly after 1951 and the arrival of adult suffrage, its electoral system was corrupted. Guyana's about-even racial divide also caused an immense battle between political parties that became race-based after the split between Forbes Burnham and Cheddi Jagan. The result of their separation was loyal and blind support for each half of the two competing racial parties, no matter how woefully wasteful the government or how inept the opposition may have been. Yet, Guyana was able to dispatch very clever and resourceful diplomats to New York and Washington, during the author's fifteen year cumulative period.

Ambassador Rudy Insanally was a deep thinker and a calming force among his CARICOM colleagues. There were times when the Ambassadors to the UN from Barbados and Jamaica would exchange cross words, the former guarding against the latter's exercise of leadership by dint of an unwarranted prejudice. The false creed holds that, in the West Indies, the bigger one's country, the smarter are its citizens. Since Jamaica's population is ten times as large as Barbados', its land surface one hundred times larger, then its Ambassador must possess a superior intellect and a better understanding of complex political issues than her Barbados counterpart. Lucille Mair was the UN Ambassador from Jamaica and Besley Maycock from Barbados, both of whom were very intelligent people; but, Maycock saw Mair as simply asserting leadership, and that would not be allowed over him, a Barbadian. It was the job of Ambassador Insanally to calm and quiet their hostile engagements.

Insanally was held in high regard by his colleagues, such that he was chosen by the CARICOM group to be their choice for the President of the General Assembly, in 1994, when the GRULAC had its chance to select the president. He went on to become Guyana's Minister of Foreign Affairs. Insanally is in many ways a detached, non-threatening, un-intrusive, soft-male personality whose very demeanor transmits calm. His counterpart to the USA and the OAS, Ambassador Odeen Ishmael is an intellectual type. His speeches were always lengthy and detailed, and his approach was always non-threatening and placid. Yet, he could hold his own well among any of the diplomats at the OAS and represented Guyana outstandingly. Ambassador Ishmael has been replaced by another diplomat whom the author does not know.

IX

Barbados and Its Diplomats

The most easterly of the islands in the Caribbean archipelago has deemed itself the place from which the smartest and the most bookish of the Caribbean peoples have come. It has also produced several of the most talented sportsmen ever in the world of cricket. On November 30, 1966, it declared its independence and set about to make its place in history, again. Barbados was peopled by about 200,000 souls then and was among the smallest of states in the world. Yet, it took its seat at the UN, and later the OAS, and began dispatching diplomats to a few capitals.

Barbados had a better start than many of its neighbors, principally on account of its topography. It is very flat and easily accessible by sea. It has had an airstrip since 1935. Barbados has achieved very high human development, consistently. In 1990, when the UN commenced a complex measurement device called the Human Development Index, Barbados was ranked 20th in a world of 169 states. Its economic success is unassailable, largely on account of its high literacy rate, its low rate of incarceration and negligible lawlessness. Those characteristics are the direct result of democratic ideals put into practice, stability born of high employment, and migration which allowed an outward flow of its excess.

Though thousands of her sons and daughters have migrated to the US, the UK and Canada since the end of World War II, Barbados had long ago exported teachers and policemen to other Caribbean countries, to colonies (then states) in Africa and, in recent years, nurses to the USA. Barbados is a model for small states, though several non-independent Caribbean countries have outperformed her utilizing their available means.

Barbados' diplomacy has been cautious but not quite unremarkable. When the author arrived in New York in August 1988, a very kind and feisty lady named Nita Barrow served as its Ambassador to the UN. She was a candidate for the President of the General Assembly, but was edged out by the foreign minister of Argentina, Dante Caputo. After acceding to the presidency, the Assembly learned of certain improprieties by the Argentine diplomat causing him to lose his job as foreign minister. Ambassador Barrow, on the other hand, went on to become her country's head of state, Governor General of Barbados. She would have been a better Assembly President.

Besley Maycock replaced the matronly and gregarious lady, and was best known for his mastery of the UN budget. He was not an intellectual type though he was very well-informed and extremely sensitive to slights. Maycock differed greatly from another Barbadian diplomat named Orlando Marville whom the author first encountered in Washington, in 1985, and then again as a special CARICOM/UN special rapporteur for Haiti. Marville spoke many languages, including Danish, and was unashamedly impressed with his abilities. He caused the Haitians a great deal of pain when he declared that there was much amiss about an election which he monitored; there was merely a disagreement over the interpretation of a statute. But his ruling led to a crisis in Haiti that was very costly to the region. One could nevertheless find that Barbados played its part in helping to bring freedom to the Haitian masses. Foreign Minister Billie Miller even led a CARICOM group of foreign ministers to Haiti after Aristede's second ouster in 2004, helping to calm the situation in a volatile Haiti.

One of the most remarkable intellectuals which the author encountered during his fifteen year diplomatic sojourn was Courtney Blackman, Barbados' Ambassador to the USA and the OAS during the final five years of the last century. He was appointed the first black Governor of the Barbados Central Bank, in 1970, a few years after understudying an Englishman. Blackman was subsequently knighted for his superb management of the country's financial resources. Ambassador Blackman was a marginally impressive diplomat since he is very slow in articulating his ideas. He was therefore not the best of public speakers; paradoxically, he is undoubtedly among the best raconteurs that this author has encountered. Whatever his shortcomings, Blackman was sound in his understanding of international politics and a good judge of character. He hated to be outdone by any of his colleagues, and frequently told the story of being an equal of the Barbadian Director of the Pan American Health Organization, Dr. George Alleyne, during their years as teenagers. Blackman did challenge the US publicly during a preparatory session for the Quebec Summit. In retaliation, one of their operatives reported to his prime minister that he was embarrassing

Barbados at the OAS; it deeply hurt Ambassador Blackman for it was not true. The lesson which he learned was that if you pick a fight with a US diplomat, not on some principle but as a show of superior knowledge, be prepared to be dethroned. Dr. Blackman also wrote several books, the most renown dwells on central banking; it is a collection of speeches and papers which he had delivered over several years.

Michael King replaced Courtney Blackman in Washington. King is remembered for his role in delaying adoption of the Inter-American Democratic Charter which is recalled in chapter seven. Barbados' neighbor can attest to the consequences of quashing democratic ideals, acting very much like a South American dictatorship.

X

Grenada and Its Diplomats

In 1979, five years following the independence of Grenada, an unusual political development took place. A group of youthful politicians took up arms against their government during the absence of its Prime Minister, Eric Gairy. They seized power and declared themselves the People's Revolutionary Government (PRG) of Grenada. The leader, Maurice Bishop, declared himself the Prime Minister and set Grenada on a path hostile to the USA, friendly to the USSR and embracive of Cuba.

Grenada's new prime minister attended several CARICOM Heads' meeting during the period of his leadership and was confronted by Prime Minister Vere C. Bird of Antigua and Barbuda or Foreign Minister Lester Bird. "You must hold general elections and allow the people of Grenada to decide whether they wish you or someone-else to lead them," Bishop was told. Eventually, this became the position of CARICOM, though the regional body would not expel or suspend Grenada as others wished. It is worth noting that following the ouster of President Aristede of Haiti on February 29, 2004, the CARICOM Heads suspended Haiti from the CARICOM until democracy was restored.

In 1979, Grenada posed a serious challenge to the English-speaking leaders' view of themselves as freedom-loving democrats. It was difficult to reconcile the military rule of Grenada with the democratic ideals which the English-speaking Caribbean embraced. Grenada's hostility to the USA was also way out of step with the approach that the newly independent island-states had pursued with their giant neighbor to the north. The USA is the very best friend of the CARICOM states.

Many English-speaking leaders hold Fidel Castro of Cuba in high esteem for being able to challenge the USA, for placing his island-country at the forefront of a battle between the two superpowers, and for playing such a significant role in Southern Africa's liberation from Portuguese colonialism and apartheid. Yet, they would not replicate his leadership style in their countries. Those leaders failed to understand why Bishop chose to act like Castro and why Grenada chose to be hostile to the USA. General elections in Grenada would have partially solved the US/Grenada impasse and the CARICOM/Grenada denouement. It appears in hindsight that currents within the PRG of Grenada forbade Maurice Bishop from taking the necessary steps to fix the problem.

At the OAS in Washington, Ambassador Lake of Antigua and Barbuda, throughout 1982 and 1983, would make Grenada's ambassador know that her government's legitimacy was not established. Lake would complain that she had a point of view on every subject and was most often wrong.

As we now know, Grenada was invaded by the English-speaking Caribbean Regional Security System (RSS) states and the USA, in October 1983, after Maurice Bishop was murdered and hundreds of innocent Grenadians were killed by mad thugs posing as a government. Many persons think of the action as US-led. In fact, were it not for the uncompromising urgings of the CARICOM leaders, especially Dame Eugenia Charles of Dominica, who turned to the US -and not to Britain- for support, President Reagan may not have been inclined to act. It was also fortuitous that the USA needed a victory, coming on the heels of 229 murdered marines in Lebanon. The Grenada invasion provided the USA with an easy victory that temporarily erased the memory of its loss in the Middle East.

The Caribbean leaders needed to end the anti-democratic governance of Grenada, fearing that it might inspire the leftist movements in the other Caribbean countries to follow Bishop's model. The murder of Bishop provided the perfect opportunity to return Grenada to democracy. The creation of the RSS by treaty in 1982 was also precipitated by the anti-democratic Grenada experiment and the need to plan to counter the undemocratic ambitions of those who could not win elections.

The English-speaking Caribbean peoples consider themselves democrats, freedom-loving and just; no military coups or undemocratic governments can survive in these tiny island-states, and none has.

The author has served with four Grenadian Ambassadors that are worthy of note. Dr. Lemuel Stanislaus was a dentist who served his country at the UN after the 1983 invasion. He was avuncular and friendly to his colleagues, but he was an unrelenting foe of Cuba. In the Group of Latin American and Caribbean countries at the UN (known as GRULAC), Stanislaus would not yield an inch to Cuba. His successor was another New Yorker turned diplomat named Eugene Pursoo. Ambassador Pursoo was inventive though at times enigmatic. After Haitian President Aristede was ousted in 1991, Aristede came to the UN and addressed the GRULAC states. He asked for questions afterwards and Pursoo did question him. The ambassador wanted to know if Aristede would forego returning to Haiti if replaced by another elected leader. The question was out of step with the CARICOM position that Aristede had to be returned. No-one knew why he appeared hostile to Aristede.

Pursoo was nevertheless a friendly type though he appeared to have dictatorial tendencies. In 1993, he led a team of his UN colleagues to Grenada and to a series of meetings with young students. Many persons in Grenada have an abiding interest in foreign policy issues as a result of the traumatizing experience of the four-year experiment under Maurice Bishop, when Grenada was thrust into world headlines. Pursoo demitted office when his party lost elections, and he has since gone on to lecturing at the City University of New York.

Francis Xavier was Grenada's Ambassador to the OAS and the USA following the end of the revolutionary experiment. He was a journalist and a very clever man who hated to be marginalized. The author recalls him in Cartagena, Colombia, in 1985 at the OAS General Assembly. A threat to disrupt the Assembly by guerrillas who had assassinated judges of the Colombian Supreme Court shortly before the OAS meeting caused most delegates to express fear for their safety. Xavier was fearless. His statement before the Assembly also conveyed the same strength of character that Grenada, two years past the debacle, was displaying.

Denis Antoine, another member of Grenada's diaspora in the USA, serves as Ambassador to the USA and the OAS under the Keith Mitchell administration. He is probably the most experienced of Grenada's senior diplomats, having lasted more than 10 years. He and the author presented credentials to US President Bill Clinton at the White House on the same day in January 1996. Antoine is remembered for his erupting hostility in September 2001 when scores of diplomats were stuck in Peru following the attacks on the World Trade Centre by terrorists. The US closed all air traffic over its skies, and so there were no flights leaving Peru to take us back to Washington for several days. When flights did become available, the mad rush led many to jostle for inclusion. Antoine made his intent very clear to his colleague from St. Kitts and Nevis with glaring eyes, a loud voice and a threatening stance. As it turned out, we were all on the same flight and safely back in Washington by September 15, 2001. He is also remembered for making numerous interventions at the OAS General Assemblies over the years. His style is clearly intended to register Grenada's presence and to demonstrate that Grenada has a point of view. He, like Pursoo, could be persuasive and he was bold.

XI

The Bahamas and Its Diplomats

The material standard of living of the Bahamas stands in stark contrast to its neighbors, Haiti and Cuba. The main islands of Nassau and Freeport seem more like an extension of Miami, just a few miles away. Tourism and off-shore financial services account for its economic standing. The Bahamian leaders are terribly afraid that an unchecked flow of Haitian refugees, stopping off on their way to Miami, could endanger their choice lifestyle; about one-third of the population is made up of Haitian descendants and immigrants.

The Bahamas' early beginnings after 1776, when thousands of loyalists were expelled from the new country called the United States of America, made the Bahamians wary of large population movements. 8,000 loyalists made their way to the Bahamas with a greater number of their African slaves and developed a colony that still has the flavor of the black/white dichotomy of yesteryear. The African population exceeded the stock of Caucasians and so when adult suffrage became the law, the blacks outnumbered the whites and took control of the machinery of government.

Lynden Pindling led his country into independence in 1973, and the Bahamas have prospered since, recording economic growth every year in their 33 years of sovereignty. Sitting in such proximity to the giant, the Bahamas have always felt a pressing need to cooperate with the USA. Hence, when the USA accused the Bahamas of harboring tax cheats, the banking laws were changed to deflect the criticism. When drug traffickers attempted to use its waters to trans-ship the illegal substances to the USA, the Bahamas permitted US Coast Guard vessels to pursue the criminals in Bahamian waters.

The Bahamas sit at the feet of the giant and understand the crushing kick which they could be dealt. Yet, Bahamian Ambassadors have been relatively active in pursuing democratic ideals at the UN, the OAS and the Commonwealth. They have not allowed their superior economic status to deter them from meaningful debate and participation, at the ambassadorial level.

One of the first Bahamian diplomats encountered by the author was a giant of a man who once served as deputy prime minister under Pindling. As Ambassador to the UN, Sir Arlington Butler was unafraid of losing his assignment or being censured by his close political ally. He therefore gladly led his delegation to criticize US policy when the USA attempted to extend its law-making capability beyond its borders, attempting to disallow trade with Cuba. When US President Bill Clinton signed the Helms-Burton bill, which clearly contravened international law, criticism from the Bahamas was loud and clear. Cubana Airlines had regular services to the Bahamas and therefore transacted normal business in Nassau, like any other carrier. The Helms-Burton bill prohibited all craft that entered Cuban airspace or waters within a three month period from unloading at US ports. The Bahamians were very clear in their denunciation of this unlawful imposition, but this may have been because Butler was a man of great courage. He was also an Olympian and served as the fourth President of the Bahamas Olympic Association. No doubt, an Olympian, who stood more than six feet tall and weighed about 300 pounds, would be less afraid than a man smaller in stature.

The Bahamian Golden Girls athletes won gold for their small country in the 2004 Sydney Olympics, and will no doubt continue to impress the world with their prowess. Another outstanding diplomat from the Bahamas assigned to the UN was a priest who was also an elected member of parliament. He was Ambassador James Moultrie, a very kind man who saw moral elements in many of the challenges which the UN had to address. Moultrie was ably assisted by a dynamo of a woman, Missouri Sherman-Peters, whose high energy and indomitable will served the Bahamas well during her tenure. Moultrie was also one of the kindest diplomats that the author has encountered; he never wished to offend. He was replaced by a soft-spoken civil servant who was prepared to ensure that his children were educated and that the Bahamian chair was always occupied. Many of the Bahamian diplomats assigned to the UN seemed unwilling to risk speaking for fear of saying the wrong thing. Yet, among the English-speaking cadre, they were among the best trained.

In Washington, a young diplomat named Joshua Sears was assigned as Ambassador during much of the author's eight years. He was very quiet, almost shy; his wife was far more outgoing and unafraid. But Sears had talented staff who prepared his statements whenever he had to speak. When I served in Miami as Consul, a talented Bahamian named Mullins served as my counterpart. I gathered from my discussions with him that the Bahamas felt a strong appeal to the democratic urge, fuelled by racial discrimination. Later on when I served in Washington, I came to the conclusion that the traditions of the East Caribbean, of labor unions and sugarcane fields, of riots and radicals, had not been duplicated in the north though, in 1942, riots and labor unrest plagued the comfortable colony. It is of interest to note that the Bahamas are outside of the geographic Caribbean.

XII

Dominica and Its Diplomats

The most intensely forested of the Caribbean islands, virtually untouched since Columbus' visit in 1493, is Dominica. In order to distinguish itself from the Dominican Republic, where its mail is sent wrongly from time to time, it is properly known as the Commonwealth of Dominica. Capable of growing bananas, but unable to grow sugarcane, Dominica has never been a place from which great wealth emerged. Nevertheless, it has had a strong intellectual movement within, partly fuelled by its placement between Guadeloupe and Martinique, two French-speaking territories, where literacy is high and ideals are on the lips of many. Dominica became an independent country on November 3, 1978, ahead of its Leeward Island neighbors and despite its less developed status. Dominica had never felt a very strong connection to the UK, but rather to France. In fact, it has joined the group of Francophone states, a sort of counterpoint to the British Commonwealth of Nations. Dominica is trapped by geography, its development severely hampered by mountains and continuous rain. Its tourism, though based on its tropical ecology, is ironically hampered by both factors. Dominica's inability to accommodate large aircraft on its airstrips has also acted as a disincentive to further economic development.

Dominica's longest serving ambassador is a very well-off businessman named Frank Baron. He was Ambassador to the UN, the USA, the OAS and the UK all at the same time, and he lived in Dominica while others acted for him in those places. He was also the first Chief Minister of Dominica. Baron told the author a tale of his attendance at a White House Dinner, accompanying Dame Eugenia Charles, the Prime Minister, in 1983. US President Reagan asked the prime minister to name something which the USA could do for Dominica; she had been so vocal in support of the RSS/USA invasion of Grenada in that year that he wished to reward her. Baron whispered "rural electrification" into her ears. A few months later, the US Army Corps of Engineers sent in the helicopters and the high tension wire and the towers; within weeks, all of Dominica was receiving electricity. Years later, Baron told the author that he wished he had said "a 10,000 foot runway".

Rapid development has eluded Dominica precisely because it is unable to accommodate large aircraft at its airports, thus discouraging tourists from visiting for fear of flying on tiny airplanes. A large number of Dominica's citizens, possibly as many as one-quarter of its population, have migrated to other Caribbean countries, including

Antigua and St. Martin, Guadeloupe and Martinique. Dominica's development still has a long way to go, despite having nurtured several outstanding international civil servants.

Dominica once assigned Ambassador Swinburne Lestrade, an experienced and articulate former Director General of the Organization of East Caribbean States (OECS) Secretariat, to Washington for about one year. When the talent pool in Dominica proved too shallow, he was reassigned in order to fill a responsible post in the Ministry of Finance. It is interesting to note that the current President of the Commonwealth of Dominica, Nicholas Liverpool, is a very able lawyer who served on a UN War Trial Tribunal, served as the Chief Justice of the Caribbean Court of Appeals, and as Dominica's non-resident Ambassador to Washington for five years after Lestrade. Dominica still does not have a resident Ambassador to the OAS or the USA.

Because of her absence from the halls of the OAS, Dominica's record in support of democratic ideals has not been remarkable. Though, whenever present at the UN, Dominica can be counted on to vote with the CARICOM states. When Rosie Douglas was the Prime Minister of Dominica, he actually visited Washington and spoke at the Georgetown University. He praised Judy Rolle, the youthful diplomat who serves as charge d'affaires in Washington, during the absence of the non-resident ambassador. The author has frequently thought of Dominica, based on its policy of not assigning an ambassador to the New York and Washington posts, as a non-dues-paying union member who benefits from successful negotiations but who does not contribute resources to the union. For the record, Dominica pays its subscription to the UN and to the OAS with regularity and on-time.

XIII

St. Lucia and Its Diplomats

The embodiment of the best of St. Lucia's diplomats is found in the erstwhile Ambassador Edsel Edmunds. He served for such a long time in Washington that his term was second only to the Prince of Saudi Arabia, who was the Dean of the Washington diplomatic corps. Edmunds is an intellectual and a man of principles. The author encountered Ambassador Edmunds in 1985 during the author's nine-month stint as First Secretary in the Washington Embassy of Antigua and Barbuda. By the time of the author's second return in 1995, Edmunds had matured fully and knew the diplomatic landscape of Washington well. St. Lucia appeared to be the most dynamic of small countries, largely because of him. When his benefactor lost power in St. Lucia, Edmunds was replaced by a youthful female who had also worked with Edmunds in 1985. Ambassador Sonia Johnny may not have brought the depth of experience of her predecessor but she is certainly a very urbane diplomat. Rather than focus on what many may regard as esoteric interests, she set out to win scholarships and other kinds of tangible benefits for her country's citizens.

OAS Ambassador of Venezuela, Layne of St. Vincent, Hurst, Johnny of St. Lucia, and Chris Thomas,2000 (Photo by Edwards)

St. Lucia has produced two Nobel Prize Winners in less than fifteen years. Arthur Lewis won a prize for economics in 1979; and Derek Walcott won a prize for literature in 1992. It is rational to conclude that the laureates represent the tip of the St. Lucian intelligentsia, concealing a learned mass of iceberg-St. Lucia in its population of 140,000 citizens. The two Nobel laureates are the amalgam of several countries' efforts and sheer genius which Arthur Lewis and Derek Walcott possessed and exposed, by studying and lecturing in Trinidad and the USA. St. Lucia nurtured them, however.

St. Lucia has produced several colorful personalities. The St. Lucian Ambassador to the UN, George Odlum was the most colorful. He chose to seek election to parliament on the opposition party's ticket while on temporary leave from his government assignment; it was indeed one of the oddest moments in the history of Caribbean politics and democracy. How can one represent a government and still stand opposed to it? He was dutifully relieved of his responsibilities. Before that end came, Odlum was determined to leave a worthy legacy after having been unable to win a seat in the parliament despite many elections. He later won an election but did not achieve an outstanding record as St. Lucia's foreign minister. He was dismissed from that post a second time for his bellicose approach to his political superiors whom he wished so badly to replace. He has since died.

The Ambassador who followed was a very charismatic type. Julian Hunte actually sought and won the Presidency of the fifty-eighth General Assembly in 2003 while serving as Foreign Minister. That is a miracle given the demands of the office of President, and knowing the small staff which the St. Lucian Mission has available to it. Yet, St. Lucia and Mr. Hunte achieved this milestone, for which they are to be congratulated. The author is wary of applauding an achievement that merely earns status without a corresponding conferring of increased material benefits to those who pay the salaries. It is unwise to spend the scarce resources of one's small country on inflating the egos of its elites while giving short shrift to the bread and butter issues that are of concern to the citizens of that small country. A diplomat must show that s/he is able to transform the position sought-and-achieved into improved conditions at home; although, it is accepted that "man does not live by bread alone." The author applauds Hunte for transforming his leadership into tangible benefits for the region and his country.

St. Lucia is one of the few countries in the world where there exists a hybrid legal system consisting of the French Code and the British Common Law. What began as a compromise following Britain's defeat of France in the 1797 Caribbean war, has metamorphosed into a very unusual system that draws attention from scholars.

XIV

St. Vincent and the Grenadines and Its Diplomats

Ambassador Kingsley Layne of St. Vincent and the Grenadines was by far one of the smartest diplomats in the Caribbean diplomatic corps. He was known for writing and dispatching lengthy press releases in order to ensure that he would never be forgotten in St. Vincent. Layne believed that Caribbean integration was an essential element of his country's diplomatic ambitions; his Prime Minister had proposed a single, unitary state of the six states of the OECS. That idea was not acceptable to his other colleagues. Layne had, however, been employed by the OECS and was thus grounded in the creed of integration.

In Washington, Layne would give pertinent speeches in the halls of the OAS, filled with a genuine belief in the magnificence of the region, especially our adherence to democratic ideals. He suffered from a physical illness that would cause him to fall asleep, no matter how greatly he resisted. When he served as the Chairman of the OAS Inter-American Committee for Integral Development (CIDI), he was assigned a co-chair, just in case he fell off to sleep. He was relentless in his pursuit of Haitian development and could always be counted on to shepherd the institutions' many resolutions on Haiti. Layne was instrumental in dispatching Sandra George, a talented Vincentian diplomat, to Haiti as one of the members of the UN/OAS team following the establishment of the UNMIH mission; she spoke French, Spanish and Creole. Sadly, Sandra George died while there of an asthmatic attack.

One of the most embarrassing moments which the author experienced during his eight years in Washington was the day that several policemen came to the OECS House which is the joint edifice of five of the six embassies of the OECS states. The police handcuffed a Vincentian diplomat who was accused by the spouse of the Ambassador of threatening bodily harm. The author insisted that the police had no jurisdiction over the Embassy and ordered the police to remove the cuffs and to allow the diplomats to solve the disagreements among themselves. The event made the headlines in St. Vincent and greatly hurt those involved.

Hurst, OAS Secretary General Cesar Gaviria, and Ambassador Kingsley Layne, January 1996 (Photo by Edwards)

Following elections in 2001, Ambassador Layne was replaced by an OAS employee named Ellsworth John; Ralph Gonsalves became the new Prime Minister. John is an imposing six-foot tall male with a keen understanding of the operation of the institution for which he worked. He also once served in the same Mission to the OAS in Washington and therefore knew well the demands of the assignment. He was ably assisted by Fitz Bramble, an athletic Vincentian educator who himself has taken up an assignment in Suriname as the OAS representative there.

St. Vincent is a hilly island with very few flat plains sufficiently long to build a 10,000 foot runway. The end result has been an inability to develop a viable tourism industry, much like Dominica. The Grenadines, which is made up of small islands that are coral based, is very much a place of white sand and gently lapping waves. Their tourism potential is better, although there are no plains sufficiently long to accommodate a large jet. St. Vincent and the Grenadines has thus been dependent upon agricultural exports of bananas and arrowroot; it has experimented with assembly plants and clothing factories, with some degree of success, manufacturing exports to the USA.

There are fewer opportunities for economic growth and wealth-creation in St. Vincent than in Barbados, its geographic neighbor, and so there has developed a penchant for migration. Large numbers of

Vincentians live in Barbados, Trinidad, Antigua, the US Virgin Islands, New York, London and Toronto. They form nationalist associations that are very active and that help to smooth the passage of more of their country folk to these other countries. In Antigua, the Vincentians tend to become policemen, a necessary part of the guarantee of good governance, but a sure indication that scarce Vincentian Government resources are expended to produce professionals for another country; primary and secondary education are for free in St. Vincent.

XV

St. Kitts and Nevis and Its Diplomats

The smallest state-member of the UN in 1983 was a Caribbean country with a population of fewer than 50,000 and land size as large as Washington, D.C. Up until 1968, three islands made up the entity then known as St. Kitts, Nevis and Anguilla. The Anguillans protested the evident attempt to include them permanently in the mix, and they forcefully put the lone policeman on a boat and declared their preference to be a colony. The British sent in paratroopers and Anguilla received its wish in 1968. St. Kitts and Nevis became independent in September 1983 but not before Nevis wrote into the constitution its ability to declare itself free of St. Kitts if it chose to, by referendum. Thus far, Nevis has not been able to garner sufficient votes to win its separation from St. Kitts, and various attempts have been made to keep them together.

St. Kitts and Nevis named Billy Herbert, a well-off lawyer, as its first Ambassador to the UN after independence in 1983, but kept him in capital. The country purchased a piece of New York City real estate for its UN Mission and Consulate which is the wisest strategy for states to adopt given the likelihood of perpetual presence in New York. No Caribbean country achieved this milestone, though many purchased houses in New York's suburbs as homes for their ambassadors. When Ambassador Herbert disappeared during a boating trip one Sunday afternoon, he was replaced by another well-known lawyer and former prime minister named Lee Moore. In September 2006, a third lawyer and former attorney general named Delano Bart replaced one Mr. Christmas as the Ambassador from St. Kitts and Nevis to the UN.

An absent ambassador severely reduced the opportunity for St. Kitts and Nevis to exercise influence at the UN. It is not possible to show up once per year for two weeks, return to capital and leave the supporting staff to make effective representation. Dominica also practiced this absentee policy in New York and Washington to the detriment of its interests. In 2000, St. Kitts and Nevis fixed that deficiency permanently.

St. Kitts and Nevis did, however, dispatch to Washington during the Denzil Douglas first term as Prime Minister a very complex man named Osbert Liburd. He was by training a plant pathologist, having earned a Ph.D. at Cornell University in New York in this obscure subject. St. Kitts was a producer of sugar from cane, and his skills as an agronomist were useful to his country. However, Liburd liked politics more than agriculture and served as chairman of Douglas' party. He won the confidence of many diplomats by his extensive knowledge of the US stock market and the riches which could be earned from wise investments; but, he did not display an identical level of interest in the issues at the OAS. He objected to the OAS employing persons who moved from their missions to the OAS Secretariat; the number was so small it hardly mattered but he regarded his position as pure and sound. He was wrong! Liburd was an admirer of the US President Clinton and showed great interest in US domestic politics; he was eventually reassigned in 2001 though he regarded his forced return to capital as a betrayal.

Liburd's replacement was a psychiatrist named Izben Williams. He was the embodiment of the best in St. Kitts and Nevis, and an effective diplomat. Though he spoke in the halls of the OAS only when the moment required it, Ambassador Williams was quite articulate and inquisitive. He brought his considerable knowledge of human frailties to the corps and was frequently a sensible voice.

Williams had very good supportive staff in the person of Jasmine Huggins, a smart young lawyer who was deeply Christian and appeared morally too pure to want to be a diplomat. She was good at crafting speeches, just as her UN counterpart, a young lady named Yvonne Dascent. Kevin Isaac, another of the country's excellent diplomats in Washington, strengthened the multilateral and bilateral strengths of St. Kitts and Nevis especially through his proficiency in languages.

The diplomatic corps of the English-speaking Caribbean is especially deficient in foreign languages; that cannot continue. Ambassador Williams recognized this weakness and he asked the Mexican Ambassador to the OAS if Mexico could help to address this shortcoming. For a year, the Mexicans paid a tutor to teach Spanish to a score of English-speaking Caribbean diplomats in Washington. The author made full use of this training.

Kevin Isaac eventually transferred to the OAS following the election of Ambassador Albert Ramdin of Suriname to the post of Assistant Secretary General of the OAS, in 2005. Isaac became Ramdin's special adviser. If there is one lesson which all West Indians learn when they collaborate, it is that the strengths and intellectual capacity of talented people bear no relation to the size of their states; small states produce giants just as large states produce idiots (though small states produce fewer of the latter). It is of interest to note that St. Kitts and Nevis was the smallest UN member-state upon its entry in 1983 up until 1991 when San Marino and Monaco became members and snatched that title from it.

XVI

Suriname and Its Diplomats

Although Suriname is Dutch-speaking, its leaders have good reason to wish to be a member of a regional group despite the absence of independent Dutch-speaking Caribbean countries. Curacao, Aruba, St. Maarten, Saba and St. Eustatius are still colonies of Holland and can therefore not be relied upon to form a regional group of any weight. Although all the Caribbean is present in the Association of Caribbean States (ACS), including the non-independent countries, the need for a closer working relationship with sovereign states is necessary and enduring. It is exceedingly difficult in an age of regionalism to stand alone, sovereignty in hand notwithstanding. In multilateral institutions like the UN and the OAS, election of a country's diplomats to office can be made less likely by standing alone; worthy initiatives are not likely to receive support without expression of a regional group's endorsement; in times of crises, the ability to turn to one's regional partners enhances the probability of finding a solution.

For these reasons, the South Americans form the MERCOSUR, and the Central Americans have formed the CAFTA, the North Americans formed the NAFTA, and the Caribbean formed the CSME. Although these are trade and economic groupings ostensibly, they are a sound basis on which to rely for political support, especially in multilateral settings. Cuba sometimes stands alone, and for this reason has sought to align itself with the CARICOM group. Suriname has found great success by joining the CARICOM.

Ambassador Albert Ramdin, former Ambassador to the OAS from Suriname, was elected by the OAS to serve as the Assistant Secretary General of the OAS from 2006 to 2010. His reliance on the support of the other 13 CARICOM states was pivotal in Suriname's ambition to fill this slot, occupied by Trinidad and Tobago for ten years in the person of Ambassador Christopher Thomas. In fact, the person who occupied that post immediately prior to Ramdin was a US citizen whose election came as a result of the support by the bloc vote of the CARICOM. When Thomas' term was at an end, a Panamanian candidate and the US candidate were both vying for the second most important job at the OAS. Usually, a small Caribbean state candidate vies for this post since a glass ceiling exists which excludes small states' representatives from becoming the Secretary General, the top job at the OAS.

The CARICOM chose the US candidate for very pedestrian reasons, despite their Foreign Ministers' liking for the Panamanian candidate. Mexico protested bitterly that the OAS was now being managed by Colombia and the USA, two of the region's largest states, despite the unwritten rule that a small state must be assured a presence in one of the top posts at the hemispheric body. No-one doubted the capability of the US candidate; that is not the basis of a vote since only worthy candidates are put forward by their governments. The issue of country-size and fear of US domination haunt the OAS.

Suriname has also experienced undemocratic moments since its independence in November 1975. The military engaged in coups in 1980 and again in 1990. By joining the CARICOM, Suriname has sent a very powerful message to its military that it must behave like the militaries of the CARICOM states firmly under the control of the civilian, elected authorities. President Venetian has been fighting off challenges by Desi Bouterse both of a violent and electoral nature.

XVII

Belize and Its Diplomats

None among the English-speaking Caribbean states faces the complexity of challenges and security threats as does Belize. Once known as British Honduras, this (geographically) Central American country, nestled in between Mexico and Guatemala with the Caribbean Sea lapping at its shores, has a pending claim on its entire territory. Guatemala would wish to gobble it up, it seems, but the multilateral institutions and the political goodwill of its neighbors prevent such an outcome. It has sought and attained membership in the CARICOM, but it also seeks Central American friendship by membership in the Central American Integration System (CICA) which it has also won.

Belize may suffer from a split identity, the converse of the Dominican Republic. It has been a strong adherent of democracy while all around it dictatorships and civil wars raged. Having avoided those resource-consuming impediments, Belize is farther along on its way to development than are its geographic neighbors. However, its small population of 300,000 souls makes its task extremely difficult. Though geographically larger than all the English-speaking states except Guyana, Belize finds itself equally situated in international affairs as its tiny CARICOM brethren. Its missions abroad are small, its resource base is narrow, and its pool of professionals is as shallow as any island-country in the English-speaking Caribbean. Belize also suffers from hurricanes that have battered its tourism and agriculture with devastating effects in years prior to but especially in the 1990s.

It has dispatched to the UN, the OAS and the US, several very experienced and intelligent civil servants who have enhanced its image immensely. Belize dispatched to New York an intelligent and articulate woman named Ursula Barrow. Single, intelligent and pretty, it was one of the smartest decisions made by the new administration. She attracted more attention than any other ambassador, and so could thrust Belize into the limelight merely by showing up. She used her many skills artfully, and did in fact promote Belize's interests. One of her stumbling blocks was a Belizean colleague named Lawrence Sylvester who is very intelligent, well-read, and enormously confident. He was a little perturbed to have a female as his boss, the author thinks. So they warred all the time. Lawrence Sylvester was eventually transferred back to the Ministry of Foreign Affairs in the capital, Belmopan, and went on to become Ambassador to the UK. Ambassador Barrow was also transferred to the UK when her party regained power after a hiatus, and she has since married a Baron in England and is known as a Baroness something.

The author can especially recall Ambassador Carl Rogers, the former deputy prime minister, who served at the UN after Barrow until his party lost the 1993 elections. "Democracy brought me, and democracy takes me away," he said at his farewell luncheon at the UN. "Thank God for democracy," a friendly newcomer in the audience of diplomats quietly responded.

Ambassador Rogers was extremely close to the nationals of Belize who live in New York City, and he never failed to invite the author to his Belizean functions. Since Belize and Antigua and Barbuda became independent two months apart, both states felt the tug of sovereignty with equal weight. He invited all of his CARICOM/UN colleagues to accompany him to Belize in 1991 when The Airline of Central America (TACA) was making its inaugural flight from Kennedy JFK Airport to Belize City. When the author arrived at JFK Airport, Ambassador Rogers was saying farewell to a family of children and a spouse. When the entourage arrived in Belize City, another family of children and a spouse were there to greet him. He was a little more than 5 feet tall, but like Napoleon, Rogers could conquer most obstacles. He died about five years following his return to Belize, but his legacy lives on at the UN, and in Belize (the author is made to understand).

Replacing Rogers was a learned diplomat named Edward Laing. He served with distinction, bringing with him tremendous experience and a worthy resume. He became famous for accusing television, from the podium at the UN, of causing an increase in violence in many countries around the world. He went on to serve as a Judge on the Court of the Law of the Sea.

Yet another Belizean Ambassador with whom the author had the pleasure to serve was a lawyer assigned to the OAS and the US in Washington, in 1993. He was saddened by the frequency with which the Ambassadors from the CARICOM to the OAS put forward their names to serve only as Vice Presidents of the OAS Permanent

Committees. "We like far too much vice," he would mockingly assert. It led the author to seek to preside over several OAS Committees successfully during eight years at that posting.

He was replaced by James Murphy, a Belizean teacher of Irish stock who was once a Catholic priest. Murphy left the priesthood so that he could marry a pretty and affable woman of Chinese ethnicity. She subsequently bore him a child. "From father to fatherhood," one of his friends said to him.

Like all Belizean Ambassadors whom the author encountered, they left their postings littered with intelligent quips that have been shared with countless audiences. Ambassador Murphy was replaced by Lisa Shoman, a fiercely intelligent lawyer who was impatient with diplomatic niceties. She brought the OAS into the Belize/Guatemala border dispute, and almost scored a success when elections in Guatemala put the two states back to square one. She is still serving in Washington and regularly makes interventions on democracy issues to the benefit of the OAS member states.

Each of the states and countries reviewed in this chapter has contributed meaningfully to Caribbean integration and in varying degrees to the democratic ideals that are held so dear by the Caribbean peoples. Haiti has had the greatest impact, both because of its history and its recent crises. Cuba, standing on a threshold as its revolution ages and its leader passes on, is the most problematic. There is no telling what will result, chaos or community of action among the CARICOM and Cuba. The overall impact of the English-speaking group on global politics is far above the region's geographic size, its economic worth, its military assets. The entire region's contribution is outstanding, the author asserts, and enables the Caribbean to claim a special place in the enhancement of democratic ideals and freedom globally.

CHAPTER THREE

THE ANTIGUAN DIPLOMATS AND THEIR ISSUES

Antigua's diplomacy has been characterized by a boldness born of the struggle against mighty forces. Vere C. Bird, Lionel Hurst Sr., Denfield Hurst, Ernest Williams, Edmund Lake, McChesney George, Novel Richards and the other so-called 1939ers formed the vanguard of the struggle against colonialism in Antigua and against the dictatorship of the privileged, monied few. These leaders lent a personality to future politicians, diplomats and even cricketers that lasts even today. Accustomed to fighting powers greater than themselves, the Antigua and Barbuda person has repeatedly sought to find the Achilles heel of the greater antagonist, exploit that weakness, and then proceed to attack the weakest points along a continuum.

EH Lake, Lionel Hurst Sr., Frederick Lee, Secretary of State for the Colonies, VC Bird in 1966 outside Ministry, London. (Photo from the Lionel Hurst Sr. archives)

In world affairs, our approach is similar. Antigua and Barbuda's small size leads inexorably to comprehending the world and seeing events with lenses that differ markedly from the large state's world view. The large state is frequently persuaded that it can shape events and compel outcomes; it has the economic and military resources to make its diplomatic will felt. A small state, like Antigua and Barbuda must shield itself from the harmful fallout of major events while seeking to exploit those weaknesses that will lead to an enhancement of its material well-being and its security. The diplomacy practiced by Antigua and Barbuda during its 25 years as an independent country has been bold and clever, precise and careful, assertive and informed. The intellectual capacities of its practitioners contributed in no small way.

I

The Antigua and Barbuda Diplomats

Antigua and Barbuda did not have professional diplomats when independence dawned. The country had opened a single office in New York in 1972 for promoting tourism and trade but not for diplomatic representation. Prior to November 1981, an Antigua and Barbuda national living in New York or Toronto who wished to renew his/her passport had to go to the British Consulate there and would receive a British passport. Upon attaining independence, Antigua and Barbuda Consulates and Embassies and Missions were for the first time established.

Lester Bird became the first Foreign Minister and was instrumental in selecting the first generation of diplomats. They were all known supporters of the ruling Antigua Labor Party (ALP) and could therefore be deemed political appointees. In large, long-established states, there are career diplomats who attend diplomatic school and take complex exams before being assigned or dispatched abroad. The young state of Antigua and Barbuda had no such assets available to it, though the UWI Graduate Institute of International Affairs on the campus at St. Augustine, Trinidad, provided some training to several civil servants who would subsequently serve abroad. In 1981, however, the foreign minister made his selections based on a mix of criteria.

E.H. Lake

Antigua and Barbuda's first ambassador to the OAS and the USA, appointed in 1981, was a trade unionist/politician named Edmund Hawkins Lake. Like Prime Minister Vere C. Bird who appointed him ambassador, Lake was a messianic figure. He was born in 1912 and grew up in an era when Britain was the world's superpower; he entered into adulthood when voting in elections required property and literacy tests, which a young Lake at first could not meet; and he lived through the early twentieth century when the blacks of Antigua were still living as virtual slaves. As a schoolboy, he too used to sing:

> *Rule Britannia, Britannia rules the waves*
> *Never, never, never, never shall we be slaves.*

Lake was a democrat to his soul, having experienced first-hand some of the worst oppression of his colonial overlords, fought to overcome them, and learned to hate dictatorship. He frequently told his OAS colleague-ambassadors that he preferred not to sit next to ambassadors appointed by governments that were not lawfully elected by their peoples. Antigua and Barbuda is seated next to Argentina at the Organization of American States, and sits in regional groupings with Grenada whose government, up until 1983, came to power by a non-violent coup in 1979. Given his frequent interventions on democracy and its practice, he was regarded as the moral conscience of the OAS at a time when dictators ruled in Latin America and several Caribbean states. All of those dictators were coddled by Washington, except for Fidel Castro of Cuba and Maurice Bishop of Grenada; the latter were hostile to the USA but the other illegitimate leaders served the US interests.

Take Pinochet of Chile. It was a US Secretary of State who said that though he was a son-of-a-bitch, "he is our son-of-a-bitch." He overthrew President Allende who was legitimately elected in a state that knew only free and fair elections; the coup plotters relied on the collaboration with and approval of the USA. The hemisphere's lone superpower could not obtain the support of tiny Caribbean countries for its actions then or now, as it compelled Latin America support back then.

The USA, during and following the tenure of Ambassador Lake at the OAS, was confronted by English-speaking Caribbean diplomats whose collective instructions are to remain the moral conscience of the hemisphere and to continue to take the moral high-ground on democracy. Cheerleading for democracy is not merely a policy option but a visceral response to history, and the determination to ensure the survival of their countries for as long as the nation-state system exists. Once there is democracy among states, the extermination of tiny, defenseless states is not likely, as we shall see.

Edmund Hawkins Lake, as the first person to receive an instrument of appointment, naming him Ambassador to the USA and the OAS, in November 1981, set the tone of our diplomacy. His service to his country had a long history. At 33 years, he was selected by the nascent trade union movement to seek a seat in the Legislature. After proving that he had property valued at more than $500 and that he was literate, Lake was elected to the Legislative Council in 1946 and had to endure the dictates of the British Governor. All major decisions prior to the Cabinet form of government in 1956 and a quasi-statehood arrangement in 1967, were confirmed or denied by the Colonial Office in London, and the decision transmitted to Antigua. Lake hated that arrangement and longed for the opportunity to make important decisions without encumbrances. The story is told of Edmund Lake and Vere C. Bird stealthily arranging for the building of a secondary school in Antigua without the knowledge of the British in 1955, and repeating the same in the construction of a post office building in 1960.

Lake lost the election to parliament in 1971 and migrated to Canada shortly thereafter, triggered by a public taunting of his school-age daughter. Lake knew how vicious oppositional politics can become and sought to protect his family. Yet, he never abandoned Antigua; he merely waited for a cooling-off and a new opportunity to serve. When independence dawned, he was among the most experienced of public servants in that cadre. He was one of the non-lawyers who wrote the 1981 Constitution of Antigua and Barbuda which survives up until today; and he was a significant player in writing advanced constitutions since 1951. Lake was very intelligent, knew the weak points of the

American giant, and would exploit them at every opportunity after he was appointed Ambassador to the USA and the OAS. He retired upon the urgings of his wife who longed to live in her own house in Antigua. Upon his death in 2005 at age 93 he was accorded a state funeral. He was as intrepid as a Zulu warrior during his entire public life.

Novel Richards

Novel Richards was cosmopolitan in appearance and with an intellect to match. He served in the parliament of the *West Indies Federation* after its founding in 1958, displaying a sound understanding of inter-state relations. Richards was appointed Antigua and Barbuda's first Ambassador to Canada following independence. He was instrumental in persuading the Canadians to build schools in Antigua, long before November 1981. Novel Richards is hardly remembered for serving as his country's envoy in Canada, at any rate; the Ottawa appointment did not then and does not now carry a great deal of status. He wanted to live there, it seems. Richards is remembered for writing the national anthem of Antigua and Barbuda, for writing the history of the trade union movement in Antigua and Barbuda in a famous treatise entitled *The Struggle and The Conquest,* and for writing several books of poetry. Novel Richards' legacy is a national treasure; his account of the early years of the trade union movement in Antigua and Barbuda will cause him to live on in history. He died while in office, having suffered a heart attack during a funeral for one of the trade-union stalwarts in Antigua. His son, Conrad Richards was appointed to fill his post in Ottawa. Unfortunately, Conrad died suddenly while exercising at home, two years later, and before he could make his mark.

Lloydstone Jacobs

Lloydstone Jacobs was appointed as Antigua and Barbuda's first Ambassador to the UN in 1981. He was an extremely intelligent educator who was very unconventional. He earned his bachelor's degree at the University of Puerto Rico, and a master's degree from Columbia University in New York, both in education. He served as the principal of the century-old Antigua Grammar School (AGS), which was the institution that attracted the brightest sons of Antigua (by exam only), before being appointed to head the New York Office after 1976. The AGS prided itself on producing good football and cricket teams. Jacobs' stint at Columbia University also taught him how schools increase their attractiveness by excellent varsity teams. He witnessed Vivian Richards, then a student at the neighboring St. John's Boys School, batting during a cricket match and was impressed. He walked on to the cricket field, took young Richards to his AGS that afternoon, and enrolled him as an AGS student immediately. Vivian Richards went on to become the captain of the West Indies Cricket Team and is known for making 100 runs in the shortest possible time in the history of test cricket. Jacobs was unconventional and willing to break rules in order to succeed. He did in fact break the rules once too often during the seven-year period he served as Antigua and Barbuda's first Ambassador to the UN. Jacobs' most important contribution to his UN posting was his role in speaking out against apartheid in South Africa. He helped to secure Antigua and Barbuda passports for South African freedom fighters who needed to travel abroad but who were prohibited by law from receiving the passports of their own country.

Ron Sanders

Although a presence was required in London, following independence, the Antigua and Barbuda Government chose to participate in a joint diplomatic mission in London that comprised diplomats from several East Caribbean states. Antigua opted out later on when it determined that to stand alone would serve its interests better. Ron Sanders, a Guyanese journalist who had won the confidence of Foreign Minister Lester Bird, became the second person to serve as High Commissioner to London in 1984. Ron Sanders had come to Antigua at the invitation of Brigit Harris, then responsible for the Antigua and Barbuda Broadcasting Services. He impressed Lester Bird with his writings and his penchant for intrigue, and was rewarded with a posting abroad of his choosing. He wanted to earn college degrees, also. Ron Sanders was one of those diplomats who believed that a small state had to be selective in the issues it pursued at the UN and the (British) Commonwealth of Nations. He was instrumental in selecting the defense of Antarctica, and the security concerns of small states, as issues to be pursued by the second generation of Antigua and Barbuda's diplomats. He served until 1987 as High Commissioner in London when a falling-out between Prime Minister VC Bird and Foreign Minister Lester Bird led to his recall. He was re-appointed in 1995 and served until the UPP was elected in 2004. Sanders will go down in history as the only person who has been awarded two knighthoods. He is a prolific writer and has penned a worthy publication entitled *Crumbled Small* that relates the region's woes in their relations with the OECD, especially the states of Europe.

James Thomas

James Thomas, an Antiguan oil executive, was appointed the third Ambassador to the UK in 1987. Thomas is a very intelligent man who speaks carefully and is very well informed. His father was a talented carpenter who did his best to educate his children and to change the social conditions in Antigua that caused so many to be poor. James Thomas is a scholar from Oxford University, dapper and very judicious in his pronouncements. His tenure in London lasted for eight years making him the longest serving Ambassador in the UK, at the time. Many states change ambassadors after three years; given Antigua and Barbuda's narrow resource base, both human and material, the leaders decided against such a course of action.

Ambassadors Hurst and Thomas in Guyana 1992 at CARICOM Heads Meeting (Photo by Murdoch)

Thomas' long tenure caused him to be appointed the Dean of the Diplomatic Corps in London, to the chagrin of many large states' representatives. The Dean performs many protocolory functions and is a position desired by the Ambassadors from the large states. Thomas was therefore a very high-profile High Commissioner who was very adept at his profession; but several of his colleagues wished to replace him. The British asked the Prime Minister of Antigua and Barbuda to allow another diplomat to serve so that Thomas would no longer be the Dean. The Prime Minister did not oblige. When Lester Bird became the Prime Minister, he re-instated his friend Ron Sanders and dispatched Thomas to the Ministry Headquarters in St. John's. The shift came shortly after Hurricane Luis in September 1995.

Patrick Lewis

Dr. Patrick Lewis, an outstanding intellectual who had taught at one of the USA's outstanding black colleges, was named the country's second Ambassador to the USA and the OAS. He served in Washington from 1992 until 1995. During that time, he made outstanding contributions to the question of hemispheric security, a debate which Canada introduced to the OAS. Lewis was quite content with his posting when a reshuffle took place under Prime Minister Lester Bird; it led him back to New York as our third Ambassador to the UN until 2004. Lewis had served at the Antigua and Barbuda UN Mission for several years and in the Ministry of Foreign Affairs during the early years of independence. During his tenure at the UN as Ambassador, he demonstrated a firm understanding of the issue of the development challenge faced by small island-states, having introduced the subject to the OAS during his earlier assignment at multilateral body. Lewis had championed the protection of Antarctica, at the UN, and freedom from Morocco for the Saharawi people, during his first years at the UN. His leadership among his regional colleagues at the OAS was outstanding. He was invited to the OAS twice, following his appointment to the United Nations, to address the OAS Hemispheric Security Committee on the subject of security. Lewis is back in Virginia as the head of a department in a highly regarded black college.

John Ashe

Dr. John Ashe became the country's fourth Ambassador to the United Nations upon the election of the United Progressive Party to a majority in Government in 2004. Ashe had served as Minister Counselor at the Mission since 1989; he was appointed as Ambassador for environmental issues in 1996, and thus brought a great deal of experience to the UN posting when appointed to lead it. Ashe and the author served simultaneously, positioning Antigua and Barbuda as a leader on environmental issues. He is a very intelligent scholar who earned a Ph.D. at the University of Pennsylvania studying science. His strongest skill, however, is in pursuing non-paying posts at the UN. He has served as the Chairman of the Sustainable Development Conference in 2003, which is quite an honor, and chaired the 2005/06 Fifth Committee of the 60th UN General Assembly. He was also elected to serve as the Chair of *the Group of 77 and China* commencing September 2007 to 2008.

Deborah-Mae Lovell

The first female appointed to serve as Ambassador to the USA and the OAS is Deborah-Mae Lovell. She is a seasoned diplomat having served in London, Ottawa, Washington and New York before being elevated to her most important assignment in 2004.

Professor Gisele Isaac, Bernie Isaac, Deborah Lovell, Lionel Hurst, Dr. Nelson in Washington, Nov. 1996. (Photo by Edwards)

She is the shortest person who has ever been appointed to the exalted position of Ambassador, but her stature has not stood in the way of her leadership. She did spend seven years as the understudy of the author, and she underwent the best training a diplomat could receive by her many postings. Ambassador Lovell also spent training time at the UWI campus in Trinidad at the Graduate Institute of International Studies.

Lionel Hurst

The second person to be appointed Ambassador to the UN, in 1988, or seven years after independence, is the author. Long before independence, Hurst had determined that Antigua and Barbuda would become a member of the UN; it would then require diplomats, and so he set about to prepare himself to represent his country at the premier multilateral institution. He earned three college degrees, including a specialty in international law and a master's degree in international business. Hurst was fortunate to be brought into the government's service in 1985, when the Antigua Labor Party was still in an ascendant position. After serving in capital, he was first assigned to Washington; nine months later, in May 1986, Hurst was transferred to Miami to set up, open and manage a trade mission. The Caribbean Basin Initiative under President Ronald Reagan promised a windfall in manufacturing opportunities in the Caribbean; it turned out to be a dud. Hurst was transferred back to Antigua after six months to lead the re-development of the capital, St. John's, serving as the first Executive Director of the St. John's Development Corporation. Six months later, he was back again in Miami, this time to a mission that was transformed into an Antigua and Barbuda Consulate. While serving in Miami, in 1988, the incumbent UN Ambassador Jacobs encountered difficulty and was asked to demit office. Hurst was appointed to fill that slot at age 37 years.

Colin Murdoch, Lionel Hurst and Patrick Lewis, September 1995, New York (Photo by Edwards)

It was quite an honor, for UN Ambassadors are the most senior of diplomats within their service. Hurst was simply intelligent and energetic, bold and unafraid, honest and plain spoken. The foreign minister recognized those traits and gave him an opportunity to prove his worth. He served for seven years in New York and then was transferred to Washington where he served for eight years. Hurst resigned in order to seek a seat in the parliament; he lost that bid in the elections of 2004, turned to hosting a radio talk show and writing articles for newspapers. The ALP secretariat was thankful for his writing skills during the two years after his electoral defeat.

II

The Supporting Staff

While the ambassadors determine the diplomatic direction of the embassy or mission, it is the supporting staff who set the level of efficiency. The Ambassador of St. Vincent and the Grenadines to the USA spent more than a half-hour in the presence of the first George Bush, when he went to present credentials to the US President. Usually, the ceremony is a five-minute exercise undertaken out of tradition and courtesy by the US President these days, and less out of a genuine attempt to welcome the holder of the office to the recipient's capital. At any rate, the extended time spent with Kingsley Layne is attributable to Bush's love of sailing and his unforgettable experience exploring the Grenadines; Bush was also a former US Ambassador to Japan. He offered newly appointed Ambassador Layne a piece of advice that was shared and which remains with the author. "There are three persons whom you must treat with great care: 1. your driver; 2. your cook; 3. your secretary." These three staff members hold your life and your success in their hands, he reportedly told Ambassador Layne, and are deserving of more thoughtful care than even one's adult children. Those are words of wisdom by which any ambassador can live.

There were no West Indian schools of diplomacy to prepare civil servants to fill the diplomatic posts abroad, following the independence of the island-states of the Caribbean. The UWI would establish its School of International relations in 1966, in Trinidad. But, the British had not invited any of our civil servants into their embassies, consulates or missions before independence; nor had the British opened their Foreign Service Institute to the colonies. The Caribbean countries had to learn from others who had gone before and to invent, which is one of our strongest cultural traits despite being labeled as "Mimic Men" by a well-known author.

In 1962, Jamaica had gone about the task of establishing a foreign service and foreign ministry that duplicated, in many ways, the arrangements of a large country. After the 1979 coup in Grenada, a similar model was adopted by the People's Revolutionary Government of Grenada, under Prime Minister Bishop. Trinidad and Tobago still retains all of the trappings of a large state's Ministry of Foreign Affairs. So that by 1981, when Antigua and Barbuda set out on this un-chartered course called independence, there were many models and styles that could have been adapted. Antigua and Barbuda chose simple and low-cost arrangements best suited to a tiny state.

One of the first persons whom Ambassador Lake in Washington recruited was a young lady named Gracelyn Henry. She had worked with two outstanding lawyers in Antigua and could manage an office with little help. She was also a very diligent and highly reliable person whom the Ambassador made responsible for the issuance of passports and the management of the Embassy's scarce resources. Dispatched from Antigua, she was appointed Consul and fills that function twenty-five years later. Dawn Antonio, who joined Consul Henry and Ambassador Lake at the Washington Embassy, would be dispatched to serve as the Ambassador's executive secretary. She was perpetually dissatisfied and was thus very close to being a perfectionist. Nothing left her desk that was not perfectly executed. Like Consul Henry, she regarded the employment opportunity abroad as a sort of work/scholarship and they each pursued higher education, earning college degrees and other professional certifications.

Hurst, Ambassador Christopher Thomas- Assistant Secretary General, Paul Spencer at the OAS 1996 (Photo by Edwards)

Paul Spencer later joined the Embassy as the second diplomat there. He took a liking to the empty gestures that characterized the OAS prior to 1991; although, the OAS did distribute small sums for projects and a few scholarships each year. Spencer enjoys intrigue and alliances; he likes to trade support in exchange for tangible diplomatic gains. He also likes gossip. Spencer now works for the OAS as a country representative in St. Lucia. Back in 1983, Spencer focused his efforts on the US Congress as well as the OAS, for the USA was increasingly interested in Antigua and Barbuda and the other East Caribbean independent states following the Grenada coup of 1979. The 1983 passage of the Caribbean Basin Initiative (CBI) by President Reagan would provide a sound reason to spend many hours "on the hill" and at the US State Department exchanging notes with the Caribbean Desk Officer.

Following the September 11, 2001 terrorist attack on the USA, the Congress made a passport mandatory for those US citizens returning to the USA following a Caribbean vacation. It was customary for Americans to rely on driver's licenses and other identification to re-enter following holidays in the Caribbean. The passport requirement places Caribbean tourism in some jeopardy after January 29, 2007; so, the diplomats have been pestering the Congress and the State Department to grant delays in implementation. The cruise tourism sector has persuaded the US Congress to delay implementation until January 2009, but not those persons traveling by aircraft. Two diplomats with responsibility for interacting with Congress are females. Ms. Anne-Marie Layne and Miss Joydee Davis are the supporting diplomats at the Washington Embassy at the time of writing; they worked at the Ministry of Foreign Affairs, are civil servants not political appointees, and are very intelligent and well-trained diplomats. They replaced Starret Greene who served as the Deputy Chief of Mission during my tenure there. He was a meticulous and prolific producer of papers. His skill at writing must have encouraged him to type, or he typed often because he could write. He was also a very good pianist and played music for a church in Washington, on Sundays. He has since been appointed to represent the OAS in St. Kitts and Nevis, and is doing a superb job. Times have changed, in 25 years. Ambassador Lake employed a driver, back in 1981. Twenty-five years later, Rahaman Aziz is still the driver/receptionist and fix-it person at the Embassy of Antigua and Barbuda in Washington.

At the Mission to the UN, Lloydstone Jacobs inherited a staff whose focus was tourism and trade promotion up until 1981. David Fernandez is probably the longest serving public servant abroad, having been enticed to join the office in 1973, one year after the opening. He is a handsome and charming man who found his calling promoting Antigua and Barbuda to well-to-do Americans and travel agents. Fernandez is part Portuguese, slender and tall. He was in many ways the embodiment of the young country. He was finally retired rather involuntarily one year after the UPP came to power, in 2005. Dornella Seth was brought on board after 1981 and also served until the UPP came to power. She served as clerical staff until Ambassador Jacobs demitted office, and then as Ambassador Hurst's executive secretary.

Seth was encouraged to enhance her qualifications in order to transform her status into a diplomat. She must be congratulated for earning both bachelor and master degrees, and becoming a diplomat assigned to the UN. Conrod Hunte has had a similar history; encouraged to transform himself into a diplomat, he went from being the Mission's accountant to being a professional, employed by the UN and the Mission, and was appointed an Ambassador in 2006. Aqeelah Akbar is a very talented and intelligent young woman whom I asked to join our staff when the need arose to add one other person. She was unlike all the other staff members in that she was born on Barbuda. Poised and eloquent, she represented Antigua and Barbuda at the UN well, especially on issues pertaining to gender. Glentis Thomas came into the mission as a driver, completed his first degree and has moved up to being a diplomat. Victor Carmichael was the elder statesman in our New York Office, working alongside Fernandez to promote tourism. He was one of the most charming persons the author has ever known. His style and self-assuredness were the perfect ingredients in serving his nation as a promoter of tourism. Another personality was Telbert King. He was brought on by Ambassador Jacobs in 1985 to promote investment. He was marginally interested in his function though he had earned a degree from New York University in economics. King eventually left the mission's employ, returned to Antigua, where he runs a fairly successful business.

Fernandez, Burton, Hunte, Knowles, Hurst, Thomas, Lewis, Francis, Edwards, Ashe, Gomes (standing) Carmichael, Seth, Akbar (seated) Photo taken in 1989 of NY Office staff and nationals who visit frequently. (Photo by Edwards)

Karen Knowles, once a Carnival Queen who possesses charm and poise, was also appointed to serve at the New York Mission in tourism promotion. She was very good at interaction with the national community and served as the de jure Consul, examining passport applications and safely dispatching them to Washington for completion. She too completed at least one college degree during her tenure. She left the Mission just before 2003 and then returned shortly after the UPP became the government in 2004. She is very talented.

Several nationals visited our New York Office quite frequently and were treated like staff. Venetta Burton worked at the Hyatt Regency in New York and was integral to our visiting delegations, securing rebates that saved us thousands of dollars over the years. Johnny Gomes, who worked for Shell in the Rockefeller Center, was also a frequent visitor who brought his musical skills to bear at the UN where he played the steelpan on several occasions. The BWIA staff, located on the first floor of 510 Fifth Avenue, were frequent visitors upstairs and also integral to our travel plans. We were very much a family.

The author takes great pride in knowing that all the younger persons with whom he served in the New York office regarded the employment opportunity as a stepping stone to higher achievement and training. That is the Antigua and Barbuda way. They all acquired college degrees and additional training during their tenure. All of our diplomats are articulate and clear about our mission, and delight in serving our country at the OAS, the UN, the Commonwealth and elsewhere.

Madeleine Blackman has served as Consul in Toronto, Canada, for more than two decades. She is a very efficient and careful person who has helped to encourage Canadians to visit our small state. She was ably assisted by a tall Antigua and Barbuda named Sam Lord who has made a home for himself in Canada. Carol Hurst also worked with the Consulate in Canada for a period but returned to Antigua when her children were grown and no longer needed her guidance. Upon her forced retirement at age 60 years, from the government's service, she returned to Toronto where her skills are in demand.

In Miami, four persons have served as Consul. First to be appointed Consul was the author, who served for a little more than one year after establishing the office in 1986. A young lady named Doralyn Millett and the author worked to establish a presence in Miami, including the creation of a nationals association. Then an x-ray technician from New York, who had ambitions to join the political fray, was appointed by the Foreign Minister. He embarrassed himself during his appointment and was asked to demit office. The third was Dr. Norman Athill, a dentist, who formed part of the VC Bird kitchen cabinet; he was dispatched to Miami. He remained for a very long time until 2004 when a Mr. Sweeney was appointed by the newly-elected UPP government.

One of the successful ingredients in our staffing and foreign policy implementation has been the Ministry of Foreign Affairs and its staff. Eric Challenger, the permanent secretary at the time of independence until his retirement in 1993, was a very sensible civil servant. He believed that the advent of cable television, the low cost of telephone and facsimile communications, the emerging Internet, all eliminated the need for lengthy reports each week detailing the work of the overseas missions. Large countries' embassies and missions began this practice when these technologies did not exist, and many small states merely copied these outdated models. Whenever he felt the need, Challenger would ask for a paper. But he frequently arranged for conferences by telephone with the Foreign Minister in order to reach decisions. Challenger died in 2003.

Two other civil servants deserve very favorable mention. They are Ena Pereira-Thomas and Colin Murdoch. Both became permanent secretaries within the Ministry of Foreign Affairs upon the retirement of Eric Challenger. Ena Thomas held responsibilities for protocol and passports; Murdoch became an ambassador with responsibility for policy implementation and staff supervision. He was also the contact person in capital for the overseas missions. These are dedicated professionals who were determined to perform their functions well and to ensure that Antigua and Barbuda managed its affairs as well as any first-world state. Cicely Solomon, who fills the portfolio vacated by Ena Thomas following the election of the UPP in March 2004, is a very capable civil servant. She has extensive experience from her years at the Ministry of Foreign Affairs, and carries out her duties with aplomb. The transfer of staff from the Ministry to the overseas missions has brought a level of professionalism which the author continues to applaud.

Our UN Mission also commenced the practice of awarding outstanding nationals living in the New York, New Jersey and

Connecticut region for their contribution to their adopted country. A number of highly regarded persons including Amelia Charles, Enid Hurdle, Johnnie Gomes, Blandina Francis-Negga, Franklyn Reid, and the several Presidents of the New York-based Antigua and Barbuda Progressive Society -more than 73 years old in 2007- have received the Independence Commendations in the presence of hundreds of nationals. The event would take place during the annual New York Church Service to commemorate the state's independence. Applauding achievement is the Antigua and Barbuda way.

III

Determining The Pertinent Issues

Multilateral organizations are places where diplomats go to speak to each other and to the international civil servants who are employed to carry out their wishes. Cynics say that we go abroad "to lie" for our countries. Very often, the diplomats select issues that are of importance to their countries' domestic populations and to the region's peoples. Ghana, it has been noted, selected the fight against colonialism in Africa and Asia, as an issue it would pursue at the UN. The US has selected democracy within states as an issue that its diplomats promote vigorously at multilateral institutions.

Antigua and Barbuda's diplomats were also required to decide which issues would appeal to its domestic population, since foreign policy planning is in its simplest form an extension of domestic politics. A former speaker of the US House of Representatives once said that "all politics is local." At the UN, the OAS and at the Commonwealth of Nations, Antigua and Barbuda's diplomats selected issues that had appeal to its population, that fascinated the diplomats, and that would elevate their country's standing. What could we do that would make us stand out? In the idiomatic expression of the British, the Antigua and Barbuda diplomats were trying to "hit above our heads."

Unlike a large state where all policy is fashioned in the Ministry of Foreign Affairs (known as the State Department in the US), among many small states at the UN, the OAS, the Commonwealth of Nations, policy choices are frequently left to the Ambassadors. The limited size of their Ministries' staff, access to knowledge of intervening events, and reading the mood of organizations, are often best undertaken by the diplomats who are present in New York, Washington and London. Many governments in small states depend on their very intelligent and well-informed UN diplomats to guide them and to be able to decide on what is best; the same is true at the OAS and at the Commonwealth of Nations.

The most erudite men and women are often posted in the missions abroad; as a consequence, policy options and determination of issues are frequently assigned to the Ambassadors. It is not uncommon when voting is taking place at the UN to see diplomats frantically trying to telephone their Missions in order to receive instructions. Before the advent of cell phones, a bank of public telephones was maintained in the lounge behind the assembly hall; diplomats would scamper to use the limited number whenever a vote unexpectedly arose. Employment at a Mission abroad is considered fortunate and so there is a tendency to make no mistakes that could cause a diplomat to lose his assignment. The Antigua and Barbuda ambassadors did not suffer this uncertainty and were thus very bold and innovative.

The COFCOR (Council on Foreign and Community Relations) is also a forum for determining jointly where the CARICOM states will proceed on many issues. At times, it is impossible for the COFCOR to meet during a crisis, in which case the Ambassadors in New York, Washington or London will meet and they jointly decide. There are Ambassadors from small Caribbean island-states who dare not speak on issues without first submitting a text to capital, nor take a position without the express permission of their ministry. Thankfully, that was not the Antigua and Barbuda experience.

One event which the author feels compelled to relate occurred at the UN in 1991, shortly after Kuwait was invaded and its sovereignty obliterated by Iraq. I was serving as the Ambassador to the UN at the time when the debate took place at the UN. I did not enquire of my ministry just how to vote or what was appropriate to say; it was late in the evening when a resolution came to the General Assembly and there could not be any consultation with capital, anyway. The Iraqi Ambassador asked for a vote on every paragraph of the resolution. At one point, all of the countries abstained when the issue of punishment of Iraq came to the vote; not Antigua and Barbuda. We were the only country voting in favor of the paragraph. The USA and Kuwait abstained. The little red, amber or green lights that go on next to the countries' name on the big screen overlooking the Assembly Hall, showed a sea of amber and only one green. It was Antigua and Barbuda.

It was a moment of great pride for the author. We never wavered in our commitment to the ideal of democracy and stood opposed to the snuffing out of a little country's sovereignty by force of arms. Four years later, when the Emir of Kuwait met Prime Minister Bird at the 50th anniversary of the UN, he handed him a check for one million dollars ostensibly to help with recovery from the hurricane Luis. It was actually a thank you for our willingness to stand alone, four years earlier.

Freeing Nelson Mandela

When Antigua and Barbuda began to call for the release of Nelson Mandela at the United Nations, not very many people outside of South Africa knew who Nelson Mandela was. The USA, under President Reagan, hardened US policy, refusing to impose sanctions and calling for "constructive engagement." Not so the newly independent state of Antigua and Barbuda. The Antigua and Barbuda Government, after 1981, granted passports to South African freedom fighters so that they could travel outside of their country freely. As poor as Antigua and Barbuda was, it awarded scholarships to several South African youth so that they could be ready for leadership upon the death of apartheid.

Ambassador Lloydstone Jacobs and Foreign Minister Lester Bird are to be credited for this initiative. But Prime Minister Vere Bird embraced the Jacobs' initiative because he knew that South Africa's freedom was ours as well. Nothing which the USA offered could cause Antigua and Barbuda to drop its vocal opposition to South African apartheid, the killing of Steven Bikko, and the murder of Soweto's youth.

The demeaning of the African person in South Africa by apartheid, no matter how objectionable it may now seem to all, conveyed to VC Bird and many other anti-colonial leaders then, the relative weakness of black nations everywhere. The Antigua and Barbuda government felt particularly weak given its size and influence, but determined that it could select an issue that could make a difference. The chorus of release of Mandela from prison was as a result of our joint effort, in no small part, we believe.

On the domestic front, the calypsonians in Antigua (and in other calypso countries) were singing about freedom in South Africa and the end of apartheid, raising the consciousness of the electorate in Antigua during the early years, before 1975, influencing their government. African Liberation Day in May 1974 is memorable because of the friction with the Royal Antigua Police. The law required police permission to stage a march and demonstration. After granting permission, the Police Commissioner was instructed by the Minister to withdraw the permit; the law actually gave the minister the final word. After dutifully attempting to disperse the marchers, the police acquiesced because of the numbers and the determination of the crowd. A calypsonian named Swallow would later memorialize the events in song which means that the events are frequently replayed in the national consciousness.

Vere Bird long embraced Marcus Garvey's African-centered philosophy. Bird was sure that his role was to continue the dismantling of "the white man's burden"; he traveled to Africa during the 1957 Ghanaian independence celebrations and was infected with the optimism that it did portend. He believed that cars, machinery and foods from Africa would soon be exported to the Caribbean. South Korea has beat Africa at this ambition.

Bird had passed a resolution of the House of Representatives as early as 1956, banning the importation of South African exports into Antigua and Barbuda because of the apartheid policies of Boer South Africa, made into law in 1948. Racism had existed ever since slavery, but South Africa's legalization of racist preferences after the end of World War II made South Africa's apartheid especially objectionable. Freeing Mandela appealed to Bird, to the Antigua and Barbuda body politic, and to its UN diplomats.

Saving Indigenous Peoples

Antigua and Barbuda also saw a link between the extinction of the Caribbean's original Arawak and Carib inhabitants by the European invaders, after 1492, and the modern threat to indigenous peoples everywhere. The author, as Ambassador, began to take an interest in the defense of indigenous peoples, after 1988, playing a crucial role to the annoyance of many. When the Colombians negotiated a watered down resolution on indigenous peoples that failed to address the serious challenges which Amazonian deforestation and industrialization posed for the indigenous of South America, the author refused to vote in favor of the resolution. He made instead a statement about the need to address the diminishing numbers and imperiled habitats that threaten the indigenous groups' survival. It was a bold step to take for the Latin Americans were certain that they had duped the rest of the world by their sophistry in the UN Committee.

When, for example, the Latin American countries attempted to keep the indigenous Americans from participating in the debates at the OAS, the author invited the indigenous peoples' representatives to join Antigua and Barbuda's delegation and to speak from our seat. That defeated the conjoined Latinos' efforts to exclude the indigenous people from the discussion and earned the Antigua and Barbuda delegation much praise from the USA, Canada and even the defeated. The indigenous peoples were later assigned a seat and a microphone in the gallery of the OAS Permanent Council and allowed to speak freely, thanks to the maneuvering of Antigua and Barbuda.

Reversing Global Warming

When Antigua and Barbuda began to speak about "global warming" at the UN in 1983, many regarded the author with the same disdain that was heaped on Grenada's head when its Prime Minister talked about UFOs from the lectern at the UN. Global warming had been treated with disdain by the Americans and their press, and the journalists have a giddy influence on diplomats living in New York. Today, the New York Times, one of the most influential newspapers in the USA, sees global warming as among the greatest moral issues of the day. In its editorial f March 10, 2007, it argued that "The greatest moral issue of our time is our responsibility to the planet and to all its inhabitants".[6]

Antigua and Barbuda's delegation, led by the author, joined with others in proposing the Framework Convention on Climate Change –though we wanted to call it *the Convention to Prevent The Ill-Effects of Global Warming*. When the first meeting to draft the Convention was held in Chantilly, Virginia, in 1989, we were forceful in making known what should be contained in the draft of the Convention, as we saw it. Today, global warming is accepted as real and threatening; but that was not the case when we took up the mantle, long before US Vice President AL Gore became, thankfully, a spokesperson for this earth-threatening issue. The instrument was called *The Framework Convention on Climate Change* upon the insistence of the US delegation, among others.

Global warming remains the most compelling challenge facing Antigua and Barbuda and other low-lying states, given its ability to cause the ocean to swallow up our island-countries. Since 1988, the author has made more than 100 speeches to universities, churches, Red Cross annual meetings, to symposia and international gatherings on its ill-effects. The author has traversed the USA with NGOs, going from city to city, to editorial board rooms, to university after university informing of the danger posed by burning fossil fuels in abundance. Unless American civilization finds a non-polluting method for generating huge amounts of energy, then it too will collapse like all previous civilizations before it. Global warming has replaced racism as the most severe challenge of the new 21st century.

Protecting Antarctica

The largest and most wealthy states have signed a pact that allows them to carve out pieces of this icy continent and to plant their flags thereon. The Antarctic Treaty Consultative Parties (ATCP) is a little known arrangement among 29 states that reflects the ideological prejudice of the Europeans who colonized the so-called "new world" after 1492. Antarctica is regarded as *terra nullius* and therefore can be claimed by any state with the power to enforce its ownership or possession. The ultimate goal of the ATCP is to divide the continent among themselves, and to proceed to mine their sovereign territory for minerals and other sought-after valuables. Antigua and Barbuda objects.

In collaboration with Malaysia, Cameroon, and any other state which we could persuade to join us, we began a campaign to reverse the division of Antarctica. Antigua and Barbuda succeeded. At least, for fifty years, no mining or other exploitation of Antarctica will take place there while scientists do their utmost to learn of the benefits which a pristine Antarctic environment bestows on the inhabited earth. We pressed this issue at the UN each month, each assembly, each opportunity, and the attention was too much for the large countries to sustain; they capitulated, agreed to our request for a moratorium so that the fight has been passed to the next generation.

Antigua and Barbuda believes that Antarctica should become a world park, and that any scientist from any country, desirous of visiting and exploring, ought not to be denied entry to, or forcibly removed from, territory claimed by a sovereign state. If parts of Antarctica become the sovereign territory of countries, the continent will cease to yield her secrets for the benefit of mankind. Our delegation saw this fight as an extension of the victims' attempt to re-define the 1492 encounter, and to set the rules governing the exploration and settlement of outer space. The benefits of the abundance of the universe must be shared by all and not relegated to a few rich states that will hoard the wealth of tomorrow for the benefit of their citizens and the people of their choice. When our colleagues would ask: "Why is Antigua and Barbuda interested in so distant a land?" Our delegation took delight in demonstrating that our tiny state's interests were never narrow and that history had endowed us with a platform that could be put to use to further more than our narrow material interests.

Independence for the Saharawi

While all of Africa has achieved independence from European colonialism, one little piece remains forcibly attached to a larger state, against its peoples' wishes. Spain ruled this piece of land as it did Morocco and the two became fused at the time of Morocco's independence. Antigua and Barbuda has stood with the Saharawi people, demanding independence from Morocco. We have hosted their leaders in our capital, and when the larger state invited Caribbean diplomats for a junket, we politely refused. There is an unwillingness on the part of all African Heads of State to discuss issues of border disputes since the Europeans drew artificial and arbitrary lines through regions that have been connected by history and tribe. If that discussion is opened, the Africans fear an unending strife among its many peoples, though the splitting-off of Eritrea from Ethiopia has not resulted in the Pandora's Box that many predicted. The African leaders have nevertheless not pushed Morocco to disgorge, though several plebiscites have told the occupying power that the Saharawi people wish to be free of their control. We pride ourselves as being the only CARICOM state to take this position at the United Nations when the issue comes up for debate. The Saharawi people have been very thankful for our support. Dr. Patrick Lewis is responsible for this position, as much as Lester Bird, then foreign minister.

Intervening in Latin American Issues:

Argentina

Each year at the General Assembly of the OAS, since the 1982 Argentina-UK War over the Falkland Islands, Argentina would remonstrate against Britain and encourage her many South American neighbors to join in the condemnation. It was an unwritten rule that no English-speaking state would intervene. The USA, Canada and the fourteen CARICOM foreign ministers would remain silent during the debate. The British, with representation present at the OAS General Assemblies, wanted it that way. In 1999, the CARICOM decided that in order to win participation and support of the Latin Americans on issues that pertain to island-states, the Caribbean had to participate in the debates that touch on Latin American interests. The author, as head of the Antigua and Barbuda delegation in 1999, made an intervention during the Falkland Islands/Malvinas issue, asking the two large protagonists to find a solution that was acceptable. The British were furious. The Argentines were gracious. The Americans were stunned. Antigua and Barbuda in one five-minute speech won support and praise from all of its Latin American neighbors by daring to intervene on the issue.

In multilateral diplomacy, merely to speak is tantamount to joining sides, regardless of the content of the speech. The author as Ambassador knew this but had weighed the benefits against the burdens and decided that the former outweighed the latter. It was sheer genius, though our Ambassador to the UK later complained of being "blindsided" by the bold move. He was summoned to the British Foreign Ministry and asked for an explanation. Now, we were more than a mere gnat; we had exercised our right to address any subject or issue and that boldness infuriated those who wanted us to shut up! The Argentines became our life-long friend. Later at the OAS, when an NGO Representative, invited by Antigua and Barbuda as Chairman to address the Permanent Council, insulted the Argentines by claiming racism in Buenos Aires, our friendship was strained. But we would repair it by speaking up at the subsequent OAS General Assemblies, to the chagrin of the British. In 2003, the Prime Minister Lester Bird asked that we not intervene on the issue.

Standing with Bolivia

The same impetus to participate in Latin American issues drove Antigua and Barbuda to intervene in the Bolivia/Chile dispute, which is brought to the OAS General Assembly each year since 1992. Bolivia once ceded a small chunk of its territory to Chile that gave Bolivia an outlet to the Pacific Ocean; this followed Bolivia's certain defeat during a war that occurred in 1878 between these two South American republics. What is the relevance of a South American war of 1878 to Antigua and Barbuda in 1998? Our OAS delegation saw an opportunity to make ourselves relevant and to win a friend by urging conciliation. Bolivia had dispatched a female television journalist, smart and pretty, to the posting in Washington. She was very persuasive. But Antigua and Barbuda was predisposed to insert itself in the annual debate. At the 1998 OAS General Assembly and for three consecutive years, Antigua and Barbuda would speak to the need to find a solution to this troubling issue.

Hurst receives national award from Bolivian Ambassador, Washington 2002
(Photo by Edwards)

The current Secretary-General of the OAS, Carlos Insulza, was Chile's foreign minister then; he would ask the author privately what he could do to dissuade us from speaking. Chile has since offered many scholarships to Antigua and Barbuda, and a score of nationals are studying at various Chilean universities. After the author's departure from Washington, in 2003, Antigua and Barbuda relented. But in 2002, Bolivia would confer its highest national honor, the *Orden del Merito,* on the author, Ambassador Lionel Hurst, for his friendship to Bolivia (Photo above).

Fighting Latin American Racism

Anyone who has traveled to South and Central America will immediately recognize the extreme poverty and ignorance in which the Spanish- and Portuguese-speaking black citizens of the 18 countries live. Throughout Latin America, only the indigenous people are poorer than the descendants of Africans. The African descendants, whose ancestors were brought to the continent to be slaves and who worked without compensation for hundreds of years, are deprived of basic human rights and dignity in the countries of Central and South America. The Antigua and Barbuda delegation at the OAS, under the leadership of the author, decided that it can make a difference and that it will address the issue of persistent racism in Latin America.

Antigua and Barbuda collaborated with the head of a non-governmental organization in Washington that supports the Afro-Latin struggle for dignity and equality. When the author became Chairman of the OAS Permanent Council in 1999, he invited Mr. Michael Franklyn to address the Council on the troubling issue of unrepentant racism in Central and South America. It was a moment that will be remembered at the OAS forever. By challenging the representatives of the governments at the OAS, we hoped that notice of their exclusionary practice would reach their legislatures and their political leaders who would act to change the circumstances. We also hoped to get media coverage that would shame the Latinos into corrective action. One can never be sure of the level of success of such a grand cultural shift; but our delegation felt absolved and that we had made our sovereignty useful yet again.

Latin American immigrants may confront the white bigots in the USA through their immigrant organizations. But in their own countries, the governments of Latin American states knowingly deny the same rights and freedoms to their black citizens that the immigrants demand in the USA. Antigua and Barbuda brought the issue of persistent Latin American racism to the OAS, repeating our displeasure at every general assembly, every summit, and every gathering of the OAS at which democracy was discussed. Antigua and Barbuda carved out a special role for itself --in the tradition of the West Indian intellectual. The author has received plaques and commendations from several groups for his leadership on this pressing issue.

For those who may remain skeptical of this claim, even the Catholic Church in Latin America recognizes its own racially exclusionary practices. In May 2007, the Pope visited Brazil where he canonized a Brazilian saint and delivered the opening address to Latin America's bishops. One of the challenges faced by the Catholic Church in Brazil, as described by the New York Times of Sunday, May 13, 2007, is "the racial and ethnic composition of the clergy...Of Brazil's more than 400 bishops, only 11 are black and blacks are also underrepresented among seminarians."[7] Yet, the vast majority of the Catholic faithful in Brazil is black. That is an issue which the leaders of the Catholic Church agree must be addressed. Antigua and Barbuda would encourage them.

Challenging the USA at WTO

Antigua and Barbuda has had an epic battle with the USA on a matter pertaining to electronic commerce. The small island-state took the matter to the World Trade Organization (WTO) Dispute Settlement Mechanism in March 2003 and won. The US Congress, pressed by lobbyists such as the disgraced Mr. Abramoff, has made Internet gaming illegal; however, US companies and states that offer internet gaming to their citizens are not in violation of any law. That approach is called discriminatory and disallowed under WTO rules. When Australia and Costa Rica, two countries with an identical interest in the outcome, were invited to join the Antigua and Barbuda effort at the WTO, they declined. Antigua and Barbuda went forward alone to challenge the USA. Canada, Chinese Taipei, the European Communities, Japan, Mexico, and China have since joined Antigua and Barbuda as third-parties.   It was not unusual for Antigua and Barbuda to send its lone lawyer and its Ambassador to the US State Department to hold settlement discussions, as the WTO rules require. The USA's receiving delegation would number more than twenty-five experts and lawyers; Antigua and Barbuda's delegation would be of two persons. Yet, we were never intimidated. We stepped forward, pointing out that the USA's regulations were discriminatory and that they foreclosed Antigua and Barbuda companies from offering its services to US residents, while US companies had access to the same US consumers. Under WTO rules this practice is disallowed.

Despite our good relations with the US and our reliance upon the US market for capital, tourists, food and machines, Antigua and Barbuda decided to exercise its right and to challenge the USA. The entire world has taken note of our boldness. Though we have won, the USA has refused to abide by the WTO ruling, in an Orwellian twist claiming that it has, and Antigua and Barbuda has appealed. The fight is not yet over and its denouement will require a more complete examination. However, the WTO challenge has already demonstrated that the US is unwilling to abide by the rules of its own making when the judgment goes against it. We continue the West Indian tradition of making the USA a better country, abiding by its core values and the rules which govern all states in their relations with each other.

The US sometimes casts aside its commitment to building democracy within states, thereby diminishing US legitimacy. On those occasions, a tiny island-state and its neighbors may step forward to fill the breach, championing the issues that the USA has abandoned out of self-interest. These small Caribbean states help to improve on US global leadership by challenging it to live up to its high ideals. History will record this battle between the mouse and the elephant at the WTO, and the resultant loss of legitimacy which the WTO may suffer, as a consequence of US intransigence. The USA has started more litigation under WTO rules than any other country and thus needs the legitimacy of the WTO much more than Antigua and Barbuda does.

When the moment is propitious, several US administrations appear willing to defy the rules; even the rules promoted by the USA. Bear in mind that the United Nations is in large part the brainchild of the USA. When it was unlikely that the Security Council would give its approval for the use of force against Iraq in 2003, the US decided to wage war against Iraq without the express approval of the UN, as the rules require. Kofi Annan, the former UN Secretary General, has said that the US/Iraq war, launched in 2003 on a variety of pretexts, is illegal. He is right. The Bush Administration diminished the standing of the USA in the eyes of many by launching a war that failed to abide by rules which the USA sensibly constructed in an earlier period. The WTO dispute with Antigua and Barbuda is beginning to make the USA appear similarly defiant since it has announced that the USA may withdraw from the WTO agreement on services that require the US not to discriminate. When the rules do not favor the USA, several administrations appear willing to abandon them.

Democratic ideals are fixed notions of civilized behaviors of states and their governments; there is hardly room for fudging. However, if the world's lone superpower intends to persuade by influence, and not by mere power, it needs to resist the temptation to disregard the principles and ideals that make it a model.

The American people must not allow their government to disregard Antigua and Barbuda's successful judgment at the WTO; the world will take note and the resulting fallout will jeopardize the future of the WTO. The January 31, 2007, WTO decision and the March 31, 2007, ruling require the strictest adherence of the USA to the findings of the deliberative body. If the US Trade Representative's office disregards the WTO order, the WTO will lose its effectiveness and the trading system will not endure.

The material well-being which free-trade promises will not inure to the benefit of poor states, either. Further, the formulaic claim that free trade and prosperity will stem the nascent terrorism which many poor states are fighting to suppress, will be hollow and empty.

Fighting to Save Bananas and Sugar

During the days when Caribbean islands were colonies, especially in the post World War II era, the UK and France established special trading regimes that allowed banana and sugar producers to ship their produce to Europe at prices that amounted to a subsidy. The banana agreements were profitable to small farmers in the Windward Islands of Grenada, St. Vincent, St. Lucia and Dominica, and to the benefit of producers in Guyana and Jamaica. But the banana plantation owners in Central and South America were not pleased with the arrangement. They saw the subsidy as an unfair trade advantage, wanted it ended and sued to do just that in 1990, when the rules governing trade --upon the coming into being of the World Trade Organization— provided the opportunity. The special arrangements were in fact ruled a subsidy by the Dispute Panel. The Caribbean countries fought this result, withdrawing any support to Central American candidates at the OAS and the UN, and treating the issue with the greatest urgency. In every forum, the issue was discussed *ad nauseam* and with resolve by the Caribbean countries determined to fight the likely harmful results. For example, as currency members of the East Caribbean Central Bank, the loss of an economic staple of three of six contributing members would spell doom for all ECCB members.

The fight to save sugar and banana was conducted primarily by the diplomats abroad, and therefore serves as a good measurement of the persuasive ability of the English-speaking Caribbean diplomatic corps. Kingsley Layne, the Ambassador from St. Vincent was especially outstanding; he had an uncanny ability to weave the subject into his speeches, no matter the forum. The WTO may have ruled against the special trading arrangements that European states had extended to their former Caribbean colonies, but the discussion is on-going. The Caribbean small island-states will continue working to ameliorate the harmful effects of the end of the trade preferences as we continue to search for alternatives that can be exported to earn foreign currency.

Shipping Nuclear Wastes Through The Caribbean Sea

The 1962 Cuban Missile Crisis, as the Americans call it, could have brought to an abrupt end the possibilities which the anti-colonial struggles created in the Caribbean, had there been a nuclear war. Cuba had permitted the USSR to build missile launchers on its soil; US spy satellites were able to identify them. When several USSR ships carrying the nuclear warheads, on their way to offloading their dangerous cargo, were blockaded by US naval vessels, a crisis of enormous proportions was foisted on humanity, but especially on the Caribbean. The USA and the USSR were in a stand-off that could have resulted in a nuclear exchange. The Russian president backed down when he received assurances that the US would withdraw its nuclear weapons from Turkey and that Cuba would not be invaded.

Caribbean countries, not yet independent, had very little say in the events unfolding on their doorsteps. But clearly, there was great danger in being within the crossfire of a nuclear exchange. The scourge of nuclear technology has continued to frighten the Caribbean people. In 1994, two years following the Earth Summit in Brazil, the Caribbean diplomats at the UN began a concerted effort to declare the Caribbean Sea a "special area" within the context of sustainable development. The 1994 UN Conference on Islands took place in Barbados, and the Caribbean did its best to carve out a special place for the issue of nuclear waste shipments that would give voice to its objection. Essentially, the peoples of the region preferred to ban nuclear weapons and nuclear wastes from entering and traversing this very fragile ecosystem known as the Caribbean Sea.

France is a nuclear power. France also processes nuclear wastes generated by Japan, and the ships carrying the materiel transit the Caribbean Sea and the Panama Canal on their way to and from Japan. This matter was brought to the UN, the OAS, the Inter-American Defense Board, the Commonwealth and any multilateral institution that would give the Caribbean a hearing. One accident in the Caribbean Sea could doom our tourism, destroy our livelihood, and end normal life on our island-states. The protest has been unrelenting and the assurances from France have been unceasing. However, there is distrust of France born of its practice of exploding nuclear weapons in the Pacific on tiny islands, proclaim their tests safe, but could not do the same anywhere in France or Europe. France has chosen a defenseless region to test their poisonous systems. In 1995, when the French exploded its device in the Pacific, Antigua and Barbuda challenged France at the UN though many chose to say nothing about France's immoral actions.

Reform of the UN Security Council

The UN Security Council is very much like a board of directors. Five of its 15 members sit there permanently, and the five regions contribute two members each, staggered on a two-year rotating basis. Africa contributes three, and Eastern Europe contributes one every other year, re-ordering the fixed formula slightly. Western Europe and other states, Eastern Europe, Asia, Africa, and Latin America and the Caribbean are the five regions into which the membership of the UN is divided. When the UN was formed, in 1945, merely 51 states signed the Charter. The Security Council was then made up of eleven members, five permanent and six rotating, with a veto power exercised by each of the five permanent members. In 1965, the Security Council was enlarged to 15, its present quotient, when the UN membership had increased to more than 120 member states. By 1991, the UN membership had increased to 179 members and there was a call to reform the UN in time for its fiftieth anniversary in 1995. Brazil, Mexico, India, Japan, Nigeria, South Africa and other large states yearn to sit permanently on the Security Council.

Antigua and Barbuda asked the GRULAC to consider the subject and to find a formula that would result in our region's selection of one member to the Council's permanent roster. We argued that the increase in UN membership since 1965 had come about largely because of the addition of small states; it would thus seem that if the Security Council warranted enlargement, the new member (from GRULAC) ought to be a small state. The increase in the GRULAC membership was entirely of small states, since 1965, and even since 1945. Further, in order to ensure that small states' issues are promptly addressed by the UN Security Council, it was necessary to have a constituency of small states seated at the Security Council table. Small states cannot relinquish their interests to the dictates of large states, nor could small states bear large states to prominent roles which the large states could not ascend to in 1945 or 1965, we argued.

Although Antigua and Barbuda has never been interested in a permanent or rotating Security Council seat –it is far too costly to justify- we knew that the large states would never vote for a small state to occupy a position for which only large states deem themselves qualified. The diplomats from large states are also of the view that small states can be bullied by large states and can thus not be relied upon to vote according to conscience; or, that small states would sell their interests, capitulating to the offerings held out by large states whenever there is a decision to render. On both counts, the large states' representatives are wrong. In Antigua and Barbuda's view, the USA and the other permanent members had no interest in enlarging the

Security Council; but, a debate was justified and, hence, our delegation made its position known. Fifteen years later, the debate goes on and the configuration of the 1965 Security Council has not been changed.

Bullied by the OECD

Many small island-states in the Caribbean rely on off-shore financial services as a third leg of their fragile economies; tourism and agriculture are the other two. Primary among the financial services offered by Caribbean jurisdictions is off-shore banking. Its attractiveness is made possible by the new technologies, especially the computer, where billions of dollars can be moved around the globe securely by the click of a mouse. The new technologies eliminate the need for costly infrastructure and legions of accountants; an off-shore bank can thus be a significant player in financial services though thinly capitalized and thinly manned. Many Caribbean governments, observing the success of the Bahamas and Bermuda in offshore financial services, since the 1950s, passed similar legislation following independence that enabled their sovereign states to participate in this lucrative business. Antigua and Barbuda passed its first law in 1982, less than one year after independence.

American and European capitalists also came to realize that the sovereignty and law-making capability of a small island-state translated into the opportunity to establish banks and to compete with large financial institutions. Many large US banks also saw merit in off-shore branches and created their own in Caribbean jurisdictions. Individual Americans and Europeans, eager to reduce their tax liabilities, saw an opportunity to avoid weighty taxes by transferring portions of their wealth to off-shore banks. The ensuing competition was healthy, for it provided cheaper capital to entrepreneurs throughout the globe, reduced the cost of operation which inured well for consumers of their products, and strengthened capitalism. Small island-states were thus improving on capitalism's claim that competition is healthy.

High tax jurisdictions in Europe found this competition "harmful" and they set their police apparatus upon the tiny island jurisdictions, bullying them into imposing new taxes and regulatory regimes more invasive than their own. Antigua and Barbuda under Lester Bird would not be bullied and so they deemed us "a rogue state." This unfinished tale is an example of the failure of the diplomacy of island-states, trampled under by the mighty weight of wealthy states combined. One erstwhile diplomat, Sir Ron Sanders, calls this outcome *"Crumbled Small"*, in a publication that is filled with details.

The Organization for Economic Cooperation and Development (OECD) is a 29 member club of wealthy European nations, Japan and the USA. The OECD launched its "harmful tax competition" initiative at the tiny micro-states of the Caribbean in 1999. It attempted to compel the heads of government to sign a letter, drafted by the OECD, promising to make extensive changes to their tax and regulatory regimes. Antigua and Barbuda refused to sign, at first, but acquiesced after so many others did.

The USA also issued a "financial advisory" warning US banks to be careful of the Antigua and Barbuda jurisdiction. A US State Department diplomat can also be held solely responsible for this act of aggression against Antigua and Barbuda. The financial advisory stemmed from confiscation of several million dollars from a US drug trafficker. The funds were to have been shared between the USA and Antigua and Barbuda. The Antiguans took all the money and then told the US official that the records were lost in a 1998 hurricane and so there was none forthcoming for the USA. That was not wise. The State Department official became unrelentingly fierce and merciless, even mentioning the incident at the OAS when a new convention was being negotiated. No matter what changes the Antigua and Barbuda Government made to its off-shore banking legislation, over three years, the US State Department official would not remove the advisory. When George W. Bush became the President of the USA, he and Prime Minister Lester Bird sat next to each other at a summit in Quebec, in 2001. After PM Bird talked privately to the US President about the US advisory, he promised he would look into the matter. Within three months, the financial advisory was gone. A Republican administration has proven more reliable an ally to a small Caribbean island-state than a Democratic administration in the US White House.

It is worthy of note that the Europeans have not relented in their efforts to bully small jurisdictions. As recently as September 4, 2006, they were again issuing lists of countries that they commanded must abide by a European Union Savings Directive, releasing banking information on EU citizens or taxing their savings account in the respective states. Colonialism has ended but the drive to dominate and to direct is still very much alive.

IV

Grading Antigua and Barbuda

After twenty-five years of practicing diplomacy, it is evident to even a casual observer that the small island-state of Antigua and Barbuda, limited in its resources and reach, has managed well its independence. Our detractors may predict our demise, as one writer did in his *Caribbean Time Bomb.* Our own may even examine us and find us wanting, as in Jamaica Kincaid's *A Small Place.* But when an objective invigilator examines what our brightest sons and daughters have done in multilateral institutions to project an Antigua and Barbuda presence and to enhance the lives of countless poor and downtrodden, the small island-state's record is unassailable. Antigua and Barbuda has wielded its diplomatic presence to achieve many outstanding accomplishments for the country, its citizens, and for countless peoples in our region, in our hemisphere, in Africa and around the world. Antigua and Barbuda's leaders have demonstrated that the success of independence is determined largely by the quality of governance, the insightfulness of government managers, the courage of citizens, and access to capital.

Our little country was ranked 29th out of 174 UN member-states in 1995, by the United Nations Development Program (UNDP) Human Development Index before the first hurricane hit in September that year. That is no small achievement, fourteen years following independence, though we have fallen to #60 in the 2005 rankings, and 59th in 2006, the latest year ranking available. Antigua and Barbuda's economy has grown on average 7% annually since independence, with the exception of 1995 as a result of the hurricanes, and there is no stopping this tiny state.

Our democracy is securely rooted. In March 2004, one government was peacefully replaced by another, following general elections. No crisis, no riots, no violence, just peaceful and orderly change took place. The newly-elected government, running on an anti-corruption platform was successful at defeating the incumbent party that had won

124

six consecutive general elections. It is now left to see what changes the new government will succeed at implementing. It has brought three pieces of legislation that it refers to as a "trilogy" which is its defining character. Yet, the new government has yet to fully operationalise the new laws. It has also revised the taxing mechanism, increasing revenues by almost 50% over three years.

The same pattern of peaceful change of government has been repeated in St. Kitts and Nevis, in Dominica, in St. Lucia, in St. Vincent and the Grenadines, Trinidad and Tobago and throughout the English-speaking Caribbean region where a culture of freedom-loving, democratic ideals has sprouted from the degradations of slavery and colonialism. Most importantly, democratic ideals have been consistently promoted by Antigua and Barbuda's diplomats in multilateral institutions repeatedly, even in the face of strong opposition from the world's lone superpower. On that score, Antigua and Barbuda, a tiny micro-state, is a hemispheric giant.

CHAPTER FOUR

CARICOM's Regional Collaboration Record

The history of the English-speaking Caribbean sub-region evidences an extraordinary ability of the sovereign states to function as a group. Although West Indian intellectuals and popular calypsonians project a region rife with disunity, the facts tell another tale. The British West Indies were treated as a single entity prior to independence; the 1958-62 Federation experiment was intended to transform the colonial entities into one state. That having failed, and upon the last of the island-countries having decided on independence, the states recognized that operating as a bloc exceeded the sum of their weight, in multilateral institutions especially. By practicing common-interest politics within the region, the small English-speaking states easily adapted to practicing the same within multilateral institutions and in far-flung capitals. Acting as a group puts the sovereign states in an enviably stronger position to exercise influence, calculably more than the singular expression of many states that are larger. The primary institution which harnesses their collective strength regionally and internationally is the CARICOM, and so that is where the author will begin.

CARICOM leaders in St. Kitts, July 2006. PM of Jamaica Portia Simpson-Miller, the only female seated. Standing to her right is the President of Haiti. The other female on the extreme left is the Director General of the OECS. (Photo by Millet)

I

CARICOM: The countries of the sub-region built upon the 1965 CARIFTA agreement by signing the Chaguaramas Treaty in Trinidad, in 1973, establishing the Caribbean Community and Common Market (CARICOM). Although regional ambitions brought about this experiment, the small states recognized that they could extend their diplomatic reach by collaborating abroad. Within the CARICOM, they created The Council on Community and Foreign Relations (COFCOR). It is as valued as the West Indies Cricket Team though not as well known. The foreign ministers of Antigua and Barbuda, the Bahamas, Barbados, Belize, Dominica, Grenada, Guyana, Jamaica, St. Kitts and Nevis, St. Lucia, St. Vincent and the Grenadines, Trinidad and Tobago collaborate on the selection of candidates, the appointment of persons to high positions in several multilateral institutions, and the coordination of policies that inure to their states' material well-being.

Suriname and Haiti joined the English-speaking team, expanding the number to fourteen.

An application for CARICOM membership from the Dominican Republic languishes as the wisdom of expansion is contemplated. Several determining factors, militating against inviting the Dominican Republic into the club, bear on language, ethnicity, symmetry and history. The Spanish-speaking republic has historically identified with the Central American states and sees itself as belonging to the Ibero-American, baseball-playing, Spanish-speaking club, rather than to the English-speaking cricket-loving peoples of the hemisphere. And, though Suriname and Haiti are Dutch-speaking and French-speaking states, respectively, their ethnic and cultural roots are more closely aligned to the English-speaking Caribbean peoples than are the Dominican Republic's. Further, tiny states like Antigua and Barbuda, with a population fewer than 100,000, feel overpowered by the Dominican Republic whose population exceeds 7,000,000. That a symmetrical reluctance emerges, to which the cricket players have not yet reconciled themselves, continues to exclude the Dominican Republic. The asymmetry is palpable and there is a fear that the nature of the club would be altered significantly by the Dominicanos' presence. A degree of collaboration exists at the multilateral level; but, where membership is concerned, the English-speaking foreign ministers have spurned the pursuing Dominicanos for almost a decade.

The CARICOM Headquarters in Georgetown, Guyana (Photo from Website)

The CARICOM remains the pivotal institution within which the collective will of the fourteen countries can be successfully harnessed. Within the CARICOM are a plethora of sub-institutions that harness that will power and convert it into tangible material and other gains for the countries of the hemisphere.

CSME: The fourteen countries have decided to converge their economies to whatever extent possible, and to encourage capital to migrate freely across their borders. The single market is being advanced immediately, and the single economy is to follow. In order to achieve these objectives, a number of other agreements have had to be forged. While they are of interest, the author is of the view that this is experimental and its success is not yet to be reported. In that regard, it is virtually impossible to predict the degree of success which this experiment will achieve. However, if the past is any guide, the future for the CSME is good. Already, the Regional Negotiating Machinery (RNM) is making the region a single trading and negotiating bloc. The CARIFORUM, a creature of the Lome Agreement, has identified the whole region as a singular trading entity. The RNM is led by Ambassador Richard Bernal and is thus in the very best hands which the Caribbean could enlist.

CDB: The Caribbean Development Bank was established by an agreement signed in October 1969 but which came into effect on January 27, 1970. However, it is significant to note that the meeting which set this Bank in motion was convened in Antigua in November 1966. The Governments of Canada, the UK, the USA met alongside the Governments of Antigua and Barbuda, Barbados, Dominica, Grenada, St. Kitts and Nevis and Anguilla, St. Lucia, St. Vincent and the Grenadines, Montserrat, and the British Virgin Islands. With the exception of Barbados, all were colonies. Yet, they determined that there was a need for a financing institution that could provide resources to contribute to the economic growth and development of the region and its many parts. The CDB's purpose then was to promote economic integration among the eighteen members of the Commonwealth Caribbean whose plenipotentiaries signed on to the 1969 document. It has been a marvelous machine that has achieved much of its historical objective. Venezuela, Colombia, Mexico, China, Germany are also members though not entitled to borrow. The Bahamas, Belize, the Cayman Islands, the Turks and Caicos Islands are also now members.

The OECS Headquarters in St. Lucia (Photo by Millet)

OECS: Another institution which functions as an addendum to the CARICOM is the Organization of East Caribbean States (OECS). Lester Bird, as Foreign Minister of Antigua and Barbuda, believing that the smallest of the states within the CARICOM required a deliberative body that addressed their specific needs, proposed the establishment of the OECS in 1981, twenty-five years ago. The OECS is made up of Antigua and Barbuda, Dominica, Grenada, Montserrat, St. Kitts and Nevis, St. Lucia, St. Vincent and the Grenadines, Montserrat, the British Virgin Islands and Anguilla. The regional grouping has collaborated in aviation, culture, education, export, economic matters, legal affairs, pharmaceutical procurement, social development, safeguarding the environment and sustainable development issues. It has achieved remarkable results in its twenty-five years, although the Economic Secretariat which once was present in Antigua was closed and the institution downsized when Antigua and Barbuda failed to provide the requisite resources required of it under the Treaty of Basseterre. The OECS Heads meet once annually, and Ministers with responsibilities that fall within its purview also meet at least once per year.

The OECS is a very successful institution. Yet, there have been times when leaders from St. Vincent and the Grenadines and Dominica have proposed the establishment of a "unitary state" from among the members. Antigua and Barbuda has not been impolite, but clearly has no interest in moving to such an arrangement. The three Antigua and Barbuda prime ministers were aware how marginalized a small state can be, without power, without influence. To arrange for further reduction of the significance of Antigua and Barbuda (and the other members of the OECS) in a multilateral setting would not be in the best interest of any of the organization's six independent states. A unitary state would certainly not be in the best interests of the states that are making the proposal, no matter what their leaders may say publicly. The small states of the OECS are likely to remain as sovereign, independent states so long as the nation-state system survives.

ECSC: The East Caribbean Supreme Court is another of the marvels of cooperation among the smallest of the Caribbean states. Knowing that the cost of each maintaining its own judiciary would be too burdensome, six of the independent states and three of the non-independent countries have pooled their resources and created a single judiciary to dispense justice. It is comprised of the independent states of the OECS plus Anguilla, the British Virgin Islands, and Montserrat. The Chief Justice and two other judges hear appeals in member states by traveling to those states and territories. The arrangement reflects a high degree of confidence and trust far beyond any regional group of states anywhere in the world.

ECCB Headquarters in St. Kitts (Photo from ECCB Website)

ECCB: The British Caribbean Currency Board has a long history that stretches back into the mid twentieth century when a single currency served the Commonwealth Caribbean islands' collective interests. The British West Indies dollar served the entire region from 1951 until 1962. It was not called a central bank but a monetary union. In 1965, the East Caribbean Currency Authority (ECCA) was established following the withdrawal of Trinidad and Tobago and Guyana from the ECCA and creation of their national central banks. After Barbados withdrew from the ECCA in 1974, to establish its own central bank, the headquarters of the Bank was moved to St. Kitts. The Bank agreed to fix the exchange rate against the US dollar, abandoning the Pound Sterling when the USA became the dominant trading partner of each of the seven states and territories that comprised its membership. Then, in 1983, the Leeward and Windward Islands established the East Caribbean Central Bank (ECCB). The ECCB has stood the test of time for more than two decades; it is one of the most intelligent and forward-looking cooperation agreements which the states have established. It earns profits every year and is the source of sound fiscal advice for its members.

ECIPS: Five of the six countries that make up the Organization of East Caribbean States (OECS) established a joint presence in Washington by purchasing a single property to serve as the embassies of their five states. The level of collaboration brought about by such geographic proximity in Washington has been remarkable. Within that embassy building the governments also placed a new investment-search entity, in 1992, known as the East Caribbean Investment Promotion Service (ECIPS). John Arrindell, an astute and gifted Antiguan, led the institution and achieved much for the region during ECIPS' lifetime.

The function of that body was to seek out and attract entrepreneurs with capital and skills to the sub-region, especially in manufacturing, electronic assembly, financial services and tourism investment. The investment-search body was unwisely abandoned in 2002 because of the cost of operation, the governments decided. The closure of the ECIPS in Washington is also attributable to Antigua and Barbuda's decision to discontinue support for that venture. Antigua and Barbuda examined the returns from ECIPS and determined that its contribution was a subsidy to the other states since the investments snared by ECIPS benefited Antigua and Barbuda very little. Even with Antigua and Barbuda gone, the ECIPS would have been worth every penny spent by the remaining five OECS countries. But, it was abandoned.

UWI: It is also a fact of history that collaboration among the English-speaking Caribbean peoples long preceded the establishment of CARICOM in 1973, though interstate cooperation has intensified in the years since independence. The University of the West Indies (UWI), for example, was established in 1948 to serve the needs of higher education within the region. It moved from a single campus in Jamaica, known then as the College of the University of London, to becoming UWI. Today, that institution produces many of the doctors, engineers, architects, lawyers, politicians, and other professionals including diplomats that the sub-region requires in order to function. The UWI has three campuses in Jamaica, Trinidad and Barbados with Centers in the non-campus countries. UWI serves the independent and non-independent Commonwealth Caribbean countries of Anguilla, Antigua and Barbuda, the Bahamas, Barbados, Belize, the British Virgin Islands, Cayman Islands, Dominica, Grenada, Jamaica, Montserrat, St. Christopher-Nevis, St. Lucia, St. Vincent and the Grenadines, Trinidad and Tobago and the Turks and Caicos Islands. It is a dynamic and intellectually robust training ground for the professionals from the sub-region.

RSS: The Regional Security System (RSS) is also another marvel of cooperation among the East Caribbean English-speaking island-states. By way of treaty, Antigua and Barbuda, Barbados, Dominica, Grenada, St. Kitts and Nevis, St. Lucia, St. Vincent and the Grenadines have pooled their meager military and police resources. Very cleverly, these seven island-states have increased their defense capabilities exponentially while keeping costs well within their small countries' means. An examination of the security dilemma faced by small island-states has been thoroughly undertaken by The (British) Commonwealth of Nations and the Organization of American States, at the request of the diplomats from the region assigned to these posts. However, the RSS exists to "promote co-operation among the Member States in the prevention and interdiction of traffic in illegal narcotic drugs, in national emergencies, search and rescue, immigration control, fisheries protection, customs and excise control maritime policing duties, natural and other disasters, pollution control, combating threats to national security, the prevention of smuggling, and in the protection of off-shore installations and exclusive economic zones." It also mandates any six of the seven members to come to the defense of any single member state whenever democracy is threatened; in other words, no military coups will be allowed to stand. Each year, joint exercises ad military games are conducted in the region with American and British forces. Mexico has indicated its interest in participating in the RSS and in the exercises.

CXC: The Caribbean Examination Council (CXC) is also one of those institutions that serves to bind the English-speaking countries. In 1972, the CXC was established and seventeen states and territories subscribe to its membership. They are: Anguilla, Antigua and Barbuda, Bahamas, Barbados, Belize, British Virgin Islands, Cayman Islands, Dominica, Grenada, Guyana, Jamaica, Montserrat, St. Kitts/Nevis, St. Lucia, St. Vincent & The Grenadines, Trinidad & Tobago and Turks & Caicos Islands.

The members fixed the curricula, the level of learning and expectation across the frontiers, publishing texts and marking exams that are uniformly excellent. The CXC replaced the General Certificate of Education (GCE) that was devised and administered in London, England, by persons who knew not the conditions of learning and the cultural relevance of education in the Caribbean. It is a superior device; but, more importantly, it reflects the coming-of-age of the region in a glorious attempt to address its own needs.

CTO: The Caribbean Tourism organization (CTO) is yet another of the marvels of cooperation. Founded in 1989, the CTO represents the entire panoply of English, Spanish, French, Dutch Caribbean entities. It contributes to branding the Caribbean region as a holiday destination, collecting and disseminating data, undertaking studies and providing a forum for dissecting thorny issues which lend for a regional solution. The following states and territories make up its membership: Anguilla,

Antigua and Barbuda, Aruba, the Bahamas, Barbados, Belize, Bermuda, Bonaire, British Virgin Islands, Cayman Islands, Cuba, Curacao, Dominica, Dominican Republic, Grenada, Guadeloupe, Guyana, Haiti, Jamaica, Martinique, Puerto Rico, St. Barts, St. Eustatius, St. Kitts and Nevis, St. Lucia, St. Maarten, St. Martin, St. Vincent and the Grenadines, Suriname, Trinidad and Tobago, Turks and Caicos, US Virgin Islands and Venezuela. Only French Guiana is left out of the mix. The countries advertise jointly and collaborate where feasible, despite their competition within the same markets, to the benefit of all. It is one of the magnificent examples of regional cooperation, initiated by English-speaking Caribbean thinkers.

ACS: A similar ambition drove the creation of the Association of Caribbean States (ACS). The notion that all the islands and mainland states that border the Caribbean Sea have a great deal in common, requiring their coming-together, is another of the embracing and freedom-loving ambitions of West Indian thinkers. The ACS is the vision of CARICOM thinkers, although the governments of many of the English-speaking states have not been as forthcoming with their annual contributions as have the Spanish-speaking countries of Colombia and Venezuela. Trinidad and Tobago hosts the institution and, flush with oil revenues, contributes more than its fair share. The focus of the ACS is limited to matters pertaining to the environment, natural disasters, trade and cultural integration; yet, it has positioned itself as a potential player in diplomatic affairs. France, Britain and the USA were invited to sit at table with the ACS members since they each have territories in (and bordering) the Caribbean Sea. The USA has not accepted largely because Cuba is present and US law prohibits the US from affiliating with Cuba. The USA's on-going conflict with Venezuela's Hugo Chavez has not affected the relationship among the Caribbean and their Spanish-speaking neighbor. However, as the temperature between those two neighbors rises, the author foresees a larger role for English-speaking island-states in reducing tension.

The Agreement establishing the ACS reads thus: The Member States shall have the right to participate in discussions and to vote at meetings of the Ministerial Council and Special Committees of the Association. The list of Member States is as follows: Antigua and Barbuda, Bahamas,

Barbados, Belize, Colombia, Costa Rica, Cuba, Dominica, Dominican Republic, El Salvador, Grenada, Guatemala, Guyana, Haiti, Honduras, Jamaica, Mexico, Nicaragua, Panama, St Kitts and Nevis, St Lucia, St Vincent and the Grenadines, Suriname, Trinidad and Tobago, and Venezuela. Associate Members are Aruba, France (on behalf of French Guiana, Guadeloupe and Martinique), the Netherlands Antilles and the Turks and Caicos.

CCJ: In 2007, there is a continuing debate about the Caribbean Court of Justice (CCJ) becoming the final arbiter of justice, replacing the London-based Privy Council for the Commonwealth Caribbean. Many of the constitutions of the newly independent states after 1962 specifically mention the Privy Council as the final court of appeal for their citizens. Will the Caribbean people abandon the Privy Council for the CCJ? Barbados and Guyana have so done but that question remains unanswered at this time for the wider region.

History would suggest that the CCJ is an inevitable reality. The CCJ will surely contribute to the development of a West Indian jurisprudence in due course, but in the first decade of the 21st century, it will likely find itself sitting on its hands. It has been accorded original jurisdiction in the interpretation of the treaty establishing CARICOM and its protocols; but very few trade disagreements are likely to arise which would employ its expertise.

II

The above-mentioned institutions are a representation of scores of plurinational organizations which exist among the states of the English-speaking sub-region. In banking, sports (including football, cricket, track and field, netball, tennis, dominoes, bridge), dentistry, HIV/AIDS, weather tracking, radar, airlines, marine, fisheries, teaching, labor, electricity production, water management, funeral undertaking and a host of other charitable groupings, the Caribbean expresses itself through organizing. Many of the groups are of non-state actors and have thus not been examined here. But their contribution to a paterfamilias has been incalculable. The private institutions and business models that stretch across the region to embrace the family of states and territories help to drive the state actors closer, cementing regional integration in measurable and long-lasting cooperative alliances. The creed of cooperation which the region practices creeps into their multilateral arena, and the English-speaking Caribbean diplomats extol the virtues of collaboration at the UN, the OAS and the Commonwealth, creating sub-institutions within that advance collaboration and cooperation. The author will point to two.

AOSIS: States sometimes brand themselves in multilateral institutions for purposes of leadership. On the global warming phenomenon, the island-states at the UN created *The Alliance of Small Island-States (AOSIS)* and proceeded to brand themselves as the world's protagonists on this issue. The AOSIS was proposed by Trinidad and Tobago, and was led by Ambassador Robert Van Lierop of Vanuatu from its 1989 inception until 1994 when Trinidad and Tobago's Ambassador to the UN, Annette DesIles, became its chairperson. In 2007, Mauritius chairs the institution. Its members are from Asia, Africa, the Caribbean, the Mediterranean.

Recall that Ghana, in the 1950s, was determined to end colonialism and so projected itself. For Malaysia and Indonesia, it was the advancement of the Non-Aligned Movement. For Haiti, it was ending apartheid in South Africa. Saving Antarctica from the chopping block and distribution among the powerful has been actively pursued by Antigua and Barbuda, with success. For the promotion of democracy and democratic principles, the panoply of English-speaking Caribbean island-states have carved out a special niche for themselves which they exploit with aplomb.

But the AOSIS is a marvelous attempt to join forces within a multilateral institution and to promote the interests of its member-states on the issue of global warming. No longer is the subject treated derogatively by the US media, thanks in part to Vice President Al Gore and his 2006 movie *An Inconvenient Truth.* For those who wish a more expansive and US-centered discussion of the issue, the movie is a must see. For those of us from islands, the end of our existence is foretold by the dire consequences to come if there is no change in our waste disposal systems. I believe that the commitment to change will be too late and that many of the low-lying Caribbean islands will indeed suffer irreparable harm. They will simply disappear from the map as islands in the Pacific have done.

Humans cannot continue to dump billions of tons of carbon dioxide and particulate matter into the earth's atmosphere each year. That reckless behavior will surely result in swollen oceans, more severe storms and hurricanes, weather extremes of droughts and floods, heat and cold, and the diminution of coastal areas where a growing number of earth's inhabitants live. For islands, the results will be deadly. Islands have not agreed to be the sacrificial lamb on the altar of Western civilization.

FOSS: The Forum of Small States is another of the institutions created within the framework of our UN experience. All willing small UN member-states have decided to collaborate, using our numbers to advance our cause in a UN setting, much as the Caribbean has done within the OAS, the Commonwealth and even in institutions like the World Bank and the International Monetary Fund. By extending our allegiance to smallness rather than confine ourselves to geographic limitations, the smallest independent states are seeking ways to maximize the sovereignty which history has bestowed upon them since the end of World War II. Singapore has led this mission with success, and the reach of the smallest UN member-states has been significantly enhanced.

III

Decisive Action

By the decisiveness of the Caribbean island-states, the USA has been pushed to adopt positions which the world's lone superpower had no intention to pursue. The advancement of democracy in Haiti through reliance on the OAS and the UN is the primary example of this shoving by the CARICOM states. The end of dictatorship in Peru with the departure of President Fujimori, through the adoption of the OAS Democratic Charter, witnessed the pushing by small island-states of their giant neighbor. The end of apartheid in South Africa brought about by internal and external pressure, including several United Nations Security Council and General Assembly Resolutions, saw several countries from the Caribbean taking the lead, including Haiti. The end of military dictatorship in Grenada, despite condemnation by scores of states opposed to US intervention, was a Caribbean initiative.

The vocal support for minorities and African descendants throughout Latin America, despite opposition from many large neighbors, is evidence of our ability to define our interests and to pursue them with vigor. The agreement by the Antarctic Treaty Consultative Parties (ATCP) to forswear mining and other exploitation of Antarctica, for fifty years, is clearly the result of the continuous campaign conducted by several states including Antigua and Barbuda. A host of other accomplishments within multilateral institutions, and the very act of independence of small island-states, have been a blessing for democracy and freedom in the post-colonial world.

For the world's superpower to respond to the shoving of tiny micro-states at the OAS, the UN and elsewhere, given the military and economic might of the USA, is a remarkable achievement which policy makers, future planners, and plain citizens cannot ignore. This significant role for the English-speaking Caribbean island-states appears to this author as an unintended and unforeseen special role for the world's smallest states.

Caribbean Diplomatic Posts

The Caribbean island-states believe that democracy within states compels democracy among states at postings in New York, Washington, London, Brussels, and wherever multilateral institutions are found. Small states avoid marginalization and oblivion within the world's multilateral institutions by insisting on democratic ideals at every juncture. The Ambassador from New Zealand used to say that democracy is our *cause celebre*. Yet, the small states of the English-speaking Caribbean have not had a long history of practicing diplomacy. November 2006 marks 25 years since Antigua and Barbuda began dispatching diplomats. Many Central and South American states have been independent for almost 200 years, and have been dispatching diplomats to far-flung capitals for generations. They have interests globally and often act to protect those interests.

Contrastingly, many island-states have very few diplomatic postings abroad in a world of 192 independent states. The English-speaking Caribbean are all present in New York, Washington and London, jointly and individually represented in Ottawa, Brussels and sparsely in Paris. Jamaica and Trinidad have a presence in Caracas, and Jamaica still has a presence in Mexico City as does Belize. Jamaica no longer has an embassy in Moscow and Addis Ababa; difficult economic conditions have forced a closure of their presence in the latter two capitals. Trinidad also established a presence in Abuja and New Delhi, but those postings have proven to be awfully expensive with very little measurable returns. Guyana has not relinquished its presence in New Delhi.

There has been some talk among the English-speaking island-states to establish a joint mission in Pretoria or Johannesburg, since the end of apartheid, but resources have not been readily forthcoming to do that. Many Caribbean island-states now have diplomatic posts in Havana since the Cubans began to seek friends in the Caribbean region after the USSR's demise. The Cubans also played such an important role in ending apartheid by defeating the South African military in Angola, that the largest Caribbean island-state won the admiration and support of their Caribbean brethren. In dispatching diplomats, therefore, the numbers have been so few that the very smartest of persons are frequently selected. Wherever they are found, the Caribbean diplomats work collaboratively to achieve goals set by their own individual government and jointly as a grouping of states.

CHAPTER FIVE

THE CARIBBEAN IN THE OAS
AND THE UN

When Trinidad and Tobago became an independent state in 1962, its Prime Minister, Eric Williams, decided against having Trinidad and Tobago join the Organization of American States though Trinidad and Tobago immediately became a member of the United Nations. Williams perceived the OAS to be a tool by which the USA controlled the states in the Americas and he wanted his state's independence to be meaningful. He did not concede to OAS membership until 1967, five years later, when Jamaica also followed suit. He was persuaded during the ensuing years that Trinidad and Tobago could assert its sovereignty even against the all-powerful neighbor to the north, whose representatives also gave assurances of their government's intent to abide by the rule of law. Canada held a similar view, refusing to become a member of the OAS until 1990, following the end of the bifurcated world and the new role which states of the Americas could play without worrying about US hegemony in Latin America.

The OAS has a long history stretching back to 1889. The institution began life as the International Union of American Republics in 1889; its focus then was rule-making for the safe shipment of international mail. In 1910, it was renamed the Pan American Union when it became evident that a larger role was required for a union of the states of the hemisphere. The Union evolved into the Organization of American States, in 1948, and will likely so remain for the foreseeable future.

In the seventeen years since 1990, the results have justified Canada's decision and Eric Williams' earlier choice forty years ago to move forward with membership. The USA does not dominate, and the superpower's will is often thwarted by even the tiniest of member states, acting in concert or unilaterally. Trinidad and Tobago and the other English-speaking Caribbean countries have established their leadership within the OAS on various issues, and they have demonstrated that size and contribution to budget make less of a difference when intellectual capacity, determination, and courage mark the diplomat's character and the country's will. The urge towards consensus has also reduced the urge to compel which held sway long before the balance shifted to a more democratic institution.

Guyana and Belize had a different problem with membership. They had been excluded by a Charter obligation which denied membership to any state that had a border dispute with any of the founding OAS member-states. Since Venezuela and Guatemala have disputes over territory with these two English-speaking states, then membership was denied them both. Bear in mind that although Guyana became an independent country in 1966, almost twenty years following the establishment of the OAS, it had to remain outside of the OAS until there was sufficient political will to change the Charter, twenty-four years after its independence. Belize and Guatemala still disagree over territory, and so when Belize gained its independence in 1981 it too was excluded from OAS membership for the same reason for nine years.

A secondary reason for exclusion may also have been the fear of dominance by an English-speaking bloc. States, like individuals, always fear being outnumbered and out-maneuvered. The Spanish-speaking OAS members knew that there would be a shift in balance with the addition of three more English-speaking countries should Belize, Canada and Guyana be added to the roster of eleven Anglo members and the USA. They were not completely wrong in their assessment; yet, the enlargement has led to a less powerful USA and a far more egalitarian institution, to their benefit.

I

The New World Order

In 1990, with the USSR facing collapse and a new world order beginning to emerge, the countries of the Americas saw new possibilities and new collaborative potential. In that year, the OAS Charter was changed, allowing Guyana and Belize to apply for and to achieve membership within the OAS. Canada also acceded to membership in that year. When crises occurred in the years after 1990, a fuller Caribbean –indeed a fuller hemispheric response -could be forthcoming.

Since Cuba had been expelled from the OAS in 1962, following its standoff with the USA over Russian nuclear missiles, it has remained outside of the hemispheric body. Only St. Kitts and Nevis has called publicly for the readmission of Cuba, at an OAS General Assembly in 1996 in Panama, despite the antagonism which the US State Department and the Cuban electorate in Miami continue to exhibit to this most genuine of Caribbean countries.

It is of interest to note that a Barbadian and then a Trinidad and Tobago citizen each became the Assistant Secretary-General of the OAS over a twenty year period, commencing in 1978. Val McCombie and then Christopher Thomas were two diplomats who won election to the post. McCombie certainly came on board at a time when the Anglo-Caribbean was not yet certain of its role in the OAS. But there was a need by the Latin states to demonstrate that they willingly welcomed the English-speaking countries into the fold of American states, and that collaboration was sure to follow. Albert Ramdin, a citizen of Suriname, was elected to that post in 2005, largely as a result of full CARICOM support. The post is regarded as CARICOM's, but acts as a glass-ceiling beyond which the CARICOM dare not ascend.

For a five-year period, the CARICOM deliberately stepped aside, allowing two non-CARICOM candidates to contest the Assistant Secretary General post. Panama and the USA both put up candidates in 1999 at the OAS General Assembly in Windsor, Canada, to become Assistant Secretary General. Despite CARICOM's certainty that it could win if it put forward a candidate, it lent its support to the American, Luigi Einaudi, at the last minute. He won, to the disgust of the Mexicans and others who perceived no need for the USA to seek out that post since Americans occupy several substantive posts within the Secretariat that determine how the institution's monies are spent; and, their numbers within the Secretariat far exceed what appears balanced. The USA made out that Einaudi was not a US candidate, just an American seeking the post. Most countries saw that as a campaign strategy rather than the real reason. Yet, it speaks to the new alignment within the OAS since 1990.

Einaudi turned out to be a very fair and exemplary Assistant Secretary General, intellectually equipped and of a warm disposition. He was unusual for an American in that he spoke French, Spanish, Italian and dabbled in a few other languages, which is very much unlike the average American diplomat who is uni-lingual. He also gathered around him professionals from a swath of states, not US citizens. His Chief of Staff was a diplomat from Trinidad and Tobago named Sandra Honore; she was another of the many talented professionals that have been produced by that CARICOM state. She spoke Spanish, Portuguese and French with the same ease as she did English, and was a very gifted thinker. Honore returned to the Ministry of Foreign Affairs in Trinidad when Einaudi concluded his term.

The prevailing view among the CARICOM Foreign Ministers during the lead up to the 1999 Windsor OAS Assembly was that it was "time" for a Secretary-General to be elected from the CARICOM states. The Ministers propose that CARICOM relinquish the post of Assistant Secretary General so that their candidacy for the higher post could be deemed reasonable. Just who their candidate might be, no-one was able to answer. The author penned a paper that was critical of this approach, seeing petulance and a lack of forethought in the strategy.

The Secretary-General of the OAS has to be someone who can command the attention of the Heads of State and Government of the hemisphere, the paper asserted. While former Caribbean Prime Ministers are well-known within their sub-region, they are completely unknown within the Latin American countries. None of them was fluent in Spanish, except for Leonel Fernandez of the Dominican Republic, and he was not of CARICOM. The strategy was ill-informed, the author wrote. It did not yield the anticipated results.

In 2005, the CARICOM returned to putting forward a candidate for election to the Assistant Secretary General post, and won easily. A Chilean foreign minister won the post of Secretary General.

The OAS is far more than elected posts and personal ambitions. It plays significant roles in making new rules and establishing public international law. There are several distinct areas where the role of the English-speaking Caribbean receives high marks and meaningful participation. An examination of those subject areas follows.

Technical Cooperation

Each year, the OAS dispenses about US$8,000,000 in direct grants for small projects that help to promote goodwill. They used to be called technical assistance. The more polite name is now "technical cooperation." The projects are economically insignificant though meaningful material benefits flow from them, and the money is well-used. St. Kitts and Nevis will have a land registry and cadastral survey undertaken using OAS money, in 2006/7. Antigua and Barbuda will finance the repair of its chemistry lab and criminal forensic lab at OAS expense, in the same year. Small sums, each year, go towards financing scores of low-cost projects that buy goodwill for the OAS, since the resources are limited and must be spread out among the states. Yet, the resources are fought over by the diplomats as though the existence of each speaker's country is at stake.

The OAS once used to have two distributing institutions called "CIEC" and the other "CIES". The inefficiency in that two-tiered arrangement drove Antigua and Barbuda's delegation under Paul Spencer's leadership to propose a single institution. Out of the discussion came the Inter-American Council for Integral Development (CIDI) which encompasses the distribution and the resource-seeking arm of the OAS, in 1996.

The OAS has been very good at attracting skilled people to the CIDI, whose primary job was to raise money. It is evident from the history of the organization that it can raise money to undertake certain tasks, and not others. For example, the OAS can raise money to pay for the monitoring of elections, and for electoral reform in the hemisphere. In fact, the OAS budget for specific projects exceeds the annual budget contributions by member-states. The regular budget has been stuck at US$78 millions for more than a decade. There is little agreement to get states to pay more to the OAS. Yet, the budgeted amount for specific projects, funded by international agencies, the US and European Governments, exceed US$78 million in 2006. But many attempts to raise money for projects that fall outside of narrowly defined band of issues, unrelated to democracy-promotion, are repeatedly rejected by donors.

There is a view among many of the OAS diplomats that the full panoply of Caribbean countries are present at meetings to participate in the discussions on distribution of the CIDI funds, but seldom find time and manpower to participate in the discussions within the other OAS committees. There is truth to this claim. Many Caribbean diplomats believe that their elected governments and their own efforts will be judged on the basis of their ability to extract resources from wealthy states and multilateral institutions. That attitudinal behavior is cultural; many private citizens regard that skill as a test of their government's ability. On the campaign trail and on the evening news, any project funded by outsiders' money receives undue media attention in many Caribbean states.

The notion that a mendicant bent should inform our foreign-policy drive is deeply imbedded from our days as colonies when getting the British to part with grant-in-aid funds was the only means to attract capital for infrastructural development. One of the remnants of colonialism is this yearning for free money, or money for which no tangible give-back is required.

The Antigua and Barbuda delegation, like several of the CARICOM better-off states, resists appearing focused on technical cooperation funding, and pays equal or greater attention to the more esoteric and intellectually demanding subjects which are placed on the agenda of the OAS.

The CIDI has spawned six inter-American committees on such subjects as ports, education, culture, science and technology, culture, labor. These committees help to make the technical arm of the OAS more complex than the original designers had in mind for the hemispheric institution, and are all possible as a consequence of the demise of the USSR, the challenge of illicit drugs and, since 2001, the threat of terrorism.

Scholarships and Fellowships

The OAS distributes at least four scholarships and fellowships each year to each of the states; Canada and the USA do not participate. Actually, the OAS assigns a sum of money to each state, allowing for approximately four students per state. Students from any of the 34 member states may choose to study at any university in any of the member-states; the OAS meets the cost of tuition, rent, books and spending money. The baccalaureate students must have already completed the first two years with a 3.5 grade point average or better to be considered. The graduate scholars must choose to study a subject area for which there is a shortage of supply in expertise in his/her country.

So, the Director of our solid waste management system, one Mr. Lionel Michael, was accepted to complete a Master's Degree in the USA on an OAS fellowship grant. He works for the Government of Antigua and Barbuda and our OAS Mission had to certify that his studies would enhance an area that is lacking in expertise. If he had been accepted to study at Harvard, the entire bill would have been paid by the OAS fellowship program.

Many Latin Americans, otherwise unable to afford US Ivy League schools, have found the scholarship and fellowship program to be an ideal vehicle to enable attendance at these schools. Caribbean diplomats have tried to stretch the monies by having scholars select low-cost educational institutions which then allow multiple fellowships and scholarships that a single high-cost institution would have made less affordable to more scholars. A more egalitarian approach informs our choices.

This program is one of the successful undertakings that provide a positive acceptance of the OAS and wins the institution much applause. There is no additional money forthcoming to expand the program but all diplomats wish that there was.

Fighting Illicit Drugs

In the post-Cold-War period, everyone was persuaded that concern for illicit drugs would replace the anti-communist rhetoric and raison d'etre of US foreign policy in the Caribbean and Latin America. Since the OAS is an arm of the US foreign policy machine aimed at the Americas, the holistic issue of illicit drugs -including production, trafficking and consumption- would surely reach the halls of the OAS, the experts predicted. But tiny Caribbean countries, caught in the crossfire of the producer- and the consumer-states, found that the drug trade was endangering their security and placed them in a position of protecting the third border of the USA. The OAS was the ideal place to which to turn. Trinidad and Tobago, the nearest of the island-states to the source of the production, felt the greatest sting from the traffickers. The drug gangs in Trinidad are a menace to her security and place her high on the list of states where murders and kidnappings are spiraling out of control. Trinidad and Tobago's diplomats sought to use the OAS to bring a solution to this difficulty and so a very well-trained Trinidadian named Lancelot Selman led the charge.

The OAS created the Inter-American Drug Abuse Commission (CICAD) for the prosecution of the challenge, in 1989, and expanded its remit when it began to appear that the USA was blaming others for the difficulties that it experienced with the drug trade. Everyone, except the USA, was persuaded that demand drove the trade, and the biggest market was the USA. Yet, US pronouncements would make out that Colombia, Mexico, and -given the enmity between the USA and the largest island-state in the Caribbean- Cuba were the source of the challenge. Even Haiti was accused of encouraging and dealing with drug traffickers. As recently as January 2007, the Haitian president, Renee Preval, was accusing the USA of doing too little to help Haiti fight the scourge of drug trafficking that is plaguing his country's capital and fueling violence in the slums of the city.

The Central Intelligence Agency (CIA) and the US State Department created an annual report by Congressional fiat that measured the efforts of states to fight the illicit trade; it is called the International Narcotics Country Strategy Report (INCSR). If seizures did not continually rise, then the report concluded that the effort to intercept drugs was falling-off. The states that were being judged believed that the fall-off in seizures came as a consequence of the traffickers' improved techniques, once detected. Recriminations led to friction between the USA and the other states. To minimize the friction, the OAS created the Multilateral Evaluation Mechanism (MEM) which evaluates all 34 states, including the USA. The MEM also makes specific recommendations to each state following a review of its strengths and weaknesses. The MEM was put in place in 1998 and has proved a far better test of the states' struggle against the evil than the CIA's skewed and politically-determined findings. The US Congress still compels an evaluation by the CIA, but when their report is stacked against the OAS' MEM, the degree of fairness is patently obvious.

Illicit drugs remain a challenge to the countries of the hemisphere, but its importance has paled next to the terrorism threat and democracy-promotion that now occupy center-stage in US foreign policy drive in the hemisphere and beyond.

Human Rights Protection

The countries of Central and South America are notorious for the degree of unkindness visited upon their populations by military dictatorships. Until Jimmy Carter became the US President in 1976, and spoke out against their wicked treatment of their defenseless populations, especially political activists, there was no voice in the US Government expressing disgust at what passed for governance in the Americas. The OAS Inter-American Commission for Human Rights (IACHR) and the Inter-American Human Rights Court (IAHRC) were the only institutions that sought to dissuade governments from inflicting death and torture on civilian populations. Today, both institutions are held in very high esteem precisely because they provided a forum for innocent civilians to prosecute their governments at a time when the activists' voices could not otherwise be heard. The jurists who listen to complaints and render judgments, or decisions, are among the bravest and most outstanding citizens from the hemisphere.

It is interesting to note that a former attorney general of Antigua and Barbuda named Clare Roberts has been twice elected to serve as the Chairman of the Inter-American Human Rights Commission. He won election to the Commission in 2002 and has continued to serve with distinction on the hemispheric body. Clare Roberts is one of the smartest and most daring Antigua and Barbuda nationals, and his country saw fit to confer one of its highest national awards on him during the twenty-fifth anniversary of independence celebrations on November 1, 2006.

Mr. Roberts had to recuse himself in 2004 when an NGO in Antigua and Barbuda, connected to the author, submitted a complaint to the Human Rights Commission, seeking redress for an unfair law that subjected young criminal suspects to incarceration for inordinate lengths of time prior to trial. The parliament subsequently repealed the law, nullifying the complaint before it was heard. That may have been one of the first times that a complaint, other than a capital punishment appeal, had been brought before the Inter-American Human Rights Commission from a CARICOM state.

The Caribbean states do not pursue the OAS mechanism in part because the electorates can change governments without fear. Because governments are aware that public opinion determines their longevity, human rights abuses are few and far between. The author is of the view, however, that the parliaments of the Caribbean are too quick to impose incarceration and long jail sentences for petty crimes. Possession of small quantities of marijuana by poor and unemployed young males results in incarceration at rates that place Caribbean small states among the countries with the highest number of inmates per capita. That approach to crime prevention and deterrence is excessive and needs to be addressed; capital punishment is also in need of urgent attention and revision.

The Inter-American human rights institutions cannot limit the states' law-making capability, but the IAHRC and the IACHR have surely stood in trial of the states of Central and South America where governments routinely arrested, tortured and sometimes killed dissidents. The planting of democracy in the Central and South American countries has not lessened the demand for the Commission and the Court; the number of complaints has risen and continues to rise as citizens become less fearful of reprisals.

Election Monitoring

The OAS has become an expert in monitoring elections in the states in the hemisphere. It has monitored more than 90 elections since this task has fallen to this hemispheric institution since 1990. It has monitored elections in the Dominican Republic, Guyana, Haiti, St. Vincent and the Grenadines, Suriname, Venezuela, St. Lucia and in many of the countries of Central and South America. The OAS not only monitored elections in Haiti but also organized, in collaboration with the United Nations, a massive voter registration drive. Many of the Anglophone Caribbean countries have a preference for the (British) Commonwealth of Nations Electoral Observer Mission and have not asked the OAS to participate as often. Yet, it is evident that there is a very special role for the OAS to play in ensuring that a primary exercise of democracy is dutifully carried out in an atmosphere of peace.

The OAS also attracts resources from wealthy donors to enable it to fulfill this task and it has the technical skill to play well the observer role. Former Dean of the Diplomatic Corps in Washington, Ambassador Edsel Edmunds of St. Lucia, has led an OAS observer team as has former Assistant Secretary General Christopher Thomas. They have only been assigned CARICOM jurisdictions, however. The St. Lucian elections of December 11, 2006, were monitored by the OAS and the CARICOM. The OAS team was led by Christopher Thomas. It is of interest to note that Prime Minister John Compton, who is 82 years old and who had retired, returned to lead his party to a successful victory in those elections.

Confidence and Security Building Mechanisms

Giovanni Snidel, a US State Department diplomat who has been seconded from the US Department of Defense, is one of the most enduring pillars in the OAS Committee on Hemispheric Security. Though the USA has used the big stick in Latin America for more than a half-century, his disarming style and pleasant demeanor since 1990 when the Committee was established at Canada's insistence, have generated more friendship and equality among the countries of the Americas than any weapons-system could have achieved.

The OAS Committee on Hemispheric Security was chaired by Mexico in 1996/7, and Antigua and Barbuda in 1997/8. Both periods saw very innovative agendas including a two-day symposium during Mexico's chairmanship that brought together experts from many universities and multilateral institutions to discuss the "Special Security Concerns of Small Island States." That conference was chaired by the Mexican Ambassador to the OAS, Ambassador Carmen Moreno, a meticulous and hard-working woman who was as prickly and annoying as she was intelligent. During the following year, sessions on the same subject were pursued in El Salvador preceding and during the Conference of Hemispheric Defense Ministers. The item has remained on the agenda of the OAS each year and has attracted many to its innovative approach to security.

The Committee has new challenges ahead of it as the focus of the USA on terrorism replaces many of the other concerns which the USA itself used to champion. Canada introduced an item it called "human security", defined broadly to mean ensuring all the conditions necessary to make a society governable and to provide its citizens with all the tools required to succeed. Canada has repeatedly demonstrated the uses to which wealth and influence can be properly put in an age when wealth accumulation has mistakenly taken center-stage above human needs. The Canadian Ambassador Peter Boehm was a very amiable and intelligent envoy whose special attention to the Caribbean resulted in an excellent working relationship, manifested in the reach of Canada within the OAS body. His role in the Summits process is very well recognized as outstanding.

The Prime Minister of Trinidad and Tobago was present in Washington in September 2006. Mr. Manning articulated many of the conclusions which the OAS has articulated as the security concerns and new security paradigm, promoted by the Caribbean states. During his September 2006 visit, the Prime Minister addressed the question of illicit drugs and small arms trafficking. The OAS Press Release from the event quotes him as underscoring his "country's firm commitment to playing its part in strengthening hemispheric security." Prime Minister Manning, when addressing the OAS Permanent Council of Ambassadors, explained the serious implications for the region and beyond "if our countries were to ignore the multifaceted security question." He emphasized challenges related to the movement of narcotics across borders, small arms and pervasive criminality that breed increased gang violence, trans-national organized crime, the spread of HIV/AIDS. He also addressed the effects of natural disasters on Caribbean countries though Trinidad and Tobago is out of the hurricane belt. Manning says that these are compelling reasons for states to cooperate on the collective security of the Americas.

One of the best positioned institutions for promoting the sought-after collective security is the Inter-American Defense Board. It remains a very significant institution in the promotion of security and confidence building measures. The institution dates back to 1948, the post World War II era. However, it has become more relevant in the early 21ˢᵗ century by addressing challenges to security articulated by states like Antigua and Barbuda.

The IADB Headquarters in Washington, DC (Photo from Author's archive)

In March 2006, the IADB became an agency of the OAS by the adoption of its statutes by the OAS. Many hail this new arrangement as a sign of improved times and the supremacy of the civilian/elected governments over their militaries.

The Inter-American Defense College is also an important part of the Inter-American system for it brings scholars from throughout the hemisphere to Washington to study a plethora of subjects related to security of the hemisphere. The College and the Board are twins. The head of the IADB is also the head of the college, with delegations from the 34 states participating in the work of both institutions. I have lectured more than a dozen times at the college to scores of professionals on Caribbean politics and diplomacy. Both military and civilian officials have enrolled in the classes over the years, enriching the two institutions while enhancing leadership in the hemisphere.

The domination by the USA ended when, for the first time, a Brazilian was elected to chair the IADB in 2006. Under the ancient rules, only the country where the institution is based could be its chair.

That appeared very colonial, and even the USA did not wish that any longer.

It was also a rule that only militaries could represent their countries on the IADB. Trinidad and Tobago, Barbados and Guyana are the only English-speaking countries that have assigned a military attaché to the IADB. Antigua and Barbuda, Bahamas, Grenada, St. Kitts and Nevis, St. Lucia, St. Vincent and the Grenadines are now represented by their Ambassadors. The rule was changed to allow non-military representation in order to accommodate the island-states that can ill-afford to send one of their officers to Washington year-round. Once per year, the IADB holds a special assembly and that is when full military representation from the CARICOM states is guaranteed. The collaboration between the military and the diplomatic, spawned by this arrangement, has inured to the benefit of the states and to their hemispheric institutions.

General from Argentina, Hurst and Commander Thomas of ABDF at 2003 IADB annual meeting (Photo by Edwards)

Environmental Protection

The OAS was persuaded to create a Department of Sustainable Development following the frequent interventions calling upon it to act to save the most vulnerable from environmental degradation. Seeking to avoid duplication of the efforts of the United Nations and other multilateral institutions, the OAS Department has a very narrow mandate. Climate change and protection of fresh water supplies are high on the agenda of the Department of Sustainable Development, working in collaboration with the many agencies of the United Nations, including the United Nations Environmental Program and the United Nations Development Program and its funding arm the Global Environmental Facility. The author has chaired the management committee and has been very vocal

On December 4 and 5, 2006, the first high level meeting of Ministers of Sustainable Development met in Bolivia, at the same place where the Summit of the Americas on Sustainable Development took place in 1996. The results of that meeting informed the process which brought climate change and other threats to Caribbean island-states' security to the fore.

When Antigua and Barbuda first brought to the OAS the issue of global climate change, tied to the hurricanes that plagued the sub-region in the early years of the 1990s, the author was scoffed at for making what appeared then to be a fantastic claim. How could man's industry spawn a change in the global climate that could increase the number and ferocity of annual storms that are injurious to Caribbean states? Many of this author's own OAS Caribbean colleagues joked that he was perpetrating a massive Caribbean joke on the hemisphere. Now that global warming has been accepted as real and the danger is described as ever present, the wisdom of the author's claims back in 1995 does not now seem so fictional. The hurricanes that began battering Antigua and Barbuda, after Hurricanes Luis and Marilyn in 1995, pushed Antigua and Barbuda to make global warming a paramount issue that required immediate attention.

Prime Minister Lester Bird saw the effects that hurricanes had on insurance premiums for hotels and residences, and he proposed a few innovative approaches aimed at keeping the rates within reasonable limits in order to grow tourism, especially the hotel industry. Support from the OAS for the Antigua and Barbuda prime minister's proposal has borne fruit almost ten years following the planting of the seed. The World Bank has agreed to a fund which, in its workings, will provide recovery resources to the disaster affected states and lower their insurance premiums. Grenada, having been struck by Hurricane

Ivan in 2004, was the first to benefit from the Antigua and Barbuda proposal.

Trade

In an era when free trade agreements and trading blocs mark the relations among states and their economies, the OAS seemed designed for smoothing the trade relations among the states of the hemisphere. The Free Trade Area of the Americas (FTAA) is the primary hemispheric agreement though there are many sub-regional arrangements that seem more defining. The FTAA was to have been operationalized in January 2006 but that date has proven elusive. Yet, the role of the OAS is not to be underestimated. The OAS was made the secretariat for the FTAA, and virtually all negotiations among the states were directed by the OAS secretariat staff. The heads of state and government of the 34 American and Caribbean states, meeting at one of their biennial summits in Chile, assigned the OAS this very important task. The leadership of the OAS, under former Colombian President Cesar Gaviria, was delighted to play this role.

In Latin America, many of the intellectuals saw the FTAA as a US ploy to continue to extend control and dominance over her South American neighbors. The US clearly saw it as means of ensuring that Latin America did not fall behind in development and that the USA would not become a magnet for people seeking to escape poverty. The CARICOM saw the FTAA as useful if it meant that the small states, reliant upon customs duties for revenue generation, did not have to abandon a cheap and effective means of collecting government revenues.

Customs duties and other charges upon goods entering ports are used to protect home-grown industries in many Latin American countries. By removing the customs duties, the theory goes, the protectionist urge will disappear and the flow of goods, services and capital will be enhanced. Since Caribbean countries were not protecting manufacturing industries from imports, there seemed to be no reason why they could not be granted a derogation from this requirement. In an era of ideological purity, the US believes that any deviation from the principle would weaken the effects which the US was attempting to achieve. There was no relenting, and many CARICOM states have in fact passed new laws that do away with customs duties and impose value-added taxes(VAT) or, in the case of Antigua and Barbuda, a sales tax to be imposed at the point of sale of goods rather than upon their entry into the country at its port. No-one yet knows how this new paradigm will work for the collection of government revenues, but there is sufficient faith based upon the experience in Dominica and Barbados that there will be compliance.

The CARICOM has its own sub-regional agreement on trade which it calls the CSME (CARICOM Single Market and Economy). For a host of reasons including the differing levels of development, the project has been divided into two parts. The single market will go first, then the single economy will follow in due course. Many of the fourteen CARICOM states report readiness for the single market but integrating the economies has proven far more difficult. The challenge posed by differing currencies and gaping values for each relative to the US dollar, for example, make the integration of the economies virtually impossible. There is no agreement, not even in principle, to do away with the currencies of the states in favor of a single CARICOM currency. There can be no single economy with seven differing currencies and central banks, each dictating a policy at variance with the partners in the single economy. It may never happen.

At the 2000 OAS General Assembly, Antigua and Barbuda proposed the establishment of a single currency for all the states of the hemisphere moving towards an FTAA. We made it clear that we were not proposing abandoning our currencies for one that now exists; rather, we were proposing that all 34 states agree on a single hemispheric currency, and asked that the OAS study the steps to be taken which would cause such an idea to be realized. We knew that the probability of a hemispheric currency was zero, but by placing the demand on the table we showed how difficult it was for all necessary adjustments to take place in order to make the economies of the hemisphere fully integrated in an FTAA. We were not mavericks, nor pie-in-the-sky theorists; quite the contrary. By placing the demand on the table, we identified a salient difficulty which even the strongest proponent could not overcome. The USA, we knew, would never abandon its currency for a hemispheric peso.

In South America, the MERCOSUR was entered into by Argentina, Brazil, Paraguay and Uruguay in 1991. Bolivia, Chile and

Venezuela have also become associate states in the MERCOSUR. The object was to strengthen trade among the southern cone countries, to the benefit of their states and their peoples. The CAFTA (Central America Free Trade Agreement) was designed for the same purpose in the Central American region. The NAFTA (North American Free Trade Agreement) was also designed to facilitate trade among Mexico, the USA and Canada, in order to ensure a free flow of goods across the borders of the three contiguous states.

All of these sub-regional agreements have the support of the OAS and its secretariat but their singular challenge is to devise rules that will not conflict with their requirement under the FTAA and, more recently, under WTO.

It is of historical importance to address the CARIFTA (Caribbean Free Trade Agreement) signed in 1965 by Antigua, Barbados and Guyana. A wealthy entrepreneur constructed an oil refinery on Antigua, beginning in 1965, with the foreknowledge that the refinery would produce far more petroleum distillates than Antigua could consume. To make the enterprise viable, it was called the West Indies Oil Company (WIOC) and it was assured of entry of its products into the markets of Barbados and Guyana. WIOC worked well for five years from the commencement of its exports, in 1968. In 1973 the price of the raw product tripled and the cost of operating a relatively small refinery made the WIOC an unprofitable venture. It is also alleged that the 1973 oil embargo against Israel was extended to Jewish businesses. Since a European Jew had a considerable ownership interest in the oil refinery, the supply of the raw product was discontinued to the oil refinery, turning it into a bunkering and distribution facility. In that same year, the CARIFTA metamorphosed into the CARICOM giving new and bigger impetus to a collaborative effort that has grown in the 34 years since.

The OAS has remained a very useful and significant multilateral institution for the countries of the English-speaking Caribbean. They have transformed the organization while being transformed themselves by membership within it.

II

The Caribbean in the United Nations

The hope for the United Nations as mankind's savior has been partly realized. Certainly, in its work in the English-speaking Caribbean sub-region, the United Nations retains its very high standing with tremendous amounts of goodwill. Its responsibility for gaining sovereignty peacefully and without rancor for many colonies is one of its major successes. The UN's responses in times of crises following natural disasters, and its contributions to helping overcome the HIV/ AIDS pandemic give it creditable marks. The UN's intervention in Haiti and its role in helping to spur development in the region have also done much to burnish its image among citizens, community leaders and diplomats throughout the English-speaking Caribbean region. Yet, having its headquarters in New York means that the major decisions which it takes, emanates from its nerve center where more than 8,000 civil servants meet its needs and are led by its Secretary-General.

The Secretariat

When the USA proposed to have the UN Secretariat located on its soil, in 1945, the City of San Francisco was the most logical choice. It had served as the place where the Charter was ratified by the original 51 members and where the final negotiations had taken place. However, the diplomats from the USSR, having flown from Moscow to New York only to transfer for a cross-continent flight to California lasting an additional six hours expressed a preference for New York. The US Government, anxious to please the USSR, quickly agreed to New York, and so San Francisco lost the bid. One of the wealthy Rockefellers donated the land and the two buildings were constructed by 1960 on grounds that were previously decrepit waterfront properties.

The 38 storied building is majestic, but the general assembly hall with its dome is magnificent. Each time I spoke in the general assembly during the annual assembly debates, my delegation would invite hundreds of nationals to come listen. The nationals were always more impressed with the building than with the speech. There is great awe and wonderment standing in the assembly hall with diplomats from the world's diverse nations sitting before the speaker.

The Secretary-General sits on the uppermost floor of the Secretariat building and most Ambassadors to the UN get to visit there only once, upon the presentation of their credentials. Kofi Annan, the second African to occupy the post, ended his term in December 2006, and a South Korean named Ban Ki-moon has become the new chief. Each newly-assigned permanent representative brings with him/her a fancy document from the head of state which identifies the bearer as the credentialed envoy, and s/he is given a few minutes of the Secretary-General's time to discuss whatever is on his/her mind. There is a continuous parade of new Ambassadors to the UN, especially during the summer months when diplomats with school-age children are given time to re-adjust.

The Office of Protocol is the first UN subdivision that a new diplomat will encounter. For a long time, an Egyptian diplomat who spoke as many as six languages served as its head. A number of Caribbean people have worked in that office, including a bright young woman from Puerto Rico. The diversity of the UN's staff is one of its strongest allure. Professionals from its 192 member-states are employed in the secretariat and carry out the varying responsibilities which the UN has pledged to undertake.

Primary among the tasks is the collection of UN dues from the member-states, and a complex distribution and spending system that many staffers do not yet grasp. The UN's budget for 2008/09 is approximately US$4.2 billion dollars, not including a near-matching sum for International Peace-keeping missions to which all member states must contribute. John Ashe, the Antigua and Barbuda Ambassador to the UN, chairs the UN Committee that determines the budget for the 2006/07 period. Besley Maycock, the Ambassador of Barbados, has also chaired this committee.

The General Assembly

Foreign Minister of Antigua and Barbuda, Lester Bird, delivered the annual address to the UN General Assembly once, prior to 1995. Then, he found the audience too scant and that not much attention was paid to his speech though he is an accomplished orator. Prime Minister Baldwin Spencer has also done the same once, in 2005, and then assigned his attorney general to make the speech in 2006. The assembly hall is filled to the brim whenever the US President comes to the UN to speak. When it is Antigua and Barbuda's or any other country's turn, the hall seems to empty out. The wealthy and large states have a sufficiently large staff to ensure a presence and therefore can pay attention to whatever is said to or about them. In fact, the statements are circulated and simultaneously interpreted into the official languages of the UN, to wit: English, French, Spanish, Arabic, Chinese and Russian.

The Antigua and Barbuda Minister, during the author's tenure, addressed this prejudice by passing the responsibility to his ambassador. For that reason, I delivered the country's primary foreign policy statement for seven consecutive years, commencing in 1988. The same behavior held for many of the CARICOM states' annual statement before the general assembly. The author is of the view that the cost of flying to New York, inflated hotel rates in the city, and the anticipated low regard of member states for the opinions of small states, except on issues that address a very narrow range of concerns, contribute to making the expenses and the effort less than worthy.

The responsibility to draft the statement was also the author's, though Ambassador Patrick Lewis contributed immensely in 1988 and 1989, and other staff members reviewed the draft for errors and accuracy, in my seven years in New York. I would invite our nationals to the UN and they would fill the gallery, giving Antigua and Barbuda an audience which only the USA and Haiti (during Aristede's visits) would enjoy.

It was always a pleasure to have the Antigua and Barbuda nationals in the gallery applaud loudly after the speech, long after the polite applause from the diplomats present had ended. The speech would also be broadcast on the country's national radio live, and national television about three days later after the cassette was flown to Antigua. The World Wide Web has made these arrangements appear outmoded since the UN streams the assembly broadcasts, both audio and video.

While speaking at the UN is an important element in the articulation of our region's concerns, employment within the Secretariat is even more important. The highest ranking persons from the Caribbean used to be Jamaicans and civil servants from the defunct West Indies Federation. The highest ranking person ever from the CARICOM was a Jamaican named Lucille Mair. The CARICOM website recalls that "Dr. Lucille Mair has been hailed as a highly esteemed international diplomatic figure serving prestigiously as Assistant Secretary-General in the office of the United Nations Secretary in 1979, from which she performed with distinction the role of Secretary-General of the World Conference on the United Nations Decade for Women in 1980. The admirable record of international service of her career includes appointment as the Secretary-General's Advisor to UNICEF on Women's Development and Secretary-General of the United Nations Conference on Palestine from 1982 to 1987."[8]

Blandina Francis-Negga, a citizen of Antigua and Barbuda, was the highest ranking national of my small state when she last served as an editor of the Daily Journal. Fifteen Antigua and Barbuda nationals served at the UN during the author's tenure, and more than one hundred and twenty English-speaking Caribbean nationals. Guyanese now outnumber the Jamaicans, reflecting a larger number in the diaspora in recent times.

Security Council

Guyana, Jamaica and Trinidad and Tobago have occupied one of the non-permanent seats on the Security Council during the 62 years that the UN has been in existence. The smallest states have determined that the cost of representation thereon would consume more resources than they could afford. A term on the Council lasts for two years and the various committees and sub-committees of the Council meet on a continuing basis almost daily. The committees do not commence their work until all members are present, meaning that a mission must have at least ten diplomats of sufficient rank and knowledge to service the UN Security Council membership. Employment within a UN Mission is relatively expensive, and a large staff is far too burdensome for many small states. Three or four diplomats are the average for small missions because of the high cost of employment in a very expensive city. For example, the cost of a driver to a Mission in New York exceeds the emoluments received by a permanent secretary in Antigua, the highest-paid civil servant. Antigua and Barbuda's Mission is not large enough to accommodate as many persons as would be required, and the remittances from our capital are barely sufficient to meet the cost of a severely limited diplomatic staff.

There is no friendship gained by Security Council membership, either. Almost every decision taken there amounts to punishing one state and rewarding another, a zero sum game. A decision involving the use of violence, authorized by the UN Security Council, is almost always objected to by the state whose territory is about to be attacked. Or, sanctions that will make life more difficult for innocent civilians who cannot dissuade their governments from taking decisions injurious to the nation, are the responsibility of the Security Council, regardless of who sits on it. The establishment of a peace-keeping force -another of the decisions which only the Security Council can take- is almost always objected to by several members. Only the Permanent Five can exercise a veto, so that if there is unanimity among China, France, Russia, the UK and the USA there is hardly a chance that a measure will not pass.

The adoption of UN Security Council Resolutions which dealt with Haiti and the establishment of several civilian or peace-keeping missions won the support of the CARICOM states. However, the CARICOM were always spectators, sitting on their labeled chairs in the gallery of the Security Council while the fifteen members deliberated. Two states from the Group of Latin American and Caribbean region (GRULAC) sit on the Council all the time, but only from the CARICOM occasionally. Guyana first sat on the Security Council in 1975 and again in 1982 for two year periods. Jamaica followed in 1979 and again in 2000 for a two year-period. Trinidad and Tobago sat once in 1985/1986 following the departure of Eric Williams as its Prime Minister. The Haitian resolutions have been a recurring UN Security Council responsibility; in February 2007, it had to renew the mandate of MINUSTAH, the UN stabilization force in Haiti.

UNDP

The United Nations Development Program is the arm of the UN that distributes development assistance contributed by the wealthiest member states. The contributions are sometimes earmarked for specific projects which the contributing state may identify. At other times, the contributed resources are not specifically earmarked and the UNDP Board will help to decide how the resources are best spent and distributed. The UNDP's total budget exceeds US $4.5 billion, earmarked contributions stood at $2.5 billion and non-earmarked approached $1 billion dollars. Spain is the largest single contributor followed by the UK. Spain's contribution in late 2006 totaled $700 millions; the USA contributed $245 millions behind the UK's $254 millions.

The UNDP has offices in 166 countries, including an office in Barbados that services St. Kitts and Nevis, Antigua and Barbuda, Dominica, St. Lucia, St. Vincent and the Grenadines, Grenada and Barbados. The UNDP Barbados office also serves the non-independent Caribbean countries of Anguilla, British Virgin Islands and Montserrat. Separate offices in the Caribbean are found in the Bahamas, Haiti, the Dominican Republic, Cuba, Trinidad and Tobago, and Guyana.

Major decisions are taken by the UNDP Board of 36 member states which now include Antigua and Barbuda, Guyana and Jamaica among the six member-states from the Latin American and Caribbean region. The Board meets at least once per month in New York in the chambers of the Economic and Social Council, the parent body of the UNDP. The elected board members sit at the front and the remaining 155 states are placed in alphabetical order behind the members. For almost twenty years, since its founding in 1971, Trinidad and Tobago sat on the UNDP Executive Board; the countries of the CARICOM repeatedly nominated that state for re-election. That has since changed.

In the Caribbean region, the UNDP has five areas on which it concentrates its resources: i. Democratic governance; ii. Crisis Prevention and Recovery; iii. Poverty Reduction; iv. Energy and the Environment; v. HIV/AIDS reduction. The UNDP is a very significant player in recovery following natural disasters which occur with frequency in the Caribbean region. It has been providing help to St. Kitts and Nevis to prevent that small state from splitting apart. Nevis has twice held referenda on separation and twice failed to reach the percentage support required.

The UNDP has been very busy providing resources and expertise to the various Constitutional Review Commissions that are examining the constitutions of several states in the OECS. There is a feeling that the constitutions need reform and the UNDP has played its part in that process. But the majority of the resources of the UNDP have gone to poverty reduction, helping to address inequalities that are gender based and that impact heavily on rural areas. It is a very useful institution that plays a significant role in development, more so in the poorest of states than in the small developing states of the Caribbean region.

There are several other UN bodies that play important but not significant roles in the Caribbean region. The UNEP, for example, has worked on climate change issues to the benefit of all states but especially so of small islands-states. The UN Fund for Population (UNFPA) has also been an important player in the region, especially in Haiti where the population challenge is great. The UN Education and Science Organization (UNESCO) and the UN Fund for Women (UNIFEM) have also served the region well.

CHAPTER SIX

POLITICAL CRISES IN LATIN AMERICA

The Organization of American States (OAS) has become the institution that responds meaningfully whenever a political crisis erupts within the states of Latin America and the Caribbean. The people and the governments of the Central and South American states have an abiding faith in the OAS. The resolutions which issue following a crisis usually make headlines in their capitals, and the word of the OAS carries weight. Even the speeches by the representatives are reported. Unlike the UN where there is a permanent press corps, the OAS attracts the Latin media only when a crisis erupts and decisions are being taken.

During the annual General Assemblies, wherever they may take place, a horde of reporters and photographers will keep watch, following the public figures around and interviewing at every opportunity. I can recall witnessing this phenomenon in 1985 when in Cartagena, Colombia, for my first OAS General Assembly. The new minister of foreign affairs of Nicaragua attracted a following of Paparazzi whenever she emerged from the meeting room. She had lured a Nicaraguan general to her bed in order for revolutionaries of the Sandinista Front to execute him. This act gained her notoriety throughout the Americas in part because she had reversed the role of the popular character from Mexican history who befriended the conquistadores and betrayed her own people. Our Nicaraguan heroine eventually died very young from breast cancer. Though her rise and fall were followed closely by the Latin press, the US press hardly paid attention.

Central American Crises

The states of Central America were involved in civil wars in the 1980s. The violence in Nicaragua spawned a crisis in governance in the USA when US Government officials conspired to disobey US law by selling weapons to Iran, then using the profits to fund "the Contras" in Nicaragua -despite the US Congress' withdrawal of funding in order to end US support for the Contras. The debacle severely undermined the Reagan presidency. A civil war in El Salvador and a similar conflict in Guatemala, severely threatened the stability of the six Central American states. In fact, Guatemala played a significant role in securing the peace in the region under the Esquipulas Agreement in 1987.

The author had the opportunity to visit the conference facilities on a little island off Panama's Pacific coast where Esquipulas II was signed among the warring parties. The English-speaking Caribbean was not very deeply involved, in large part because the USA defined the conflicts in cold-war terms and that foreclosed participation by other hemispheric parties. Although the foreign ministers from the CARICOM applauded the parties during their UN general assembly speeches, there was no role for the Caribbean states whose inabilities prohibited them from bringing resources to the table. Once the Cold War came to an end with the demise of the USSR, political capital became a "commodity" that carried weight, and the Caribbean states had a storehouse of that.

Cuba as a Challenge

There are hardly any crises between the states of the OAS anymore. The International Court of Justice (ICJ) during the 1950s ruled on a number of cases involving borders and territorial disputes between several of the Central American states, and one decision between Colombia and Nicaragua over islands in the Caribbean Sea. There is also a dispute between Uruguay and Argentina over traffic on the Uruguay River which has been halted by activists seeking to discourage a pulp mill from exploiting the forests of Uruguay. That dispute has also reached the ICJ. If one considers the friction generated by Venezuela's President Hugo Chavez towards the USA under President George W. Bush as a crisis of sorts, then there is an ongoing crisis between the USA and Venezuela. President Chavez's announcement that he plans to nationalize the property of US firms in Venezuela has also set off several alarm bells in Washington, and filled the newspapers with reasonable stories about Chavez's anti-democratic bent.

The Venezuelan president won re-election to an additional six-year term on December 3, 2006, thereby ensuring that he will be around during the term of another US President. That may allow for a different relationship to emerge after 2008.

The frailty and mortality of Fidel Castro is also being deemed by US thinkers as an opportunity to fix the relationship between the USA and Cuba, following Castro's demise. That may be wishful thinking. There is no guarantee that the Cuban people will surrender the gains they have made under the revolution, though many Cubans are anxious to enjoy many of the consumer items to which even the poor in the USSA have access. Universal education and healthcare are two of the Cuban revolution's primary gains; they may not withstand winds of change if the Miami Cubans became the new leaders of a reformed Cuba. The end of Fidel Castro may also cause Cubans to want to partake of the political freedoms which their Caribbean neighbors enjoy. Talk radio, for example, is not a staple of Cuba's airwaves but flourishes in every other Caribbean island-state and territory. Were the USA not playing such a frontal role in trying to end Castro's rule by its 46 year-old embargo and threats against Mr. Castro's life, the Cuban people may have seized the initiative many years ago. The USA has unwittingly been the best ally of the Cuban revolution after 1961, driven largely by the exiled Cuban community of South Florida.

The political crises that have attracted the OAS have occurred within states, prompted by a breakdown of the political process and, usually, the looming intervention of militaries. Bolivia, Chile, Ecuador, Paraguay, Peru, Venezuela all experienced threats to democratic governance when their presidents were removed either by a military coup, as in Chile, Paraguay and Venezuela, or by protests that immobilized governments and set in motion a chain of events that resulted in riotous situations, as in Bolivia, Ecuador and Peru.

Since 1990, only Haiti among Caribbean island-states has experienced a breakdown that was brought about by violent overthrow of its government. That occurred twice; once in 1991 when a military coup took place, and again in February 2004 when the President was chased from his country by violent thugs. Except for Haiti, one could say that the Caribbean seems immune to political crises that endanger democratic governance. Democracy is deeply grounded in the English-speaking Caribbean, and even the treaty establishing the 1982 Regional Security System (RSS) seems to reflect this reality. The signatory states to the RSS Treaty have given permission for military intervention by any six of the seven whenever the military steps out of line in the seventh state. Because the English-speaking Caribbean projects a model of democratic stability, the states occupy a superior platform that enables them to add their voices whenever democracy is threatened in the Americas. The states have political capital to spend.

It was on those crisis occasions in Latin America that the CARICOM diplomats stuck to their high democratic ideals in the face of US willingness to shepherd a course of action that departed from the nurturing of democratic standards.

Paraguay

Step back a little to 1989 when the President of Paraguay, the military dictator Alfredo Stroessner, was deposed and a political crisis erupted there that made its way to the OAS. The CARICOM representatives were certain that his departure would be good for Paraguay; but they also surmised that the manner of his departure was hurtful to building democracy and that the resulting leadership vacuum would lead to more dictatorship −not to representative democracy. Privately, US diplomats suggested that Stroessner brought stability to Paraguay over his 35 year rule. He had been welcomed to the US White House by President Johnson for his strong anti-communist stance. However, President Carter spurned his advances, believing that his human rights record and his coddling of Nazi officials made him a poor model for the region. The Reagan administration was also not embracing of him. It seemed that his six rigged elections offended even the strong anti-communist Reagan regime.

When the military in Paraguay unseated Stroessner, the moment was right to introduce democratic practices. The US was convinced that transition to democracy would take time and suggested that the military coup plotters be given an opportunity to establish the systems that would lead to free and fair elections. On the contrary, the CARICOM states were persuaded that Paraguay needed to have free and fair parliamentary elections immediately; political parties could be encouraged to compete freely for support and an election date fixed, in order to declare Paraguay an adherent to democracy. The USA prevailed, in 1989, and it took four years for the military there to step down from political leadership and to allow open presidential elections.

Paraguay's transition to democratic rule has been torturous and long delayed. Since 1811, when it declared its independence from Spain, it took more than 180 years for democracy to sprout in Paraguay. The deep cultural proclivity of that country's anti-democratic history was for continued dictatorship. When small states' representatives in Washington made clear their preferences, there were many Latin diplomats who saw the interventions from the Caribbean countries as "pie-in-the-sky" theorizing. Yet, the elections in Paraguay just four years after Stroessner's departure made clear the ability of people, freed from fear, to exercise wisdom and good judgment. In 1993, Paraguay's first democratically elected President took office.

After 1951, when adult suffrage became the law, the English-speaking Caribbean peoples began to exercise the wisdom of which all people are capable. Bear in mind that there were high rates of illiteracy within Caribbean countries at the time. In fifty-five years, the Caribbean people have remained true to the rule of law and democratic ideals except for the one instance in 1979 when Grenada experienced a coup. No matter the history and the cultural bent, when afforded the opportunity, the author has come to believe that Latin Americans will choose the freedom of representative democracy over military dictatorship every time. That is the lesson of Stroessner's departure. The rule of law has begun to shine.

The role played by the US Ambassador in Asunción is also of relevance, during and after 1989. The South American states expect a leadership role for the USA and so very often turn to the resident

US Ambassador to play a mediating role whenever crises erupt. CARICOM states do not have a presence in these countries, except in Venezuela, Cuba and Mexico. Antigua and Barbuda, Belize, Jamaica and Guyana have honorary consuls in several capitals, but these are nationals of the countries and have been appointed for commercial benefit, not political. Hence, any impact which the English-speaking Caribbean will have during these crises will almost always be limited to their roles at the OAS or the UN where the hemispheric states are represented. It is within these institutions that the CARICOM states have successfully worked to enlarge the freedoms which Paraguayans and others have enjoyed. The USA thus enjoys a decided advantage, given also the military role which they have played. The Lain Americans purchase their weapons largely from the USA, and the military attaches dispatched from Washington to their several capitals carry tremendous weight among the receiving Latin states.

Ecuador

The crisis in Ecuador in January 2000 provided another test of the OAS' ability to bring calm and peace to a tortured democracy. President Jamil Mahoud Witt was duly elected to office for a six year term and had served almost one-half of his term when he was unconstitutionally removed from office. The events in Ecuador provided an opportunity for the states of the hemisphere to stand with a duly elected President, to defend democracy and to marginalize the military during a political crisis.

The Clinton administration was then demitting office, and a wrangling in the USA over a presidential race which seemed likely to drag on for months, left decision-making in the State Department to the career diplomats and not a politically appointed cadre. Had the Bush administration been securely in place during the Ecuador crisis, the results may have differed.

The CARICOM states at the OAS expressed the view that Mahoud's vice president should step forward, given the absence of any recall provisions in the Ecuadorian constitution, but only as a temporary measure until new presidential elections could be reorganized. The US State Department was among the strongest of foes against the unconstitutionality of the anti-democratic forces in that country, and warned the military to stay out of the fracas which came about as a result of street demonstrations.

The CARICOM states and the other members of the OAS Permanent Council on January 21, 2000, sent a strong message to those forces that there would be no tolerance for any undemocratic replacement of the President. Mr. Mahoud stepped down and allowed his vice president to fill his post, and new elections were scheduled.

Ecuador has been locked in a battle with the Caribbean states over the banana quotas and special pricing arrangement set by the European Communities. Ecuador brought the issue to the WTO Arbitration Panel, declaring the arrangements as discriminatory. Despite the undermining of a preferential agreement that brought significant benefit to the Caribbean, the small-island states yearned for democratic ideals to take root in Ecuador. They believed that a stronger trade union movement could only emerge under a democratically elected government, and that the workers on banana plantations could not expect better wages and improved working conditions under dictatorship. By improving the wages and benefits of Ecuadorian workers, the cost of their bananas would likely increase and make Caribbean bananas more competitive. Under the oppressive conditions extant in Ecuador, the pittance paid to workers would remain inordinately low, making the produce more competitive than Caribbean bananas produced on small, private farms at far higher labor costs. Democracy is good for strategic as well as purely altruistic reasons.

Ecuador is also an exporter of fossil fuels. It is of geo-political importance to the USA whose reliance on its fuel exports lessens reliance on Mid-East oil.

Ecuador has continued to show instability, and the OAS remains very much seized of events there. It is of interest to note that Ecuador has changed presidents six times in the past ten years, suggesting that the Ecuadorian people see their President as pivotal in achieving the high economic standards that they expect in their country.

Venezuela

In April 2002, President Hugo Chavez of Venezuela was removed from office by a military coup. The USA was willing to allow Chavez's unlawful removal from office to stand by failing to denounce the coup plotters and from rumors that the rebelling soldiers received support from sources connected to the opposition forces. Since Chavez had been extremely critical of the USA and was deemed a threat to US interests, his ouster was not unexpected. The CARICOM countries stood opposed to the USA and to the policy option which it shamelessly articulated. Democratic ideals cannot be abandoned because the US State Department dislikes a leader or views his statements with mistrust. The comity of nations cannot be based on personable qualities of their leaders.

The Chavez plotters seemed to be aware that US State department support for their actions was forthcoming; Chavez subsequently charged that US operatives engineered his removal. He was actually escorted from the presidential palace by the coup plotters, taken to military barracks, and seemed deposed. Millions of Venezuelans flooded the streets, insisting that he be released. Fearing for the destruction of their capital, and having heard the voices of democratic support from the states of the region, including the CARICOM, the military yielded. Chavez overcame the coup plotters.

At the OAS, despite the waffling by the US representative, the CARICOM states were vocal in their support of democracy; and, the OAS Permanent Council of Ambassadors adopted a resolution on April 21, 2002, that clearly disavowed the anti-democratic forces. It is necessary to note that resolutions are adopted by consensus at the OAS, and there hardly ever is a resolution these days subject to a vote. The USA is thus compelled by the overwhelming number of voices in support of a resolution to yield. Though the US Ambassador to the OAS may make a statement for the record in which his government will share with the Council those parts of a resolution with which it disagrees, it is forced by consensus to abide by the majority will.

To many with an abiding interest in Latin American affairs, the evolution which has taken place at the OAS where the states can resist the USA and where tiny island-states openly express their opposition to US preferences are signals of a fundamental shift from decades earlier. Before the demise of the USSR, when the USA lent its support to a particular outcome, the member-states of the OAS seemed compelled to follow. Now with the Soviet Union gone, communism destroyed, democracy on the rise, even the USA is compelled by these circumstances to bend to the will of the majority.

Yet, I would assert that a lot of the courage which even the Latin American diplomats display is an infection spread by the fearlessness of Afro-Saxon diplomats from the tiny island-states of the Caribbean. "If they can be so bold, then so can we," the Latin diplomats have thought to themselves. The tiny island-states can be bold because they view democracy as necessary to their survival. If democracy fails among the states of the hemisphere and within the multilateral institutions of which they are members, then they will disappear as sovereign states. It is democracy or death! If their membership within the multilateral institutions is not proven useful, they may be squeezed out and compelled to congeal- as the British were attempting to do in 1958. The small island-states have become the conscience of the institution which is a burden their Afro-Saxon diplomats gladly bear.

The OAS resolution of April 2002 clearly contributed to saving Chavez from a successful military coup and to safeguarding democracy in Venezuela. The Secretary General had been dispatched to Venezuela weeks before and so was present during the debacle which continued almost down through December 2002. The strong support issuing from the OAS fortified the Secretary General and allowed him to play a useful mediating role. Along with the UNDP and the Carter Centre and the CARICOM, the OAS caused democracy to survive in Venezuela.

Chavez also survived a referendum on his leadership engineered by the opposition. The analysts in the USA credit the high price of oil -upon which rests the economic success of Venezuela- as being the root cause of Chavez's political success. He has had resources to spend on anti-poverty programs that have won him support among the vast numbers of poor. The US analysts often speak as though that approach to governing is antithetical to democracy. Sharing the wealth of a country with its underclass is the promise of democracy, and Chavez's determination and ability to deliver have endeared him to the millions of Venezuelans who are participating in the fruits of their state's oil revenues. That is as it should be though I fear he may go too far.

The major news publications in the US view Chavez's sharing of the oil revenues with skepticism and abhorrence. They look upon his approach as antithetical to good governance because it increases reliance upon the state, at a time when their ideological preference is for a decreasing role for the state and a bigger role for the private sector. That is a warped view of good governance.

The private sector in Venezuela has shown an unwillingness to act in the interests of the people of Venezuela. The private sector in the USA once behaved this way but the revolution in attitude spawned by the activism of the 1960s caused the US private sector to display what is called "corporate responsibility." That revolution never reached the states of Latin America.

Administrations in Venezuela also acted in the interest of the very wealthy, to the detriment of the vast underclass. Like most South American countries, the distribution of wealth in Venezuela is extremely lopsided with a small minority controlling a significant proportion of the nation's wealth, while the vast majority of the urban and rural poor dwell in abject and extreme poverty. Chavez has vowed to reverse this situation, and the elites feel threatened. Although there is a very wealthy class of persons in the USA, the wealth is spread in such a way that a vast middle class exists in the USA. That is the experiment that Venezuelans wish to see in their own country, I believe.

The USA is too long removed from 1776, the author concludes, while the CARICOM states are still living with the memory of 1951 –the year adult suffrage was made law. Many of the diplomats and leaders in the CARICOM were alive when colonialism existed in their countries. There is more than a historical understanding of exploitative practices by those in authority. For these reasons, many CARICOM representatives understand the struggle which President Chavez faces, and view the neo-conservative bent of the USA as harmful to development in Latin America. The idea of transferring even more wealth to the wealthy has appeal in the USA, but not among the poor of Latin America and the Caribbean. The CARICOM states and the people of the USA believe that sharing the wealth is good social policy and ensures development that is equitable.

Chavez has thus been very generous in his use of Venezuela's wealth to help his CARICOM neighbors, Cuba, Argentina, Ecuador and Bolivia. He has made loans to those states utilizing the revenues from oil, freeing Argentina from the shackles of the IMF and those lending institutions that dictate policy in exchange for resources. What could possibly be wrong with sharing wealth among poorer neighbors? The major US press, on this issue, displays its hubris, its unbelief that a small country in South America does what a very large and wealthy USA will not do or, in their view, has justifiably ceased doing. US President Bush made a visit to five Latin American states in March 2007 and began addressing the challenge of poverty. The US press has noted that the US Government is acting to challenge Chavez's leadership in Latin America; they wonder out loud if the US can match Venezuela's petro-dollar diplomacy.

The elites in the USA –in the press and the government- are persuaded that under-development and poverty in poor states are not urgent issues that require immediate attention. They suggest that developed countries are "aid-weary", having budgeted large amounts for development assistance since the end of colonial rule, to no avail. Underdevelopment and poverty are seen as the warranted results of thievery and mismanagement which the populations suffer because they permit bad government, the elites posit. Jamaica Kincaid has done a masterful job of articulating this ideology in her *Small Place* when writing of her native Antigua and Barbuda; the facts prove differently upon examination.

One sometimes can conclude that the elites believe that misery and poverty are conditions in which the Third World peoples should dwell until the world's non-white, dark-skinned peoples can figure out how to fix the systems of wealth-creation themselves. "The white man's burden," the quip popularized by Toynbee, is not the USA's, the elites believe. After all, the USA never colonized like the Europeans. Yet, an ancient US State Department did encourage dictators and embezzlers to undermine democracy in the countries of Latin America ever since its articulation of its "big stick" approach more than one century ago. The ghosts of the past have returned to do some haunting.

USA's Diminished Diplomacy

Diplomacy has diminished, and military solutions have taken prominence in the administration of the second President Bush. The US is clearly the world's lone superpower and it has led the Bush administration to announce a policy of pre-emption. The USA, the

Bush team has made public, will launch a military attack against another state if the USA believes that the enemy state is about to attack it. International law disallows this pre-emptive use of military power for it knows how subterfuge and lies can lead ambitious leaders to invent reasons to launch attacks against weak neighbors or unfriendly (defenseless) states. Under Article 51 of the UN Charter, a state may use force to defend itself without seeking authorization from the UN. The use of military force against a UN member-state that has not launched an attack against another requires the authorization of the United Nations Security Council. That was a US invention that now seems to be set aside by a subsequent US administration in a world where US military power is supreme.

Reliance upon military solutions was not the preferred approach of the USA in 1945 when the UN was founded. The US State Department, through its financing arm, used to rely upon the material richness of the USA to bring states within its influence. USAID would help build schools, hospitals, clinics and other infrastructure, and give helpful material assistance to poor countries during an earlier period. Aid is cheaper than war; and, aid is diplomacy. That is not the thinking among US policymakers in the Bush administration, in 2007, and so it is not the way aid is distributed these days.

The USA spent about US$24 billion dollars in foreign aid in 2006; but that is less than 0.7% of the US budget. Though that many billions of dollars still represent a considerable contribution to development efforts, the manner of its distribution is such that many militaries, consultants and people in the aid industry will benefit more than the people of the poor countries for whom the aid is ostensibly intended. Egypt and Israel benefit inordinately from the USAID programs in an attempt to ensure peace among those two neighbors, as does Colombia in Latin America, fighting an insurgency for almost two decades.

The rationale now holds that aid money is usually stolen by the elites within the poor countries and the intended poor fail to benefit by the spending of US taxpayer dollars with their governments. This view has led to a warped spending pattern that benefits the consultants and the aid professionals, and hardly ever reaches the poor. The Japanese, the Chinese, the British, the Canadians and the Venezuelans have figured out how to spend aid resources that reach the intended target;

it is amazing that the US State Department would publicly proclaim that it is unable to fix its shortcomings.

When the US military decides to engage in humanitarian works, it is remarkable how it succeeds in getting the benefits directly to the intended beneficiaries. US military assets have been deployed into countries following a disaster and have helped to reconstruct public buildings, provide medical assistance, deliver clean water and undertake a multiplicity of good works. Their record in the Caribbean following hurricanes is remarkable. After the Tsunami in Malaysia in December 2005, the US military saved hundreds of lives and brought order to a chaotic situation.

Only the elites within the US State Department, relying on accountable political gain or quid pro quo, can spend as it does to avoid corruption and in so doing confer benefits on hordes of consultants and private enterprise operators, while claiming that the process is intended to avoid unjust enrichment of poor-states' elites.

In the English-speaking Caribbean island-states, USAID has not made any claim of corrupt dealing. Our populations and governments are fairly honest and transparency is honored in practice; clearly, a consequence of democratic ideals being expressed in governance. In more difficult terrain, whatever may obtain, it is hard to believe that the challenges cannot be fixed by both the US and receiving governments.

In March 2007, the US President made a five-nation tour through South and Central America, shoring up US support against the diplomatic gains made by Venezuela in its anti-American, petro-dollar campaign. The US President was unable to promise any increased aid flows, only bilateral trade agreements and the purchase of bio-fuels from Brazil. It is of interest to note that the media cast the trip as an anti-Venezuelan venture, attesting to the change in circumstances since the end of the Cold War and the phenomenon of emerging power centers outside of Washington.

Venezuela's Expanded Diplomacy

When Venezuela shares its wealth, it goes directly to the poor. Like its ophthalmic program in the Caribbean and Latin America since 2004. Venezuela flies several thousand poor people each year to Cuba, where they are treated -at no cost to them- to specialist eye care unavailable in their own countries, and returned to their countries. The program is enormously successful and has won Venezuela many friends at the local and regional level.

Then there is the Venezuelan oil financing program called PetroCaribe. Venezuela offers oil at market prices but will finance that portion of the sale that exceeds US $40 dollars per barrel over a twenty year period at 1% annual interest. The governments must pledge to spend the amounts which they saved on social programs, investing as it were in their populations. That investment will put the states in a position to repay the amortized amount over a twenty-year period. It is simply brilliant.

The US elites argue publicly that Venezuela ought not be generous for that violates a core principle of capitalism. Each state, the theory goes, should sink or swim depending on its own wherewithal rather than rely upon a helping hand from a wealthier neighbor. They accuse Venezuela of giving away its people's money for extravagant and revolutionary, anti-American reasons. That claim is rejected by the CARICOM states and they therefore have befriended Venezuela and defended Chavez against unreasonable attacks by the US State Department.

It would also be important to note that Venezuela's friendship with the East Caribbean goes back more than thirty years, to the 1970s, when Carlos Andres-Perez was President and made many gestures of friendship to the Caribbean people. It was Andres-Perez who established embassies and cultural commissions in every independent Caribbean country capital. He initiated a series of exchanges that have caused thousands of Caribbean people to live and work in Venezuela, learning Spanish and the ways of the Venezuelan people. There are communities of English-speaking Caribbean people in towns facing the Caribbean Sea. They have made Venezuela their home just as immigrants from the same islands once made Santo Domingo, the Dominican Republic, and Cuba their new home as well. The Venezuelans have also established cultural institutes in their embassies, teaching Spanish and Venezuelan history to those who have an interest.

Chavez has stepped over the line on occasion. In taking the podium at the UN General Assembly debates in September 2006, Chavez called US President Bush "the devil". It lost him his country's bid to sit on the UN Security Council, and antagonized the Americans for no apparently good reason. Of course, when President Reagan called the USSR the "evil empire", and George Bush called Iran, Syria and Iraq "the axis of evil", that was mere hyperbole!

The US elites argue that Chavez wants to inherit the mantle which Fidel Castro's imminent departure may leave unclaimed. He is a close ally of what the US press dubs "leftist leaning" politicians of South America, including President Morales of Bolivia, President Ortega of Nicaragua, and President Lula DaSilva of Brazil. Whatever their view of Chavez, he remains very popular within his own country, winning re-election on December 6, 2006, for six more years.

Bolivia

Move forward to October 2003 when the elected President of Bolivia, Gonzalo Sanchez de Lozado, was under attack; there was violence in the streets and representative democracy, a relatively recent development, was endangered. Since its declaration of independence in 1825, Bolivia had experienced coups and counter coups that exceed in number its 180 years as a sovereign state. It was not until 1982 that the first civilian government came to power in Bolivia. It did not last its full term before it was displaced by unlawful means.

The OAS Permanent Council of Ambassadors in October 2003 nevertheless was made aware of the unrest in Bolivia, it consulted with the delegation and issued a resolution which repeated the representatives' resolve to support democratically elected governments. The CARICOM states again were adamant in their support of democracy, despite the lukewarm response of the USA. Shortly after the OAS acted, the President resigned and he was replaced by his vice president who lasted almost two years, only to be replaced by the Head of the Supreme Court, in July 2005. In December 2005 an election was held and Evo Morales emerged as the new President. He is from the indigenous population and has promised radical reform, especially in land reform and in the distribution of the benefits from its fossil fuels sales. He was sworn in for five years in January 2006 and has befriended Venezuela's President Chavez. The US sees the Bolivia, Ecuador, Venezuela troika as inimical to US interests. Given the power and reach of the USA it is difficult to imagine that three South American republics could harm its long-term interests. I am of the view that the US has grown accustomed to exercising control over the South Americans and may now be experiencing anxiety since it has lost the ability to control them exclusively. Venezuela's new found wealth, and the purposes to which that wealth is put, is the real worry of the USA policymakers. Yet, the Bolivians have set out on a new path which can only inure to the majority of the Bolivian population.

The CARICOM foreign ministries and their diplomats abroad were very aware that Bolivia had historically engaged in a system of exclusion of its large indigenous majority population from the economic mainstream and the politics of the country. The 2003 protests were in part about the land, the use of the gas and oil reserves, and the dominant role which foreign corporations were playing in determining the uses to which the resources were being put. Brazilian firms were especially involved in exploiting the natural gas fields for export. The USA was nevertheless Bolivia's largest trading partner though its exports to the USA were marginal by US standards. Except for the trade in cocoa leaves for inclusion in cocaine, for eventual export to the USA, Bolivia would be of even lesser importance to the USA. The material interests of the US were simply not that great. Those factors may have determined the degree of interest which the USA exercised, and its willingness to spend political capital on Bolivia.

In 2005, the OAS again dispatched missions to Bolivia and Ecuador to help manage crises that threatened political stability. By this time, the Caribbean states had established their leadership and their preference, so that the states of South America are not puzzled by the policy choices expressed by their Caribbean neighbors.

It is of interest to note that there are no reporters from the Caribbean stationed at the OAS to convey impressions back to the capitals. The diplomats are completely reliant upon their own missions and the OAS Department of Public Information (DPI) to promote their work throughout the hemisphere. Each day,

Vorn Martin and Ian Edwards, two CARICOM nationals from Trinidad and Jamaica respectively, bear the responsibility for selling the English-speaking Caribbean publics on the usefulness of the diplomats from the region, and on the issues that attract the diplomats' attention. They both do a remarkable job. But a score of journalists and editors from throughout the hemisphere, working at the DPI, keep the OAS in the media and on the minds of citizens of Latin America.

CHAPTER SEVEN

THE INTER-AMERICAN DEMOCRATIC CHARTER

On September 11, 2001, when Americans were focused on the 9/11 terrorist events unfurling in New York, Washington and Pennsylvania, the ambassadors assigned to the OAS were in Lima, Peru. The US Secretary of State, Colin Powell, was seated at table there, several chairs away from the author who was the head of the Antigua and Barbuda delegation. The OAS had convened a "Special General Assembly" in order to bring into being a Peruvian initiative that had its birth in Quebec, a few months earlier, when 34 of the thirty-five heads of state and government convened at a Summit of the Americas to sign *The Quebec Declaration.*

The former United Nations Secretary General, Javier Perez de Cuellar, a Peruvian, had proposed during the preparatory sessions preceding the Summit, the creation of a Charter that would articulate the obligations of states in a hemisphere that was committing itself to democracy. Peru had been severely traumatized by a political crisis involving President Alberto Fujimori, who fought the Shining Path guerrillas with such ferocity that he placed democratic freedoms in jeopardy. Once he had strong-armed the terrorists with little resistance from any domestic source, it was easy for his intelligence services to apply similar techniques to his political opponents. Fujimori fired and then selected Peruvian Supreme Court judges who were obedient to him, blackmailed opposition parliamentarians by spying on them and holding the evidence of their wrongdoing over their heads like Damocles' sword, and bribed many politicians whom he videotaped accepting the bribes. President Fujimori found that with an opposition squelched, he could then engage in corrupt acts that enriched himself and his cronies.

The lesson taught by the Peruvian experience is that seeking to acquire absolute power leads inexorably to absolute corruption and there are no circumstances under which a civilized society can permit un-democratic means to be applied even to fighting terrorists. This law of politics applies to the USA as well, whose diplomats repeated that refrain to Peruvian diplomats prior to the September 2001 events in the USA. Sooner than the guardians of democracy would expect, the same undemocratic methods applied to fighting terrorists in Peru seemed to creep into US domestic policies against legitimate opposition forces and innocent citizens who criticize the ruling regime. The passage of the Patriot Act in the aftermath of the September 2001 terrorist attacks against the USA, followed by an unlawful war in Iraq, the elision of constitutional rights in the USA, and the illegal seizures of private citizens whose rendition to secret jails in several countries where they are tortured and may even be killed, have begun to turn the USA into a brutal Latin American republic where people disappear and are never heard from again. The USA is beginning to look more like Peru.

Two important films which tell the tale of Fujimori's conversion to undemocratic means and his lasting impact on Peruvian democracy are "State of Fear" and "Fall of Fujimori". They can be accessed on the World Wide Web, but need to be viewed in order to get a broader picture than can here be provided.

The impact of CARICOM countries on uprighting Peruvian democracy is related here because it shows the impact which even a small state's diplomats can have on reforming democratic ideals in a much larger state. Size then is irrelevant when equally sovereign states apply moral pressure to bring about lasting change.

As history demonstrates, when Fujimori's political machinations were exposed, a crisis erupted and he eventually had to flee Peru. An interim President was selected, and democracy's survival in Peru was threatened. The OAS Permanent Council, as is customary whenever a crisis erupts in the Americas, convened an emergency session. The Ambassadors of the member-states made strong pronouncements that were reported in their own countries' press and in the press of the affected state, condemning the undemocratic events that were unfurling.

The diplomats from small Caribbean island-states, determined to be more than spectators to these events at the OAS, and certain that the militaries and elected members of legislatures or congresses can be sent strong messages that would permanently discourage unlawful plotting and *coups d'etats*, joined the debates. Months later, the CARICOM supported Peru's efforts vigorously in the lead-up to the Quebec Summit. When the Peruvian initiative came to the OAS permanent council for implementation, in the post-Quebec period, strong support was forthcoming from the CARICOM representatives.

I

Battling the USA

The US Ambassador to the OAS, at the time in 2001, was a Cuban émigré who believed that he could lecture his counterparts from the hemisphere and that, as the lone superpower in the house, he could compel his counterparts to achieve his ends. It was rumored that he was demitting office soon and that he wanted to leave a lasting legacy. Whatever his reasons, he pushed hard, even bullied, to achieve full acceptance of the draft Inter-American Democratic Charter in Washington for onward transmission to the annual assembly in Costa Rica, where negotiations to conclude the document continued. His manner and style alienated his allies.

The CARICOM representatives, the strongest supporters of democratic ideals, felt that the USA was attempting to dictate an outcome rather than arrive at a consensus by negotiation. The US lost the CARICOM delegations.

The US Ambassador to the OAS thus came up against a few Caribbean diplomats who saw the need to teach him a lesson in the practice of democracy among states. Ambassador Michael King from Barbados, leading the charge, sought to prevent what would be a rushed-job if the draft Charter were adopted by the OAS General Assembly in Costa Rica, without time to reflect on its terms. In consultation, the members of the CARICOM, represented by their foreign ministers at the General Assembly, rebelled against the shoving by the US Ambassador.

When these 14 tiny sovereign states publicly resisted the USA, larger states followed the rebellion. The large states, noting the implacable resistance of the CARICOM, joined the throng. The OAS General Assembly, meeting in Costa Rica that June afternoon 2001, agreed that there would be additional consultation and that a special session of the General Assembly would be convened to adopt the new Inter-American Democratic Charter, later that year. The USA lost a battle.

It is unusual for the USA to lose, especially when fighting against states that are considered its vassals by US policy makers and media specialists, and when the USA is determined to achieve its ends. Yet, here was the USA, as determined as a state could be, to adopt a document that was being painstakingly negotiated by the OAS Ambassadors. Standing opposed to rushing into adoption were 14 tiny states. They did not object to the worthiness of the draft or the ideals expressed in the document; they objected to the manner in which the Charter was being shoved at sovereign states, and the US delegation had to back down. It was a moment to savor for it was a milestone in US/Caribbean international relations that would continue to define the future among OAS member-states in the post-communist period. Though friendly to the USA, when the moment was propitious, the CARICOM delegations rose to defend democracy among states and in so doing improved the quality of US decision-making.

As equal sovereigns, the USA learned that in a public forum where the world is watching and listening, it too had to bend to regional opinion. In a bipolar world, it would have summoned the ministers to a private meeting and threatened; then it would have taken the public rostrum and invoked the communist threat. Freed from these forces, the USA had to behave as if it were one of many legislators in any domestic parliament: It had to compromise, despite the source of the pressure had been fourteen small states. That was a revelation and one important enough to recall.

II

The Context

The Inter-American Democratic Charter contains many lofty ideals which will be tested over time. However, in arriving at the Charter, the test of democracy-in-action among states was confirmed in Costa Rica that June 2001 afternoon. The diplomats went back to Washington and, at the behest of their foreign ministers, fine-tuned the document over several weeks. Then, since it was a Peruvian initiative, the foreign ministers were invited by the Peruvian government to Lima for the signing and for public display of our commitment, in September 2001.

On the morning of September 11, 2001, when the adoption of the document was planned, CNN broadcast live the attack on the World Trade Center, with coverage of the attack on the Pentagon and the crash in the field in Pennsylvania. It was a disconcerting morning in which the feeling of powerlessness was magnified by our distance from the centre, our inability to affect outcomes, and the dread which the events portend. The irony of our presence in Peru, for the purpose of defining the appropriate course for states when fighting terrorism, was certainly not lost. No-one knew then what the USA would do, although we were certain that those who committed the acts were sure to feel the wrath of the world's lone superpower. Afghanistan's Taliban government was subsequently routed by a combined NATO force led by the USA. Operatives within the US Government tried to extend culpability to the regime in Iraq in order to end the rule of Saddam Hussein. The latter proved to be an error of painfully large proportions.

After September 11, 2001, the Inter-American Democratic Charter was not applied to the USA in the same way that the US would hope to apply its terms to the other 34 countries of the hemisphere. While the USA would regard the document as binding on the states of the hemisphere, the same document could not win acceptance by the US Senate that has the authority to ratify treaties and other agreements to which the US executive has given its assent. The Charter therefore remained advisory, rather than compulsory; it seemed to many lawyers that it was not worth the effort unless formally adopted like a treaty.

Despite its advisory nature, the author takes great pride in knowing that many of the ideas contained in the document emanated from Antigua and Barbuda's delegation, before and after Costa Rica. Our delegation was never absent from, and always participated in a meaningful way, in the preparatory meetings. Where the drafters were likely to overlook many of the seminal ideals that translate into a practicing democracy within a state, the author was privileged to bring those ideas and ideals to the attention of the working group and they were readily incorporated.

At the September 11 meeting in Lima, the author, as head of his country's delegation, expanded on several of the themes that were incorporated in the document as a result of his own contribution in the months preceding. For example, speaking on behalf of Antigua and Barbuda, the author again reminded the Latin Americans that exclusion of their black and indigenous populations from the benefits of growing economies constituted a failure of democracy in the eyes of the excluded. A special effort had to be made to ensure that the remnants of racism were excised from their national psyches and that the benefits of democracy were spread as evenly as possible among all, including the historically disenfranchised, the meeting was told.

Again, if Lester Bird, the Foreign Minister of Antigua and Barbuda at the time, had exercised his prerogative and attended the Lima meeting, the author would not have played so prominent a role. Yet, Antigua and Barbuda would still have emphasized the issues that guarantee a fairer world and a better hemisphere; that is our state's historic mission and one of the purposes of its independence in twenty-five years. It is also the practice for the Caribbean Ambassadors to prepare the written speeches which the foreign ministers deliver at multilateral meetings, such as the Special General Assembly in Peru; the speech which Lester Bird would have made would likely have been the same.

III

The Disagreement Among The CARICOM Representatives

The Inter-American Democratic Charter is made up of twenty-eight articles. All of those articles reflect varying degrees of importance to democracy which the CARICOM states support. The articles evidence our states' mission, and the inclusion of several was the result of Antigua and Barbuda's efforts; although, in a multilateral setting all inclusions can be jointly claimed by all participants.

Although representatives from the CARICOM attended many of the preparatory meetings, they were not active participants. This silence may likely have been on account of the many interventions by Antigua and Barbuda which the English-speaking diplomats and the Latin American representatives may have regarded as CARICOM interventions. There was no agreement in advance that Antigua and Barbuda would speak on CARICOM's behalf, and thus the contributions can be legitimately claimed as Antigua and Barbuda's.

Furthermore, during the May 2001 debates, the Ambassador from Barbados came to one of the meetings and announced that the CARICOM bureau of foreign ministers had decided that the CARICOM felt aggrieved by the fast pace at which the negotiations were proceeding. He seemed to have been suggesting that the whole process cease until such time as the bureau was satisfied that the emerging document could be reviewed. Antigua and Barbuda regarded that as Barbadian hubris. Three foreign ministers, consulting by telephone at the insistence of Barbados, could not decide how much work could or should be done in Washington in late May by 34 delegations, prior to a general assembly scheduled for early June 2001. That debate would have been properly taken up in Costa Rica, during the Assembly. If the intention was to raise the issue in Washington so that it would have traction in Costa Rica, it worked.

Once in Costa Rica, weeks later, a different result obtained when the CARICOM foreign ministers jointly decided that they could put the brakes on the document. Antigua and Barbuda's delegation, led by Minister Gaston Browne, argued for the adoption of the Charter at the Costa Rica General Assembly, noting that to carry over the document to another assembly would be costly, that further improvements would be marginal, and that the Charter was not intended to become law by way of adoption by national legislatures like a treaty or convention. It would thus be a resolution, no more binding than all the other resolutions which the OAS Assembly would adopt before the three-day meeting ended, Minister Browne asserted. He did not carry the day. Antigua and Barbuda therefore joined in the CARICOM consensus and their insistence led the OAS to Lima, Peru, in September and caused the US Secretary of State to be outside of the USA when the attacks occurred on September 11, 2001.

IV

Three Poignant Articles

Although the Antigua and Barbuda delegation had an input in all twenty-eight articles, the delegation took great pride in knowing that it introduced three very poignant articles that reflect the sub-region's history and yearnings.

> Article 9 reads: The elimination of all forms of discrimination, especially gender, ethnic and race discrimination, as well as diverse forms of intolerance, the promotion and protection of human rights of indigenous peoples and migrants, and respect for ethnic, cultural and religious diversity in the Americas contribute to strengthening democracy and citizen participation.

The commitment by governments and member-states to end ethnic and racial discrimination is present in the Charter because of our delegation's insistence. Lengthy explanations were required in support of every proposal and only by being present and by full participation were the interests of states included. Caribbean diplomats continue to believe that the hypocrisy which parades in "equality talk" must be reflected in actions that lead to greater inclusion of black and indigenous people in the governments of their countries. We have another fundamental reason for echoing this cry. The Latin Americans can be fierce and unkind when they are openly criticized by the CARICOM representatives, believing our small states to be less than worthy of sovereignty, hence un-worthy of a presence as equals sitting next to them. Their attitudes are also informed by race; they are all white and many of the CARICOM diplomats are black.

The author recalls a placid Wednesday morning in October 2000, when allocation of the OAS Budget was being hammered out. The delegation of Antigua and Barbuda was adamant that allocations for the OAS overseas offices could not be further trimmed; we were not backing down on this demand since to compromise would mean the disappearance of the OAS Offices in the countries of the East Caribbean.

The OAS has three-person offices in Grenada, St. Vincent and the Grenadines, St. Lucia, Dominica, Antigua and Barbuda, and St. Kitts and Nevis, or in each of the smallest states-members. That the OAS has an office in Guyana, Suriname, Trinidad and Tobago, Barbados, and Jamaica is regarded as justified. Even the US has chosen to place embassies in these larger countries but has one embassy in Barbados that serves the needs of the other identified states in the East Caribbean, Grenada excepted.

The United Nations has done the same; placing a UNDP office in Barbados that serves the other six states of the East Caribbean. PAHO has also done the same, placing one office in Barbados that serves the other six countries. Only the OAS and ILCA, among multilateral institutions, have individual offices in the countries of the East Caribbean, and the entire CARICOM wish to retain the OAS offices.

Brazil volunteered to give up its OAS office. Brazil's representative to the Budget Committee chose to ask the author about his country's contribution to the OAS budget, drawing attention to the measly $5,000 annual contribution of Antigua and Barbuda and, by extension, of the other East Caribbean states to the OAS budget. The Brazilian was attempting to de-legitimize the very presence of Antigua and Barbuda in the discussion on allocation. The author, unusually active for an ambassador in the debates of the Budget Committee, coolly responded that the subject of discussion at that moment was not about "contributions", but rather about "allocations." I promised that I would therefore respond to the Brazilian's question when that debate was the subject. The author has no way to prove that race was also a factor. However, white Brazilians are unaccustomed to being denied their ambitions by persons with black skin. The Brazilian diplomat had to be resisted.

One method of sending a strong reminder to each of the Latin American delegations about race was to include the reference to non-discriminatory treatment in the Inter-American Democratic Charter.

Another article that the Antigua and Barbuda delegation insisted on including was focused on workers' rights and the freedom to engage in collective bargain, a fundamental right present in every English-speaking Caribbean country's constitution.

> Article 10 asserts that: The promotion and strengthening of democracy requires the full and effective exercise of workers' rights and the application of core labour standards, as recognized in the International Labour Organization (ILO) Declaration on Fundamental Principles and Rights at Work, and its Follow-up, adopted in 1998, as well as other related fundamental ILO conventions. Democracy is strengthened by improving standards in the workplace and enhancing the quality of life for workers in the Hemisphere.

Our delegation explained that all English-speaking Caribbean countries gained control of their legislative arms of government and, ultimately, their independence as a result of the agitation of trade unionists and the strengthening of the trade union movement by legislation. The role of trade unions in shaping the English-speaking Caribbean states compelled the Caribbean to share the benefits of its social experiment with the states of the hemisphere that were struggling to defend democracy.

A deep-rooted democracy in the English-speaking Caribbean was not the result of military battles or violent revolution; rather, democracy was achieved because the trade unions to which many workers in the sub-region belonged were themselves bastions of democracy and depended on the continuation of democratic governments in order to survive. That assertion rings true since every political party in the English-speaking Caribbean has its support base in a trade union. Those negotiating the Charter permitted the entry.

Yet, it is incumbent on me to note that trade unions in the English-speaking Caribbean are suffering terribly from an unwillingness of workers to support their institutions. Many workers today, in the English-speaking Caribbean, view the union as a kind of cheap lawyer. Only when a crisis erupts at the workplace is the union consulted. Or, when salary increases are to be negotiated is the union relevant. Unions have very little capital on hand and are usually poor, unable to reward their employees adequately. Though Caribbean people have benefited from the union and the political parties that emerged from them, the same people are not so willing to provide the economic support that will guarantee the unions' nor the political parties' survival far into the future. It may be that unions will have to negotiate to collect pensions and to manage pension funds in order to have capital available to them. But far too many Caribbean trade unions are without adequate resources to do a good job and to hire talented people; they are supported only by dues-subscriptions which are a pittance.

The political parties are also far from being adequately supported by their constituents. Unable to finance a campaign by voluntary contributions, the political parties are thus compelled to seek support from businesses that in turn demand their pound of flesh as compensation. Until campaign finance reform is instituted, there is every possibility that "political investors" --as Prime Minister Baldwin Spencer of Antigua and Barbuda called them shortly after his victory in 2004-- will continue to exercise more undue influence over government policies than is warranted.

> Article 5 states: The strengthening of political parties and other political organizations is a priority for democracy. Special attention will be paid to the problems associated with the high cost of election campaigns and the establishment of a balanced and transparent system for their financing.

Again, this third article was proposed by Antigua and Barbuda drawing on the rich history of the sub-region and the knowledge of conditions that seem to impair democracy in the hemisphere. It is interesting to note that the US delegation insisted on changing the verb from "shall" to "will" thus weakening the commitment in the second sentence. Antigua and Barbuda argued that the mandatory "shall" was necessary to give meaning to the commitment. The US delegation fully understood that it could not persuade its Congress to adopt changes to its legislation that, during those very months, were being discussed in the US press to no avail. Big money and fat cats, now evolved into PACS (political action committees) still dominate giving in political campaigns in the USA. In the English-speaking Caribbean, corporations and wealthy individuals still dominate giving, in political campaigns.

The Inter-American Democratic Charter is available on the OAS website and need not be reproduced in its entirety in this publication; however, there are several commitments that reflect the basis on which this Charter will proceed forward in history, and a number of assertions that will test the willingness of the lone superpower and other states to abide by the agreements so meticulously worked out.

V

The Application of The Charter

Primary among the Charter's terms, though appearing as Article 21, is the threat to expel a member-state from the OAS when democracy has been "interrupted." This idea was lifted from the OAS Charter:

Article 21 reads:

When the special session of the General Assembly determines that there has been an unconstitutional interruption of the democratic order of a member state, and that diplomatic initiatives have failed, the special session shall take the decision to suspend said member state from the exercise of its right to participate in the OAS by an affirmative vote of two thirds of the member states in accordance with the Charter of the OAS. The suspension shall take effect immediately.
The suspended member state shall continue to fulfill its obligations to the Organization, in particular its human rights obligations.
Notwithstanding the suspension of the member state, the Organization will maintain diplomatic initiatives to restore democracy in that state.[9]

When in February 2004, Haiti's President Aristede was violently chased out of his country and forced to seek refuge in South Africa, the interim government was not suspended from the OAS. The CARICOM did suspend Haiti from its organs, despite no rule requiring suspension; it chose to allow Haiti's re-entry in mid-2006, months after President Rene Preval was elected in a free election more than two years later.

Another article which owes its presence in the Charter to the insistence of the Antigua and Barbuda delegation focuses upon the preservation of the environment.

Article 15 reads: The exercise of democracy promotes the preservation and good stewardship of the environment. It is essential that the states of the Hemisphere implement policies and strategies to protect the environment, including application of various treaties and conventions, to achieve sustainable development for the benefit of future generations.

Here again, Antigua and Barbuda was insistent that the climate change phenomenon imperiled its very existence and that of every low-lying island and coastal region in the hemisphere. The USA was opposed to identifying any single convention or treaty though the Antigua and Barbuda preference was to speak directly to the United Nations Framework Convention on Climate Change and its Protocols. No matter what arguments the delegation raised, the USA objected, paving the way for the compromise which resulted in rather bland language. Protection of the environment is a staple of the foreign policy of the CARICOM, hence it was not so difficult for Antigua and Barbuda to introduce this idea and to win support for it, even if weakened.

In the article following, the language was not at all bland but very pointed. It concerned education, the principal method by which inter-generational poverty is vanquished.

Article 16 reads: Education is key to strengthening democratic institutions, promoting the development of human potential, and alleviating poverty and fostering greater understanding among our peoples. To achieve these ends, it is essential that a quality education be available to all, including girls and women, rural inhabitants, and minorities.

The Antigua and Barbuda delegation did not have much difficulty in persuading the delegations to accept the tangential ideas inherent in the second sentence of this pronouncement about minorities. That there was easy agreement on inclusion of education in the Charter was a reflection of the Quebec Summit and its declaration. The improvement on the idea came from the inclusion of "minorities", again focusing on the black and indigenous populations in the Americas who are repeatedly excluded, especially from tertiary-level educational institutions. In a country like Bolivia, the indigenous population is not a minority; however, their exclusion from the mainstream entitles them to be so regarded. The idea in the conditional sentence is to give life to the notion that it is not enough to be included in football teams and in entertainment groups. Afro-Latin Americans and indigenous people need to be included in engineering and diplomacy schools and in a host of other disciplines in education that lead to a better life, we insisted.

Antigua and Barbuda did not emphasize "girls and women", which appears as a category in Article 16. Girls and women in the English-speaking Caribbean are outperforming boys and men; in fact, the challenge faced by Caribbean civilization in 2001, and continuing in 2007, is to ensure that boys receive better upbringing so that they evolve into better men. 75% of the graduates at the University of the West Indies are female. Women are having a difficult time finding men of equal intellectual capacity as husbands.

It is ironic that the major ingredient in several Caribbean states' economic success is also in part responsible for this gender failure. Tourism has spawned successes and failures. Taxi drivers earn more than teachers in tourism economies. Tour bus drivers can accumulate more than nurses or as much as doctors. It is very difficult to persuade young men to strive hard in school, foregoing readily available material rewards, in order to emerge as teachers, only to discover that schoolmates who become masons and plumbers are sure to earn more money in their lifetime than teachers. The diversion by men to easier trades is quite easily understood. In a rational, material world no attempt to inculcate a higher value for non-material rewards is likely to succeed. It is exceedingly difficult to persuade young men to seek out higher education that will ultimately cause them to earn less than taxi drivers and tradesmen. The contradiction which that produces in an ever increasing materialist world leads to a skewed distribution of status which distorts the desired societal model. There is no easy solution to this conundrum.

The Inter-American Democratic Charter is a very useful document which is very much a statement of the thinking of the hemispheric leaders at the start of the new century. Its importance will be tested over time should the states of the hemisphere suffer any interruptions of the democratic process. Its negotiation taught the states of the English-speaking Caribbean that they could halt the effort of the USA when the USA strayed from the democratic ideal practiced among equally sovereign states. Whether the USA learned a lesson or merely conceded because it was clearly unjustified in its yearning for an early adoption of the document, I cannot say. The author is not privilege to the discussions which take place within the US delegation. However, the events were for the CARICOM a useful lesson in how to oppose the USA when that superpower overstepped appropriate bounds.

CHAPTER EIGHT

THE USA, THE UK, CANADA IN THE CARIBBEAN

The wealthiest and the largest states in the world have an interest in the English-speaking Caribbean. Their interests do not always converge but the Caribbean states are also interested in expanding their relations with the wealthy and the large. The wealthy states are interested in markets and capital, security and political concerns, but so too are the small states of the Caribbean. The English-speaking states of the USA, the UK and Canada have a long history of relations with the Caribbean countries and their friendship merits a special examination.

I

The USA in the Caribbean

Unlike the Europeans who were interested in empire, the USA was far more interested in securing markets for its goods and in seeking security, by its acquisition of Caribbean territories. Puerto Rico was acquired by military conquest in 1898; the Virgin Islands were purchased from Denmark in 1917. There was an unsuccessful attempt to purchase Cuba from Spain, followed eventually by the invasion in 1898 and the commencement of a trusteeship system for four years before Cuba's independence was won. The invasions of Haiti, the Dominican Republic and Grenada in 1915, 1965 and 1983 respectively were not for the purpose of territorial expansion. Even the construction of military bases on several English-speaking Caribbean

British territories, during 1941, was a defensive enterprise. Maybe the very breadth of the US mainland, stretching from the Atlantic to the Pacific Ocean negated the need to seek further expansion. It could also be that small islands would not add much to US prestige and could become a drag on the US Treasury. It could also be that the Monroe doctrine, characterized as "speak softly but carry a big stick", was sufficient for all of Latin America and the Caribbean.

It would not be possible to deny US history on its mainland. The US did have an expansionist history, grabbing Mexico's territory and supplanting Native American tribes in territories that eventually became states, in the 19th and 20th centuries. In its relations with small island-states of the Caribbean, the USA has been fairly charitable and its policies benign; it has provided quantifiable assistance of both a military and a non-military nature, and millions of immigrant Caribbean peoples have made their home in the USA. There is a love and admiration of the USA for its generosity and its freedoms that continue to draw Caribbean immigrants to it long after colonialism in the Caribbean has disappeared. Caribbean people love and admire the USA.

In the years 1995 to 2003, when the author served as Ambassador in Washington, the USA seldom made any requests that would have impinged on Antigua and Barbuda's sovereignty. At the OAS, whenever the CARICOM states believed that they could be helpful to the USA without compromising their democratic ideals, they would lend the USA their support. One incident which causes the author some grief, even today, stems from a moment of great generosity by the USA.

Back in 2000, the USA indicated that it was prepared to increase the OAS budget by paying more. The other states had to agree to an increase for the USA's commitment to become reality. There had been scores of papers written about reforming the OAS, and budget reform was high on the agenda. The CARICOM states decided that they would not be prepared to pay more, although the amount would have been negligible. Antigua and Barbuda pressed to have the CARICOM increase its contribution, to no avail. Quite frankly, the paltry sums which the CARICOM states pay to the OAS annual budget are insufficient to meet the salary and allowances of the Assistant Secretary General, a CARICOM national. It seemed like a perfect opportunity to express a growing maturity and responsibility by contributing more, if not a larger share. Virtually every CARICOM state cried difficult economic times, though the CARICOM states all registered significant economic growth since the date of the last increase. That was a shameful moment in the CARICOM's history of involvement in the OAS, triggered by an act of US generosity.

Once, while serving as Ambassador to the UN, and seated on the committee that determines the UN General Assembly's agenda, the US Ambassador did ask the author to take an action to help block an initiative that Cuba was putting forward. The action followed the invasion of Panama by the USA, in 1989, and Cuba's attempt to add an item to the UN's agenda which would allow discussion of the invasion by the Assembly. Antigua and Barbuda collaborated with the USA, and Cuba's effort was thwarted.

When states are unwilling to act during crises, their senior envoy will send an underling who can say that he has "no instructions." But when the Ambassador (Extraordinary and Plenipotentiary) is seated, there can be no reverting to excuses. As the Ambassador, the decision fell to the author and an immediate decision was required. Antigua and Barbuda supported the USA, though a discussion of the invasion and the resulting loss of lives and property in Panama would now not be discussed at the UN. A moment to further codify international law and norms was lost. I was of the view that the Latin American states showed no interest in discussing the matter. The CARICOM countries also had little interest in even appearing to defend Manuel Noriega, once a CIA operative in Panama. Cuba was therefore the only country desirous of a debate; though Cuba's arguments against the US action were already telegraphed, a debate would have allowed for a replay of the history of US military action in the hemisphere. At a time when the US was facing down the USSR, it appeared to me the right decision. Following the meeting, I relayed the tale of the request to the Antigua and Barbuda Foreign Minister. He was of the view that we should regard our act as a debt owed to us, and that sometime in the future we should "collect" on it. The time never arrived.

On another occasion, in 1994, when thousands of Haitians were fleeing Haiti for Miami, and the USA wanted to discourage the mass migration, it sought to have Caribbean countries pledge to accept a fraction of -what the US press referred to as- "the Haitian boat people." Antigua and Barbuda's Foreign Minister, Lester Bird, had already publicly proclaimed in the parliamentary debates that Antigua and Barbuda intended to allow a small number of fleeing Haitians to settle on Antigua. When then-UN Ambassador Albright enquired during a CARICOM meeting of Ambassadors whether she could make public Antigua and Barbuda's commitment, the author gave her the ok. As soon as the author communicated the content of the discussion to the Foreign Minister, he saw danger in the pronouncement and asked that the promise be withdrawn. It was an embarrassing moment for the author, as ambassador, whose ability to commit the government he represented was severely eroded. However, a month later, President Clinton sent his personal envoy to several Caribbean capitals to persuade them to accept a few boatloads of Haitians. When Antigua and Barbuda's foreign minister agreed, the author was asked to join a panel of experts in the capital to help explain Antigua and Barbuda's volte-face, to the discerning public. It was a moment to relish but it sent an important signal to the Caribbean about the persuasive abilities of the USA. Even when an elected politician senses danger and calibrates the extent of an electorate's disapproval, the elected leader could be cajoled into adopting what could be a vote-losing policy, by offers of US assistance.

The CARICOM states -and Antigua and Barbuda specifically- have more frequently challenged the USA, in multilateral institutions, than has the USA attempted to undermine Caribbean sovereignty. The battle over the Inter-American Democratic Charter, the support for Haitian President Aristede, the condemnation of dictators in Latin America while the US coddled them, the fight against the racism in South and Central America all point to a region whose small size belie their courage and their adherence to high democratic principles.

The US military has a closer working relationship with its CARICOM counterparts than the US State Department has with the embassies and Ministries of Foreign Affairs of the CARICOM states. Maybe the very fact of the militaries' differences in size and power leave no doubt in the minds of the Caribbean commanders that the relationship is lopsided. In diplomacy, however, there are times when the public interaction puts US diplomats in a position that compels them to be polite and not to appear overbearing, when the sovereignty of large and small is equally on display. Those are the times when the corps of diplomats from the CARICOM made the most of their leverage, pushing the USA to support positions that it would prefer not to.

The US has another arrow in its quiver which it can use to persuade, that does not involve a show of force. It is USAID, and that is addressed next.

USAID

The USA used to be far more generous; especially in the immediate post-colonial era when it competed with the USSR for hearts and minds. It envisioned its assistance programs as a means by which it could exert influence and win friendship. When Antigua wanted to dredge its shallow harbor so that it could bring the big ships alongside the warehouse, in 1968, the US Export/Import Bank was induced to help by the US State Department. When new electricity plants required improved machinery, the Export/Import Bank and USAID would come to the rescue.

In the aftermath of US President Reagan's election and the Republican revolution came an emphasis on small government, the private sector, and development by private initiative. In that frame of mind, the US government has been far less charitable. It pledged to give 0.7% of its GDP towards development assistance but has never reached even 10% of that figure; yet, in absolute terms, no other country is as generous as the USA.

Spain has actually contributed more to the UNDP in 2006 than the USA, but overall the US gives more; there is no more generous country than the USA. Its people are also among the most generous in the world. But the US population is extremely wealthy, treating as garbage material possessions that others would gladly hope to possess. Bear in mind that the military expenditure of the US Government is greater than the total expenditure of the next fifteen largest states combined. Although the US claims only 4% of the world's population, the USA's economy is twenty-five percent of global economic activity. The US Government and people have enormous quantities of wealth at their disposal.

Maybe the increasing demands made of the USA by the newly liberated states that once made up the USSR have sucked up a considerable portion of official assistance which it once spent on Caribbean neighbors. Certainly, that is the reason given for closing its embassy on Antigua in 1994. USAID has spent more than US$450 million on Macedonia since 1993, its website boasts. But the USA has been less willing to spend on its Caribbean neighbors, and USAID's budget for the region has not grown significantly in recent years. Many in the USAID see the English-speaking Caribbean as relatively well-off and thus not as desperate as many other poor states around the world. That is not a warped view.

Nevertheless, USAID has financed the upgrading of the justice systems by helping to publish the laws of several of the East Caribbean states in single volumes. In the era of HIV/AIDS, the support from the US has been remarkably consistent. Former President Clinton has also established a fund from which drawdowns are made by professionals who service the needs of infected persons. Some drugs and prophylactic devices are also provided. In tackling disasters and preparedness, the USAID has also been very generous in recent times, providing a considerable portion of the resources that go into scientific research to determine the precise measurement of sea-level rise and increases in ocean temperatures, for example. In tracking hurricanes and storms, the US has also utilized its own aircraft and scientific instruments, knowing that the storms can affect its own territories and the East Coast of the US mainland. The Caribbean is an incidental beneficiary; but the cost accounting systems place that assistance squarely in the column of a handout to the Caribbean.

The Fulbright Scholarships still provide a once-in-a-lifetime opportunity for the very brightest among the Caribbean youth. Karen-May Hill, one of the brightest of her generation from Antigua and Barbuda, has demonstrated the worthiness of the grant by her performance in the UK on a Fulbright Scholarship during the early years of the century just beginning. The OAS scholarships and fellowships, though provided for by OAS resources, are sometimes expanded with USAID and Canadian money.

The USAID website announces that "in the Caribbean the United States is the largest donor at $109 million followed by the EU at $80 million. All figures are for 2001. USAID continues to collaborate with other prominent donors including the Inter-American Development Bank (IDB), the World Bank (WB), the Pan American Health Organization (PAHO), and the Organization of American States (OAS)."[10] These figures include the Dominican Republic, Haiti and hurricane relief efforts.

The New York Times reports that "of the nearly $24 billion requested by the State Department for foreign aid this year [2006], a little over $1 billion is devoted to democracy programs, including training legislative staffs, helping reform courts, and working with women's and business organizations. Privately, officials say that number is likely to rise substantially in next year's budget request, while the roughly $3.7 billion devoted to antipoverty programs — fighting disease, promoting education, providing microcredit loans — is likely to fall to make up the difference."[11] So resources are transferred from one source to make up for the shortfall in another.

USAID is an arm of the US State Department and hence acts in a manner designed to further the policy interests of its government. The British have discontinued this link between assistance and political objectives, finding that corruption of the ends also flows back to the means. Yet, given the objective of the USA in international affairs, it cannot appear to be penurious or the United States will lose to other states whose governments are more generous and are not strictly rewarding friends only. Back to the NY Times. "Promoting democracy and fighting terrorism are laudable goals. But such work needs to come on top of — not instead of — financing antipoverty programs, which save hundreds of thousands of lives and earn untold good will for the United States. There is also little indication that America knows how to build democracy."[12]

Power

States are organized for power purposes and the United States is no exception. Power and control determine the policy options of the USA. When the USSR became a countervailing global power, following World War II, and it acquired nuclear weapons, the US developed a rationale for its foreign policy objectives. While the USA has successfully branded itself as a promoter of freedom and democracy following the end of the Cold War period, the US Government has always weighed the benefits to democracy against its own interests, and invariably came down on the side of interests. In January 2007, the USA was seeking to win support from Egypt by abandoning its interest in support of democracy in Egypt for a political calculation of an alliance against Iran and Syria. Democrats in Egypt are very disappointed with the choice of the US Government.

Yet, there is a great distinction between the US Government and the American people, even its soldiers. Americans bring with them as tourists, business-persons, teachers and military professionals, behaviors that convey a sense of magnanimity and a love of justice. It is impossible not to like the egalitarian Americans. But their government and diplomats are of another sort; they deal in power relations. During the debate on the 2003 invasion of Iraq, France stood opposed to the announced US invasion. The US (Republican) Congress removed everything French from labels in the capitol; they even refused to call French fries by their proper name, referring to them as "freedom fries." By November 2006 when the congressional elections resulted in a routing of the Republicans over the Iraq War, the prior condemnation of France barely earns the apology which France deserves. US politicians can be unforgiving when one disagrees with them and US diplomats can be extremely polite in multilateral institutions but very aggressive when they are attempting to carry out their instructions.

When the USA decided, under the first President Bush, to have repealed the UN resolution that equated Zionism with racism, many of the CARICOM Ambassadors advised their governments that it was best to abstain should it come to a vote. The CARICOM states were not all members of the UN in 1974 when the resolution was adopted, and the disagreement among Israel and her warring Arab neighbors, even at the UN, would not likely cease with the adoption of a counter resolution. Small numbers of influential Arabs in the countries of the English-speaking Caribbean also preferred not to have their adopted countries act in a manner that would irritate the Arab states (that were likely to vote against the US resolution). Unbeknown to the UN Ambassadors from the CARICOM, the US sent its ambassadors to each and every prime minister, indicating that the decision was of vital importance to the USA. The prime ministers all supported the resolution, setting aside the advice of their ambassadors. One could argue that their decision was cost-free and therefore amenable to acceptance. But when the USA wants to enforce its will, it relies on all of its strengths and seldom encounters failure.

In 1984, the US unlawfully mined the harbors of Nicaragua. The World Court has ruled against the USA for this act but the Nicaraguans have not pursued any remedies, in an effort to keep the relationship with the US free of recriminations. A newly elected President Ortega, having taken office in January 2007, may choose to pursue damages for that act twenty-three years ago though the USA is likely to ignore any award. But in 1989, shortly after the ICJ's decision made headlines, the CARICOM foreign ministers, meeting in St. Kitts and Nevis, issued a statement condemning the mining of the harbor. When the USA learned of this CARICOM act, it contacted the Antigua and Barbuda Prime Minister, VC Bird, and he in turn issued a statement to the effect that the Minister representing Antigua and Barbuda at the CARICOM meeting, who had joined in the statement of condemnation, had no authorization so to do. The USA was able to drive a wedge in between the CARICOM states when the USA's interests were at stake.

In a previous chapter, the author pointed out that Antigua and Barbuda's recognition of Cuba could only take place after VC Bird was no longer the Prime Minister, since he held the view –not unlike the USA's- that Cuba under Castro is a dictatorship. He also believed that the Sandinista Government of Nicaragua was not practicing democracy and had no difficulty in distancing his government from it. VC Bird was always more pliant and helpful to US causes than his successor prime minister, Lester Bird.

The USA had also kept open one of two bases on Antigua that the Defense Department wished to close, back in 1985. The base pays $1 million dollars in lease fees each year and spends several million more in rents and other expenses for its civilian personnel. The drive to save those bases was deemed important to Antigua and Barbuda's vital security interests; lobbyists were hired. Through their efforts, only one base was closed. There were a few who wished to see the departure of the American bases, believing that the very presence of such a facility served as a reminder of our subjugated status prior to sovereignty. They did not have public opinion on their side, like Eric Williams in

Trinidad thirty years earlier; most Antiguans and Barbudans wanted the Americans to stay. Stay they did!

II

The UK in The Caribbean

In the post-colonial period, the United Kingdom has shown staying power and generosity in its relations with its former and continuing colonies in the Caribbean. The UK has an embassy in every sovereign country, and a governor in the non-independent territories. In November 2005, I was invited to London to participate in a round-table with the Governors and Chief Ministers of the non-independent British Caribbean territories, and to address the issue of global climate change. I witnessed the open and frank relations which the governors have with the chief ministers and thought that the non-independent Caribbean countries were led by very able people. Their show of strength may have been induced by the existence of sovereign, former colonies in their neighborhood, by the once-every-two-years visit by the UN De-Colonization Committee, and by the very willingness of the UK to abide by the wishes of the majority in their colonies. What I witnessed during my two days at the Royal Institute of International Affairs is clearly a changed attitude and behavior, vastly different from what obtained in a previous era.

That the UK has a presence on each of the sovereign states may not appear as measuring much; however, the presence of an embassy signals a sufficient regard for the long history of involvement and a willingness to spend resources to be present. The USA, on the other hand, has placed a single embassy in Barbados that is intended to serve St. Kitts and Nevis, Antigua and Barbuda, Dominica, St. Lucia, St. Vincent and host country Barbados. That US Embassy also serves the non-independent Caribbean countries of Anguilla, the British Virgin Islands and Montserrat.

It is difficult to believe that the UK, China and Venezuela can afford embassies on each of the English-speaking Caribbean states but the USA cannot. There is disbelief in the USA's claim that its diplomatic presence in each of the sovereign states of the Caribbean is too burdensome for US taxpayers.

The UK has remained very much involved with the development efforts of the English-speaking Caribbean. It may just be that since the Head of State of all, with the exception of Guyana, Trinidad and Tobago, and Dominica, is Queen Elizabeth II, it is impossible for the UK to escape involvement with the Caribbean. There is a deeper level of connection, stemming from the similarity of the parliamentary practices, the adherence to the Sovereign's Privy Council and English case law as precedent, the reliance on Scotland Yard Detectives whenever the crime requires improved forensic technology, and the trading regimes that allowed bananas and sugar to enter the European market by special arrangement. The UK has remained an important partner of the sovereign states of the region, and is indispensable in the governance of the non-independent countries.

The militaries of the Caribbean have also found ample training opportunities at the military academies of the UK. Officers and youthful soldiers from every English-speaking Caribbean country have been trained at The Royal Military Academy Sandhurst, to the benefit of many a Caribbean Defense Force. That academy is the equivalent of WestPoint and thus is a celebration of our worth. In professionalizing their militaries, the leaders have found that training in England has been very helpful.

The same is true of the young West Indian cricketers who used to get lengthy contracts to play for county clubs all over England. They honed their practice skills and learned a new discipline in England where many more opportunities obtained. Virtually all outstanding West Indian cricketers of the 1970s and 1980s got an opportunity to play county cricket in England. New rules now limit the participation by the "territorials" and the absence of the exposure has caused the excellence of West Indies cricket to decline. Sir Allen Stanford, a Texan billionaire who has shown a love of the Caribbean people, has provided millions of dollars to start an intense competition called the "Stanford 20/20". It promises to provide a similar incentive as the British once did, and the superlatives that once attached to West Indies cricket may soon return.

International Collaboration

The UK has worked closely with the CARICOM states at the UN. I can recall in 1989 when Hurricane Hugo pummeled the Caribbean, our delegations sought to bring news of the disaster to the UN and to provide the UNDP with the authority to spend additional resources to assist with recovery by way of a resolution. Martinique, Dominica, Montserrat, Guadeloupe, Antigua, St. Kitts, St. Maarten., St. Thomas and St. Croix –in that geographic order- all suffered huge losses of housing, hotels, livestock, wildlife, and beaches as a result of the winds and the waves, the rain and the economic fallout. Antigua and Barbuda was circulating the draft resolution to seek the support of the states that were adversely affected.

The British, upon learning that such a resolution was in the making, called to ask if Montserrat could be included among the places affected. The Dutch subsequently asked if we could include St. Maarten. The Americans asked us to include the USVI. So, we thought we would ask the French if Martinique and Guadeloupe could also be listed. The French Ambassador said to me, in French and with an imperious tone, "Mr. Ambassador, Guadeloupe and Martinique are France." That ended that idea. The UK always sought to collaborate. It may have been their method of atoning for the sins of their ancestors who once enslaved and colonized the peoples of the region. 2007 marks two hundred years since the end of the slave trade in 1807, and a film which tells of William Wilberforce's role is playing in theaters across the US at the time of writing. It is called *Amazing Grace* and is worth seeing.

Since the UK sits as a permanent member of the UN Security Council, her Ambassador carries far more weight at the UN than does the lowly representative from any of the CARICOM states. Yet, when issues come to the General Assembly where numbers matter, 14 CARICOM states' votes can weigh far more than one single UK vote. Under those rules, the relationship with the CARICOM at the UN was warm and even friendly. Crispen Tickell served as the UK's Ambassador to the UN for much of the time while I served, and he would always stop me to chat whenever he saw me strolling to or from the general assembly hall. His deputy was also a very amiable diplomat who was constantly extending invitations to his Park Avenue home for Caribbean dinners.

There was also collaboration with the Observer Representative of the UK at the OAS. The British provide hundreds of thousands of Sterling Pounds each year to the OAS for support of very specific projects. Although the UK sends a lowly representative from its Embassy to many of the OAS meetings, from time to time it steps up the ante and dispatches its Ambassador to the US. However, it also sends a representative to the OAS General Assemblies wherever they are held. I recall the first year that my delegation made an intervention on the Falkland/Malvinas Islands issue which Argentina has introduced at the OAS. The British representative followed me into the men's bathroom when I left the meeting room to enquire if I had been given instructions to speak or whether I was speaking on my own. "I am the foreign minister," I told him. That answer stunned him. I did believe that once I was asked to substitute for my foreign minister at the general assemblies, that I inherited his authority; the decision of the foreign minister is the decision of the government.

Since the UK sits at table in the Commonwealth of Nations, headquartered in London, the collaboration there between the UK and the CARICOM states has been excellent. The Commonwealth has been active in elections monitoring in the Caribbean. The institution has also been very useful in defining a new security paradigm for small island states. Their staff and their standing have been put to use to produce well-argued treatises that have won favorable consideration among other regions.

The UK has been a source of support for Caribbean banana and sugar exports to Europe, at a time when those commodities face increasing competition and new WTO rules that almost certainly will ensure the end of their export life. During the tenure of Prime Minister Thatcher, there were ample signals that the preferential treatment which Caribbean exports enjoyed was coming to an end. The rulings of the WTO and the decisions by the European Commission have virtually ensured that cheap bananas from Latin America are likely to gobble up the 3% market share of the Caribbean exporters.

The UK has also provided technical assistance with police, military, and a host of issues that make for a fairly respectful relationship between it and the Commonwealth Caribbean. In fact, several police officers from London now spend months in the Caribbean countries where crime has proliferated, teaching many of the crime-reducing skills which the policemen from the UK have burnished in London and other British cities. Each summer, the UK joins with the US to put on military exercises known as "Trade Winds" that help to enlarge the training of the militaries of the Caribbean.

Cable and Wireless, the UK giant telecommunications firm, is ensconced in every English-speaking Caribbean territory. It has been challenged by the Irish firm Digicel, and US firms (Sprint and AT&T) have come knocking. Despite the small populations of the Caribbean, Cable and Wireless earns more than 50% of its revenues from these island territories and therefore has much to protect. Many island-governments have signed monopoly agreements which will last until 2020 in one case, and so there are good reasons for the British to continue to be present in the Caribbean.

The UK was instrumental in arranging for the Commonwealth of Nations to provide rented office space for several small former colonies in New York, so that their UN posts can be filled. Among the Caribbean small island-states that utilize this arrangement are Dominica, Grenada and St. Lucia. In a few capitals where the Caribbean has no presence, the states rely upon the UK Consulates and Embassies to issue visitors' visas to prospective tourists.

The relationship between the UK and the independent Anglo-Caribbean is respectful.

Immigration, Remittances and UK Assistance

Following World War II and for almost two decades, Caribbean people made their way to England to find employment where shortages of labor required brawn. Many of those workers have now retired and pockets of them are returning to take up residence in their home countries. They are a considerable source of remittances that contribute to enhancing the prospect of development in the English-speaking island-states. The World Bank is beginning to pay attention to the value of remittances from immigrants to their home countries. Families with parents abroad have always appreciated the remittances dispatched to their children and guardian-grandparents; the economic consequences are now being measured but have always been highly regarded.

The UK also has provided resources for infrastructural strengthening through its Department For International Development (DFID). The UK first tied aid to trade, in the 1960s, when the precursor to DFID was created. Consequently, a foreign government which awarded private contracts to UK firms used to receive larger portions of assistance from the UK. The corruption in such a system became evident to UK lawmakers and after DFID was created by law in 2002, aid was divorced from trade.

When the volcano on Montserrat erupted in June 1995, thousands of Montserratans fled to Antigua and were warmly received in households by generous families. So impressed was the UK with the Antigua and Barbuda Government's willingness to accept the displaced colonials that it offered to make additional resources available to the government for infrastructural development. Several clinics were built and several schools enlarged with the help of the British in order to accommodate the enlarged population requiring those services.

The UK has pledged to achieve the Millennium Goals set by the UN, to halve poverty by 2015. In the case of the Commonwealth Caribbean, the UK considers these small states to be fairly well advanced, as measured by high literacy rates, low infant mortality rates, longevity rates that match many developed countries', and availability of the instruments of modern civilization such as electricity, computers and cell phones.

The DFID has constructed several technical schools that train young men and women in the trades; they have yielded immediate employment in the growing economies of Antigua and Barbuda, St. Kitts and Nevis. In 1994, the DFID decided that Antigua and Barbuda and St. Kitts and Nevis no longer qualified for assistance and has stopped providing it to the two states. The incomes and level of development caused them to be graduated. Guyana and Jamaica continue to be provided resources because of large pockets of poverty within their capitals and in identified rural areas; so too have the Windward Islands of St. Lucia, St. Vincent and the Grenadines and Grenada, the banana producers that have felt the sting from the WTO rulings. The CARICOM estimates that more than 300,000 people in the English-speaking Caribbean are living on less than US$1 dollar per day. Those numbers include pockets of elderly who can no longer earn an income, as well as young men and women who have not been able to find employment. The UK has pledged to help to remove those conditions that trap these two age groups.

The expectation is that the UK will continue to nurture its friendship with the English-speaking Caribbean to the mutual advantage of the parties. Whatever the history may have been, the time has come to re-arrange the relationship to the benefit of the UK and the Caribbean. History and sovereignty are making that possible.

III

CANADA In the Caribbean

Canada has been one of the very best friends that English-speaking Caribbean countries can boast. The relations between both have been based on mutual respect and shared values. Despite its size as the second largest state on the planet, Canada is very much like a small state with a mere 30 million people. Living next to the giant, both Canada and the Caribbean know the weight of influence which the USA can exert without even trying. US television, movies, books, magazines, radio, businesses and practices, legislation and regulations can have enormous impact on the states which with it trades and that fall within its sphere of influence. For these reasons, the Canadians have sought to lessen US influence by courting Caribbean states in multilateral institutions and within the region.

In multilateral institutions like the OAS and the UN, the Canadians have found the Caribbean states and their diplomats to be allies on whom they can count for support and to show leadership. When Canada joined the OAS in 1990, one of its proposals was to create a Committee on Hemispheric Security. The Canadian proposal was supported by the English-speaking Caribbean states. Knowing the Canadian emphasis on universal education, universal healthcare, job creation, good governance and peace-keeping rather than militarization of its foreign policy objectives, the Caribbean was persuaded that the Canadians wanted to address underlying causes of insecurity. That OAS Committee has proven to be very useful in re-defining security for small island-states, and for significantly increasing confidence and security building mechanisms among the states of the hemisphere.

The Canadians used their state and its resources to place a ban on the use of landmines in conflict areas. Only three countries in the world continue to export landmines, and Canada is largely responsible for the success of this prohibition. The lady who won the Nobel Peace Prize for this effort, Jodi Williams, is sometimes thought to be a Canadian; she is actually a US citizen. But she supported Canada's efforts wholeheartedly, as did the Caribbean states. Many of our states have ratified the Convention to Ban Landmines and applauded Canada for her unstinting courage.

Canada has not made the promotion of democracy central to its foreign policy objectives, as has the USA. It has focused on reducing poverty by providing primary and secondary education. In several East Caribbean countries, Canadian taxpayers' money has built schools and, for many years, provided Canadian teachers to fill the teacher shortage gap that once existed in primary and secondary education in Caribbean island-countries. The author, in 1965 thru 1968, was taught by Canadians who volunteered to teach in Caribbean countries, much like the US Peace Corps. It is of interest to note that the Canadians acted even before the island-countries gained their sovereignty and still provide varying assistance to the non-independent English-speaking Caribbean.

Canada has not been hostile to Cuba, despite its close friendship with the USA. Canadian capital and tourists are staples of the Cuban economy and the two countries have very friendly relations. This humane approach to Cuba has warmed the hearts of Caribbean leaders to Canada, giving her additional credit in their relations with the English-speaking island-states.

The provision of university scholarships to young students from the English-speaking region was also made possible by Canadian generosity. My brother-in-law Kenrick George, who earned an accounting degree in 1968, in Winnipeg, Manitoba, related a tale of one of his professors who consistently gave him a low grade no matter how well-written his papers. He collaborated with one of the sympathetic white males who agreed to submit Kenrick George's paper as his own. Sure enough, the Kenrick George paper attracted the highest grade and the other student's paper, submitted by George, received a low grade. They then marched to the administration and registered their claim of racial discrimination. George prevailed, attesting to that university's determination to eliminate racial discrimination and to the fairness that characterizes Canadian ethos.

The same unpleasant experience was duplicated at several universities in the 1960s where, for the first time, non-white students from the English-speaking Caribbean were in attendance. This discriminatory practice created quite an embarrassing revelation of racial discrimination in Canada -a country that had accepted many runaway slaves from the USA and had been the destination of the Underground Railroad for generations of African-Americans. To the benefit of Canadian legislators, they took swift action to end discrimination and to transform Canadian society into a more race–blind place than any other majority-white, New-World state in the hemisphere.

The Canadians also enacted their version of a Canadian/Caribbean Free Trade Agreement called CARIBCAN, in 1985. It sought to enhance trade and export from the English-speaking Caribbean to Canada in the hope of improving the subregion's development. CARIBCAN sought to enable Canadian investment to find root in the subregion and by so doing further the integration of existing trade and export earnings, improve the trade and economic development prospects of the region, promote new investment opportunities and stimulate growth in the region. CARIBCAN has proven to be a marginal success in part because of the failure of manufacturing in the Caribbean.

In Jamaica with its very large pool of labor, and in Trinidad where energy is inexpensive, manufacturing has thrived. But in the many tiny states and territories dependent upon tourism and services, manufacturing has not been very successful. Tourism draws on the shallow pool of prospective employees and pushes up the price of labor beyond a range deemed reasonable by manufacturing firms. Energy prices have been rising and have thus made the cost of production higher than in competing jurisdictions, especially the maquilladoras of Northern Mexico. The NAFTA has also dealt a blow to competitiveness by making Mexican exports to Canada even less expensive than Caribbean exports. States dependent upon agricultural exports as a major economic activity have had greater success with manufacturing, in part because that line of work is more socially acceptable than agricultural labor. But the pull of tourism and the ease of migration have also put in jeopardy manufacturing enterprises in those states.

Canada's business interests in the region have also been reflected in the tourism and banking industries that dominate the economies of many of the states. The Royal Bank of Canada has a special place in the hearts of Antiguans and Barbudans. When VC Bird proposed to purchase the lands and buildings of the Antigua Syndicates Estates, the owners of more than 75% of the land surface of Antigua, he turned to that Canadian bank in London. Within a 24 hour period, the Canadians assured him in writing that they would provide the five million Pounds Sterling he requested. In 1965, VC Bird bought the entire enterprise with Canadian capital, averting the bitter struggle over land that Zimbabwe has experienced since the end of apartheid in (what was) Rhodesia. The Canadians hate poverty and prejudice; they do their best to see injustice eliminated.

The Canadians have a continuing interst in Haiti on account of language similarity but also because Haiti is the poorest state in the Western Hemisphere. Haiti is French-speaking and so is Montreal. Many Haitian professionals have studied or lived in Montreal. In fact, Canada recently named a Haitian descendant to the post of Governor-General of Canada, the highest post which one can attain in Canada outside of the ballot box. The Canadians are a very warm and welcoming people despite the vast icy areas that make up a considerable portion of their geographic space.

The Canadians have also provided resources to reduce the incidence of disease among the very young in the Caribbean. Believing that childhood diseases are treatable and would result in fewer child deaths, the Canadian International Development Agency (CIDA) has been very helpful in treating diseases.

When I served at the UN, Louise Frechette was one of the first Ambassadors whom I encountered. She was tough and ambitious. We sat on the Board of the Commission for Sustainable Development as elected representatives from our regions. At all times, she seemed ready to do combat. Yet, she recognized the fragility of Caribbean island-states' economies, their precarious position in a warming world, and the unrelenting struggle which the Caribbean would face in overcoming the environmental challenges caused by the industrial world. She was a dependable ally in our effort to help Haiti to overcome its underdevelopment, like every Canadian Ambassador whom I subsequently encountered. Frechette became the first Deputy Secretary-General of the UN when that post was introduced.

The Canadian diplomats at the OAS were also very welcoming and often made it patently obvious that along with the Caribbean they constituted a group. It may have been language because Spanish dominated the OAS meetings and the English-speaking Canadian and Caribbean diplomats at times seemed like interlopers. Whatever the reasons, the two shared a common set of values as reflected in the identical head of state, the structure of government, the adherence to democratic principles, the love of freedom and, at times, resistance to the USA. Canada was always interested in demonstrating that it was not a "colony" of the USA. The Canadian Embassy and OAS Mission in Washington, D.C. sit on Constitution Avenue and the building looks out to the US capitol in a defiant and majestic stance. Its architecture is symbolic of Canadian pride and a witness of its determination to separate itself from the US while welcoming US trade and commerce. Peter Boehm, who served for many years as Canada's OAS Ambassador simultaneously with the author, was the embodiment of the best that Canada offered to the world of diplomacy.

Canada is also determined to set aright its relations with its indigenous peoples. Nearly one-third of its geographic territory has been returned to the indigenous Canadians. The Museum of Man in Ottawa is an architectural marvel and its contents mind blowing. The Canadians have come to grips with their past and look to the future with great anticipation. The Canadian Mission to the OAS frequently invited leaders of the indigenous people, called the First Nations, to the OAS to speak from Canada's seat. In the final chapter, I argue that global warming will be catastrophic for Caribbean island-states and that it is in their best interest to negotiate a treaty that would allow them to move their populations to safe ground when the swollen oceans inundate them. Canada is the country to which the Caribbean would want to move their peoples, although Guyana is more likely to be the country of rescue.

The relationship between the Canadians and the English-speaking Caribbean is good and getting better. Hence, the future of Canada-Caribbean diplomatic collaboration can only be excellent.

CHAPTER NINE

FACING AFRICA, INDIA, THE MIDDLE EAST AND JAPAN

The Caribbean has been earlier described as a polyglot, peopled by human cargo from Africa, China, Europe, India, the Middle East and a smattering of émigrés from virtually every continent on the planet, including Australia. There are also pockets of indigenous Caribbean people living in glorious isolation in several island-countries. Because of this mix, the Caribbean governments tend to look to all of these geographically distant lands out of sentiment. The primary sources of trade, remittances and international affairs are the US, the UK and Canada. However, as sovereign states, the need to broaden the base of friendship and to establish interests outside of the Western Hemisphere has led to the establishment of diplomatic and other relations with states in Africa, Asia and the Middle East.

When the Ministry of Foreign Affairs in Antigua and Barbuda totaled the applications for citizenship awaiting approval, in 2006, there were persons from more than eighty separate countries hoping to become citizens of Antigua and Barbuda. Everywhere in the Caribbean, when the economies are buoyant and expertise is scarce, outsiders who have a love of the tropics will seek to remain, just as the colonists did after 1600.

Despite the addition of recent migrants, the vast majority of many of the independent Caribbean states are persons of African descent whose ancestors came to the Caribbean to create wealth for others at the tip of a whip. The next largest group is the East Indian; those persons who came after 1834 with the intention of returning to India upon completion of their period of servitude. Boatloads of Chinese followed in the mid 1800s, as did Portuguese middle managers. Civil wars and political strife led many Syrians and Lebanese in the early twentieth century to depart their homelands and to follow the lead of the earlier newcomers to the Caribbean. All have prospered. The poorest among the Caribbean newcomers are the vast majority of people of African and Indian ancestry. There is a smattering of poor whites in Barbados, St. Vincent, St. Kitts who are known by various names. The Kittitians call them "Frenchies"; they tend to inter-marry and so their gene pool has shrunk considerably. There are also very wealthy whites in places like the Cayman Islands, Bermuda, Barbados whose ancestors have been in the Caribbean for as many centuries as the blacks. Recent immigrant whites who have come from the USA, Canada, England and a smattering of European countries help to make up the population today.

The African descendants sought to control government after adult suffrage, barely a half-century ago, and yearned to become civil servants whose tenure guaranteed an income, a pension and status. Business or entrepreneurship was surrendered to the Portuguese and also the Arabs following the decline or departure of the European population. Actually, because the Arabs spoke little English, they were compelled to make a way for themselves. That group brought its knowledge of trading and credit which significantly enhanced the Arab success throughout the Caribbean and the Americas. The Chinese also looked to doing what they knew best, which was providing food and goods. The Caribbean Chinese started restaurants and small shops that have mushroomed into fairly large businesses, by Caribbean standards. In many places, the East Indians remained as agricultural workers, harvesting sugarcane, rice and other commodities, which kept a large number in poverty. Many East Indians also started small shops and other businesses that have mushroomed into bigger enterprises, in Guyana and Trinidad. Immigrant women from the Dominican Republic have found a place in many of the English-speaking countries of the Caribbean. They too have started small businesses and carved out niches for themselves within the economies of the states they now call home.

Because of this mix of peoples, the Caribbean states have an abiding interest in Africa, India, the Middle East and other places where their peoples' roots are deeply buried.

I

Foreign Policy
While the foreign policy of the English-speaking Caribbean sub-region is determined mostly by the material interests that concern their people and governments, the ever-present issues of size and history, including the origins of their populations, help to inform the officials responsible for foreign policy design. The leaders have not forgotten that their states were recently colonies; that sovereignty and democracy for colonial subjects in tiny places were unlikely prior to the birth of the United Nations; that the states' material insufficiency came as a result of the role played by colonies and the paucity of natural resources of most small islands; and that to erase the conditions that defined the past, Caribbean governments and people had to apply ingenuity in reconstructing their societies. Yet, the Caribbean people are haunted by their past and the conditions of the present.

Coming to terms with the inabilities of the African states is probably the most arresting of the socio-psychological challenges which the Caribbean states face. When Ghana won its independence in 1957, VC Bird who was then Chief Minister of Antigua and Barbuda returned from the celebrations. He asserted that a new day had dawned for Caribbean countries as well. Airplanes and cars built by Africans would come on to the market, displacing the European and American manufacturers. African universities and technical institutes, he proclaimed, would open up to the people of the Caribbean. The Afro-Saxons of the Caribbean wanted to believe that they could be rescued by Africa, for it was clear that the colonialists showed little interest in reversing their plight in more than three centuries. Surely, if assistance was forthcoming -and development could not take place without the friendship of large states- it would sail in from those whose blood the majority shared and whose history placed Africa and the Caribbean on an equal plane.

Since independence, the assistance has come from the USA, Canada, the UK, Venezuela, Cuba and the multilateral institutions in which English-speaking Caribbean states claim membership. Most recently, cooperation has come from Mexico, Chile, Greece, Malaysia, India, Malta and Nigeria. Additionally, the task of development turned out to be easier for the Caribbean precisely because the states are small, the people no longer identified themselves along tribal lines, racism and sexism were in retreat, industrial states were within easy reach, the Afro-Saxons spoke English albeit littered with idioms, and the future seemed to be determined more by brain than by brawn.

Africa

Having arrived at a stage of development that is somewhat advanced, can those small Caribbean states make a difference to African development? Some may think that for small Caribbean states to even ask the question is to engage in delusion. Surely, a group of tiny island-states that can barely defend themselves against better-armed drug traffickers and mercenaries, whose economies are fragile and subject to reversal following annual hurricanes, could not possibly hope to impact huge states meaningfully an ocean away, many of them larger than the states of Western Europe. In order for a state to make its will felt that far away, military assets and wealth must be brought to bear on the task, the reasonable would assert.

The author is certainly not proposing that Caribbean states become new colonials, sending their treasure and their sons to far-flung places in the hope of changing conditions on a continent thousands of miles away. Rather, the author proposes that in multilateral institutions where the two groups of states interact that the Caribbean lend support to the causes that would spur development, reduce conflict, and improve conditions in those African states. That has certainly been the formula brought to bear on the Haitian experience since 1986, or for the past twenty years, with varying degrees of success. The CARICOM has indeed sent its soldiers and its professionals to Haiti under the UN's agency, following the Security Council Resolution establishing UNMIH in 1993. But the major contribution by the CARICOM to Haiti has been the friendship in multilateral institutions by the group, and the willingness to step forward with political support.

One difficulty, which involved the author, stems from the inherent competition for available resources for development, wherever they originate. An anecdote will help to explain. When Bosnia-Herzegovina burst onto the world stage, in 1991, the United Nations Development Program (UNDP) was asked to help the new state to come to grips with the enormous challenge that it faced. In order to assist, the UNDP had to divert its fairly fixed resources from more developed states, like the English-speaking Caribbean, to Bosnia-Herzegovina. The author tried to explain to an Antigua and Barbuda public, by way of a press release, why our allotment of resources from the UNDP had declined in that particular budget cycle. The journalist in Antigua who had responsibility for getting the release on air misunderstood the content of the release and transposed the explanation to mean that Antigua and Barbuda had "given millions of its UNDP allotment" to Bosnia-Herzegovina. The Chamber of Commerce in Antigua called on the Ministry of Foreign Affairs to explain why Antigua and Barbuda would (stupidly) give away its UNDP development assistance allocation to Bosnia-Herzegovina, a country that its citizens could not even identify on the map. The author stepped in and explained that there was an error in the interpretation lent to the release. Appearing on radio, the author elaborated on the events in Bosnia-Herzegovina and showed how goings-on in a part of the world with which the Caribbean had little knowledge could adversely affect the speed with which development is hurried along in our region.

It is in the Caribbean's interest to try to end civil wars and strife in places far away so that resources are not stripped from one region to address more pressing concerns in another. Our foreign policy reflects this understanding and urgency.

Another anecdote will help to strengthen this claim. In 1994, the USA closed its small embassy on Antigua in an attempt to spread the limited resources of the US State Department to the newly independent states of Eastern Europe, we were told. Since the US Congress would not enlarge the State Department's budget, that US Government arm had no other alternative but to redeploy its assets; that was the explanation offered. The US Embassy on Antigua was deemed marginally important and was thus closed. Despite VC Bird's support for the USA, at times when such support seemed abnormal and out of step, the Embassy shut its doors. Events far away can affect a tiny island-state in a manner which bears no relation to any decision it has made. Now, the Antiguans and Barbudans who wish for a US visa must travel to Barbados, stay in a hotel, and pray that they have not overlooked some requirement that will cause them to have to return at great expense to themselves. It is as expensive to travel to Barbados from Antigua as it is to travel to Miami; airline ticket-prices bear no relation to distance.

These two anecdotes demonstrate why it is extremely difficult for small Caribbean island-states to pledge the use of resources earmarked for them to help African states that need help also. The help which the Caribbean can offer is of a political nature.

African schools are overcrowded. This came partly as a consequence of conditions imposed by the IMF and the World Bank on several African countries during the difficult years of the 1980s. These institutions, acting out of ideology imposed from Washington, mandated the African states to reduce government spending on social programs. Spending on education decreased significantly.[13] But no country can sustain economic progress if its children are illiterate. In their relations with the IMF, the World Bank and UNESCO, Caribbean states can make known their support for African development, especially the education of primary and secondary students. That kind of political support is cost-free and would improve the lives of millions of African students.

Since September 2006, at the start of the UN General Assembly, Sudan has refused UN peacekeepers in Darfur to bring protection and security to a civilian population that is under threat. Millions of black Sudanese have been displaced and thousands have been killed by militiamen of another ethnic group. Although merely speaking out at the UN may not discourage the violent thugs who have murderously displaced the villagers of the Darfur region, it is incumbent on the Caribbean governments to speak loudly and frequently to that issue for the purpose of establishing a moral platform by which the Caribbean can be seen and measured.

The December 2006 invasion of Somalia by Ethiopia has raised a few very critical issues about the use of force to settle disputes between African states. In this case, the USA has been supportive of the Ethiopians, fearing that Somalia would become a hotbed of Islamic radicalism since the Islamists there seized power in the capital. The Caribbean states need to chart their own position. The African Union (AU) has established a position on the issue which the Caribbean states could endorse publicly. The AU calls for an end to hostilities and a negotiation of the differences that would lead to fewer civilian casualties. These positions and pronouncements are cost-free and would clearly demonstrate the region's continuing interest in a continent that still holds answers to the Caribbean's future in the century just beginning. Africa will overcome many of the disabilities that plague it today and several of its very large and very small states will become models for discharge of greater responsibility in the evolving international political arena.

Barbados established in 2000 a government commission that focuses exclusively on Africa, whose responsibility is to develop ways in which there can be greater collaboration across the Atlantic. "The Commission for Pan-African Affairs has been mandated by the Government of Barbados to address and rectify [the] deficiency in Barbadian institutions and national life which is manifested in the relative dearth of relationships, exchanges and interactions with the nations, population groups and institutions of the continent of Africa and the world-wide African Diaspora. In pursuing such an agenda, the Commission will also be assisting in developing the Africa derived segment of the Barbadian cultural landscape," its website declares.[14]

The focus of the English-speaking Caribbean interaction has been increasingly on cultural exchanges, allowing West African singers, dancers and performers to visit the Caribbean. There is a heightened awareness in Barbados of the cultural roots which Africa has played in its music, art, religion and inventiveness. Barbados has produced four of the best cricketers the world has ever seen –Walcott, Worrell, Weekes and Sobers- and scores of other cricketers, politicians and entertainers who took pride in their African origin. But it is Prime Minister Owen Arthur who, above all, has translated his love for his ancestry into a tangible policy with resources to match. There is much which the other English-speaking Caribbean can learn from the Barbados experience.

In another chapter, the author addresses the role of Cuba in Africa where doctors, soldiers and other professionals were deployed to fill a need that no other state seemed willing to meet.

II

India

The sub-continent has become a major contributor of engineers and other professionals to the USA, Canada and Western Europe. The engineers have gone mainly to the USA because of higher pay and a larger receiving population of Indian nationals. However, Indian nationals have found their way in recent times to other Caribbean countries as businesspersons who sell goods originating in India (and elsewhere). A number of Indian doctors have also migrated to the Caribbean, as have Anglican priests. The relationship with India is defined by these population movements and the export of Indian expertise and capital.

After Idi Amin expelled large numbers of Indians from Uganda, back in 1979, many chose places where they were comfortable living, including several English-speaking Caribbean island-states. So that the population that has been nurtured by the Caribbean for almost two centuries is now being buttressed by an inflow of new immigrants with capital and expertise that contribute to furthering Caribbean development and integration.

As noted in a previous chapter, Guyana and Trinidad and Tobago are the two countries with the largest Indian populations. Suriname has a significant mix of Indians and Malays. Jamaica has also been fortunate to have this additional gene pool on which to draw, giving its people and country a cosmopolitan mix. The Jamaica national motto screams "Out of Many, One." But the overwhelming majority of its African population, unlike Suriname, Guyana and Trinidad, makes the motto an overstatement.

In January 2007, the Prime Minister of Antigua and Barbuda, Mr. Baldwin Spencer, set off for a visit to India for what the national radio stations called "official". It appears that with India's rise, many states have an interest in tapping into India's expertise. It turned out that the security person who accompanied the prime minister packed a firearm in the baggage. When the bags were x-rayed in Bangalore, the pistol was discovered. It appears that the Head of Government had no documentation to permit such a weapon on an aircraft, nor on his person. The prime minister was questioned for several hours, the Indian newspapers reported, and the weapon confiscated. He went on to several Indian cities and may have had a meeting with the foreign minister of India before returning to Antigua. It was a very embarrassing moment for most Antigua and Barbuda citizens. But the trip to India is an indication of the growing importance of that country to trade, finance, and learning.

The Middle East

The English-speaking Caribbean is wary of touching the conflict in the Middle East, especially the Israeli/Palestinian sovereignty issue. The region has long adopted the two-state approach to which the US has recently warmed up, following the Oslo Agreement. But the CARICOM states will not make themselves an active partner in finding a solution. Mythology has it, among Caribbean theologians, that the descendants of Abraham, today's Jews and Arabs, are destined to fight each other until God's kingdom come.

In July 1988, when another Middle East flare-up occurred, a CARICOM Heads meeting was taking place in Antigua and Barbuda. Several Prime Ministers urged that the Heads issue a statement. Prime Minister VC Bird, then an octogenarian and host of the meeting, would slowly say: "Leave those people alone." He believed that the difficulty between Israel and her neighbors was insoluble. The CARICOM accepted his urgings and no statement was issued at that time. Although the Caribbean island-states have established diplomatic relations with Israel, they have also deliberately established relations with her Arab neighbors. The object is to send clear signals that the region remains a friend of both peoples.

Were it not for their oil reserves that make up almost 66% of all known global reserves, the Middle East would get little if any attention from the major powers. As a hotbed of radical Islam and the source from which the 9/11 terrorists came, the Middle East remains a very important region in US and international politics. Because Arabs live in the Caribbean and have an abiding interest in the land of their forebears, the Middle East holds an interest for the Caribbean. The

Syrians and the Lebanese in the Caribbean are friendly to each other but there is an underlying tension brought about by the politics in the home countries. Syria's domination of Lebanon, including the alleged role of Syria in the 2006 execution of a former Lebanese Prime Minister, has adversely affected the relations between the two groups. Though the Middle Easterners play a role in shaping the foreign policy of several of the English-speaking Caribbean states, their focus more often is on the opportunity for expanding business and ensuring the immigration of more relatives from the troubled region to the peaceful Caribbean.

It is common knowledge that far from embracing democracy, the regimes of the Middle East are autocratic and unelected. There is a surrendering to this reality. The Caribbean could attempt to spread democracy by way of the same diplomatic tools as utilized in Latin America but the likelihood of success is very slim indeed given our absence from any of their regional institutions and the geographic distance that separates the states. Guyana has joined the Organization of Islamic Conference. Though a small percentage of its population is Islamic, Guyana sees benefit in membership.

Japan

Many observers see the Japanese interests in the Caribbean as based on two peculiar issues. The first is the sale of machinery, especially cars, trucks and other motorized vehicles. Japanese vehicles dominate in the Caribbean where British and American cars and machinery once held sway. The Japanese are not interested only in large markets, unlike the Americans. They are quite willing to pursue tiny markets in places like Antigua and Barbuda, St. Kitts and Nevis. A brisk trade takes place with a vehicle container ship discharging its contents in Caribbean ports at least once per month. In Bermuda, the number of vehicles allowed on the streets has been restricted to one per household. On small islands, an excess of vehicles is easily reached but that does not slow down the demand for more as material conditions improve.

The second issue which draws the Caribbean and Japan closer is whaling. The Japanese are interested in permitting their fishers to harvest whales and in reversing the ban on that activity engineered by the International Whaling Commission. Many Caribbean countries have been pursued by the Japanese to lend support to their ambitions for their fishers. To entice the Caribbean states to lend support, the Japanese International Cooperation Agency (JICA) has constructed several fisheries projects in the countries of the Caribbean. Antigua and Barbuda can boast three new facilities built at a cost of more than US$3 million dollars that have elevated fishing in Antigua and Barbuda. St. Vincent and the Grenadines has also benefited from their active support of whaling. Anti-whaling activists in a number of developed countries, wishing to dissuade the Caribbean island-states from supporting Japan, have begun to talk about a tourism boycott of the Caribbean. The material benefits conferred by the Japanese far outweigh any impact which the anti-whaling activists could hope to achieve.

The Japanese are now discovering that the small states of the English-speaking Caribbean exist and that economic and other opportunities abound. Japanese capital is making its way to Caribbean off-shore banks, and Japanese expertise is following. Several Japanese construction firms and architects have found profitable contracts in the Caribbean though Chinese firms are fast outpacing them. University scholarships are now being offered youth from the Caribbean, preceded by one year of language studies for the successful applicants. The relationship between the CARICOM states and Japan is deepening and taking on a mature appearance.

III

POLICY RE-ALIGNMENT
The fourteen states of the CARICOM are discovering the existence of the wider world beyond the traditional Western European states, the USA, Canada and the countries from which their populations come. Russia, for example, has become an important source of energy for much of Europe and a significant exporter of arms to many states around the world. The former USSR at one point attracted students from Jamaica and Guyana when the competition for hearts and minds created allies of the Caribbean; today, the ideological interest in Russia has diminished greatly. Caribbean governments must seek out ways to enhance their relations with non-traditional allies. We must re-align

our foreign policy to attract new capital, non-traditional expertise and new industries, and we are doing just that.

When my household in Antigua held a party to celebrate my young son's fourth birthday, in October 2004, among the invited guests was a young Russian of equal age. His parents had been dispatched to Antigua to manage a branch of a Russian bank that had chosen to establish its offshore branch on Antigua. I subsequently learned that an Ukrainian family, a Malaysian couple, a Korean family, and scores of Caribbean parents of multiple nationalities had –over the years- also enrolled children in that school for tots. Their reasons for being in Antigua all differ, suggesting that the Antigua and Barbuda state was becoming attractive to businesses and people from all around the world.

The foreign policy of the Caribbean states must begin to reflect this reality. Only by realigning their foreign policy will the English-speaking Caribbean states succeed in making their economies less dependent upon the USA, the UK, Canada and other traditional partners. It is in the interest of the Caribbean states to make themselves as immune to the potential despotism of their traditional neighbors as far as is possible. Too often, Caribbean citizens will make out that fear of retaliation by the USA should be a major consideration in designing foreign policy. While no state can be immune completely from the weight of the USA, to the extent that immunity is possible it ought to be pursued. Although, I repeat, the US has been generous to the English-speaking Caribbean and benign in its policies as it pertains to this group of states.

For almost ten years, the Antigua and Barbuda Government has been holding more than twenty-five millions US dollars of a former Ukrainian President, in a bank in Antigua. The money has been confiscated since he has been convicted of money-laundering; the money is awaiting a distribution plan to be agreed upon by all the states involved. The Ukrainian delegation in Washington has invited me to lunch at their Embassy so often that I began to feel as though we were friends. In fact, they wanted to have more than 80% of the confiscated funds returned to Ukraine. The USA wants to have a portion; and, the state who will receive the former head of state does not wish to have a pauper who is dependent upon its taxpayers' handouts, so that it too wishes the former president to be released with sufficient money in hand to support himself. The USA cannot return him to Ukraine where he is likely to face death, and Antigua and Barbuda does not wish to have him resident there either. The impasse continues.

Clearly, complications will arise from stretching out one's hand of friendship to non-traditional friends on the other side of the globe. The larger the risk, the larger the pay-off, goes the truism in capitalism. So too is the reasoning in the foreign policy maxim. But one lesson is certain. On the issue of democracy promotion, the Caribbean island-states have been faithful moreso than the lone superpower that has made democracy-promotion a major plank of its foreign policy. By challenging the USA to live up to its announced ambitions, the Caribbean island-states have caused an enlargement of freedoms in places far removed from their shores.

CHAPTER TEN

I

THE FUTURE OF THE CARICOM IN INTERNATIONAL POLITICS

On the basis of the knowledge which is now available, it appears to the author that the system of nation-states and the institutions that serve them will not survive the 21st century. The inability of the USA, Europe, Russia, India, China, Brazil, Nigeria, South Africa and a host of other large developed and developing states to discontinue dumping billions of tons of unwanted gases and particulate matter into our skies, will cause the earth's weather systems to go wild. Even if the states stopped emitting the gases today, the effect would continue to wreak havoc for seventy more years. It is not possible to halt the destruction in one generation; the results which we are witnessing today stemmed from emissions which commenced in the 1940s.

Small islands in the Caribbean, the Atlantic, the Pacific, the Indian Oceans, the Mediterranean, Oceania, along with coastlines all along North and South America, Europe, Africa, Asia and the coastlines of the continent of Australia will disappear under swollen oceans. Although we have not agreed to be sacrificial lambs on the altar of Western industrial civilization, the small island-states will die like the canary in the coal mine. Many will disappear under a swollen ocean, lost forever to generations of the 22nd century.

World trade will be severely disrupted since many ports, built on the assumption of existing sea-levels, will disappear under the sea and thus be unable to receive vessels. Airports built at sea level within sight of the seashore will also disappear under the swollen oceans. Many populations that now live within easy reach of coastlines, around the world, will suffer displacement which will be traumatic for many states. Unable to feed, house and provide security to their homeless populations, many states will collapse under the weight of the violence and displacement that will be engendered by the global climate catastrophe.

The earth's mighty ocean currents, that now provide ideal growing conditions to places that currently export their surplus food, will change direction. The directional change will result in unpredictable weather that will cause crops to fail, livestock to go hungry, energy supplies to dry up and millions to die from violence, starvation, lack of medicines, shortage of doctors and other healthcare professionals; hospitals will become overburdened and systems of delivery will collapse.

What occurred in New Orleans during Hurricane Katrina in August and September 2005 will be duplicated in many places around the globe in countless great catastrophes. The events will be large and immediate, making recovery impossible for small islands. Large continental states like the USA, Australia, China, South Africa, Brazil will be able to move their populations further inland and guard their borders to prevent hordes of refugees from crossing into their fragile states. Democracy will disappear as countries use violence to control their populations who will be ill-fed, ill-housed and very likely returned to a savage state.

Island-states will still have small populations dwelling on what are now remote hills, with survival precariously perched on sheer cliffs and a raging sea that will simply not settle down in a lifetime. Power plants and other infrastructure necessary for a civilized life will have disappeared under the swollen sea, and many people will revert to living like cavemen. Unable to survive by tourism and the other services they now provide, many small island-states will simply crumble and die.

The United Nations will also collapse as diplomats become an un-necessary appendage for the world's small states, and too expensive a proposition for states that would have come close to collapse. Any decisions taken by forlorn and disconnected diplomatic detritus sitting in New York, or wherever the UN may be, will have no consequence. Bear in mind that much of Manhattan Island will also be engulfed by swollen rivers, so that even the very buildings occupied by the United Nations will be submerged -the Secretariat partially, but still not useful for human habitation. The sewers and water delivery systems, the underground cables and the underground trains that keep New York alive will be under water. The City will collapse, looting and rioting will decimate its population during the incipient stage of the disaster; its economy will not survive and Manhattan will be no better off than New Orleans was, or than Antigua and Barbuda and many other low-lying island-states are following a devastating hurricane.

Now is the time for the governments of the sovereign island-states to negotiate resettlement of their populations on to continents and, with some skill, the continuation of their states' sovereign status in new lands. There is often a snicker when the following proposal is made public. I would propose a new UN convention which the states could call *The Convention for the Orderly Surrender of Habitats in Island Territories* (the O-S-H-I-T Convention). Such a legal instrument is best negotiated now when there is no crisis. When the crisis is upon the world, there will be no generosity. Although many will argue that, at a time when order has collapsed, there will be no enforcement mechanism, wisdom dictates that it is better to begin negotiations now, accepting of our fate, rather than later when our states would have disappeared. The proposal would also get the world's attention today.

There is no need for the CARICOM states to be foolishly optimistic about the likelihood of a switch from fossil fuels to a new kind of energy source. The USA, the Europeans, China and a host of others have demonstrated that they have no interest in pursuing another course of energy production. Maybe they have determined that there is no other energy source that could produce the high standard of living which the developed countries now experience and which the developing states can safely emulate. Caught in the energy trap, human civilization will collapse on itself just as all other previous civilizations did. Because we live in a globalized world, the failure will also be global.

The Global Warming Challenge

During my tenure at the UN, I came to the conclusion that the world's large powers see small islands as appendages to civilization; places where people go to frolic. Yet, anyone who has strolled along a white-sand Caribbean beach just before sunrise on a calm morning knows that God is present in the universe. And anyone who has stood and watched a Caribbean sunset, from the shores of a Caribbean island, knows that God's paintings and canvasses are magnificently pure. Spiritual rehabilitation and communing with nature are the delights which many a Caribbean island offers to its visitors.

Those magnificent island-states are in a uniquely dangerous position at the start of the 21st century. Because of their reliance overwhelmingly on tourism as an economic development activity, the English-speaking Caribbean must guard and protect their environment, a vital interest. That means an unrelenting struggle against those who would use the skies as a dumping ground, disposing annually of billions of tons of unwanted gases and particulate matter by emissions that endanger these vulnerable states' survival.

The global warming phenomenon is an ever present threat, not a distant future concern. It threatens to swell the oceans and to return the shorelines of islands to the bottom of the sea; to trigger violent and destructive storms and hurricanes every summer; to bleach and kill the coral reefs which serve as the first line of defense against massive wave energy during storms; to make tourism impossible because of the wholesale destruction wrought by hurricanes. Caribbean island-states thus face a future of certain destruction since the major polluters have failed to address the challenge immediately and to reverse their unlawful and harmful behaviors.

The evidence thus far indicates that there is little likelihood that the USA, the Europeans, and the large developing countries will find alternatives to fossil fuels in time to save civilization; it appears that they are not even seeking those alternatives, and so the polluting will continue. The massive long-term investments in coal-fired, diesel and other fossil-fuels electricity plants portend a future of immense destructive powers. Failure to address the energy challenge is sure to result in the destruction of Caribbean islands and their unsuitability for human habitation and tourism. That is an outcome that the citizens and leaders of Caribbean island-states refuse to contemplate but which this author forecasts. Caribbean diplomats bear the burdens to save our island homes.

The tropical rainforests in Caribbean islands and their characteristic bio-diversity make them a unique laboratory for plants and animals.

The medicines to be discovered that will cure diseases and relieve human pain are among the many benefits which rainforests and tropical shorelines have yielded and continue to provide to the human race. The joy and intelligence which the Caribbean islands' citizens contribute to civilization, to international politics, and to democratic ideals ought not be brutally extinguished.

The rich history and the defining character of Caribbean peoples are worthy of future generations' awe and wonderment. Slavery in our Caribbean is regarded as one of the most daunting challenges to have been overcome by the people of the Caribbean. The global warming phenomenon is a bigger challenge. While the moral wrong of slavery is today self-evident, the indiscriminate dumping of unwanted gases and particulate matter into the skies is not now deemed morally repugnant. The leaders of the island-states declare this dumping wrong! To act in a manner that will destroy these island-states, when alternatives to fossil fuels can be developed and are within reach, is a sinful act, worse than slavery.

Antigua and Barbuda chose to define the global warming challenge in moral terms. It is immoral to destroy the handiwork of God for no apparently good reason. *The earth is the Lord's and the fullness thereof, the world and they that dwell therein*, the Psalmist wrote more than two thousand years ago. That truth remains irrefutable today. The earth does not belong to the United States, Europe and China; all of God's children have a claim on the earth and its resources that go beyond states and borders. We all have a responsibility as stewards, to bequeath our earth to succeeding generations in a better condition than we inherited it. To act to preserve the earth's life-sustaining systems is a moral challenge.

Morality is always evolving. Slavery was once considered acceptable in God's sight, and denying women the right to inherit property and to vote, seemed oh so morally acceptable in democracies that today consider such denials as barbaric. Spewing filth into the skies in order to generate electricity and to make our transport systems work may seem amoral acts to the generations now alive. But to regard it as an immoral act is to elevate our thinking about our stewardship of the systems that preserve life. The author shares the view expressed by Richard Dawkins in *The God Delusion* which holds that morality is not fixed and unchanging, but ever evolving.

There is a larger reason for embracing global warming in moral terms. The destruction of the Caribbean island-states by violent climate change will only foreshadow the greater harm which will come to human civilization as a consequence of the deliberate choices of the USA and Europe, the large developing states, and industry. In the view of Caribbean people, there exists an unlimited supply of ingenuity which civilization can and must tap into in order to save earth's varied habitats.

Ocean thermal energy, geo-thermal energy, wave energy, hydrogen cells, coldwater fusion, in addition to the well-known wind and solar energy systems, and an array of science-fiction-like energy sources await humanity's discovery. At the moment, the modern-day Pharaohs have hardened their hearts and refused to provide the resources to encourage experimentation, research and development of the nascent systems. The modern Pharaohs accept no moral responsibility for the destruction of our global weather systems; those systems have taken billions of years to evolve to their fairly placid state, allowing agriculture and human civilizations to flourish over the past ten thousand years.

Our earth has been in existence for at least 3 billion years. Our sun is at its half-life, meaning that it has another 3 billion years left, give or take a few hundred million years, before it will become a white dwarf and consume its planets. During the interim, humans must do all that we can to ensure the survival of the planet in a manner that can continue to support life, human and animal, plant and insect. To act in a manner designed to ensure that our very life support systems will be destroyed within a generation makes little sense and is cruelly immoral.

Each civilization has had planted within it the seeds of its own destruction. For that reason, great civilizations that once flourished in Africa, Asia, North and South America, Central America and the Caribbean have grown up and then died. The European and American civilization which has emerged within the past century is among the greatest ever created by human ingenuity. The automobile, the airplane, the telephone, the computer, refrigeration and gas stoves, central heating and central air conditioning, space travel and satellites, the computer and the i-pod, are all modern marvels occurring within the past 100 years.

Yet, this marvelously inventive civilization has the seeds of destruction planted within it also. The energy challenge threatens to destroy the great European and American civilization which has become the dominant mode in the new century. But there is an air of inevitability among the Americans (though less so among the Europeans) who believe that what now is, will always be. There are many who see nothing wrong or immoral about their systems of energy production and the manner in which energy generation takes place. For the uninformed, forgiveness can be granted. But for those who are in a position to understand and to act, there is no forgiveness. Deliberate ignorance is no excuse.

The burden imposed by history on Caribbean countries is to persuade the rest of the world that civilization's global energy future is uncertain and that there is an urgency requiring a revolution in systems of energy production. The United Nations, the Organization of American States, the Commonwealth of Nations and every multilateral institution of which the Caribbean states are members will continue to be pressed into action by the urgency which the Caribbean leadership and people feel.

In 2006, former US Vice President Al Gore played a starring role in a film entitled *An Inconvenient Truth*. His earlier publication entitled *Earth In The Balance* also conveys an urgency which cannot be ignored. The hope of the CARICOM is that Americans will begin to pay attention to Al Gore, the United Nations and the Non-Governmental Organizations that have been pressing this issue. If the changes which are so urgently needed do not become a reality by 2020, if Mr. Gore's message is not heeded, the great civilization which has delivered so many marvelous gadgets and created such vast quantities of wealth will decline precipitously, causing massive destruction and displacement by the end of this century.

The world must act now if it is to save itself from the consequences of our actions. Global warming must be addressed now, not later.

Nuclear War

The likelihood of a nuclear winter, caused by a nuclear war between the nuclear powers, is less likely in 2007 than it was in 1967, forty years ago. Forty years hence, in 2047, it may be even less likely though a few more states will posses nuclear weapon capability. The "mutually assured destruction" approach which the USA and the

USSR took during the Cold War period provided many European states with protection. Under NATO and the Warsaw Pact, the states were provided umbrellas of military protection. The East Europeans have given up the nuclear weapons which the Soviets placed on their soil. But acquisition of nuclear weapons by India and Pakistan, North Korea and Israel, have encouraged smaller powers to seek to acquire the weapons as a kind of "insurance" against military invasion by hostile neighbors. Whether or not that particular frame of mind will encourage other nations, perceiving a threat from a neighbor, to move to acquire nuclear weapons, cannot be predicted. Size and wealth foreclose this approach to Caribbean states. Further, the Caribbean island-states have long foreworn possession of both nuclear power and nuclear arms; they have even tried to ban nuclear materials from passing through the Caribbean Sea.

The states of Latin America have also signed the Nuclear Non-Proliferation Treaty. Brazil and Mexico, in the Western Hemisphere, are quietly working to develop nuclear power as a means of partially supplanting fossil-fuel electricity plants. When that power becomes available, it is not a very lengthy step towards nuclear weapons, though both states have foresworn nuclear arms. Many leaders regard possession of those weapons as a badge of status for their states; the five permanent members of the UN Security Council are nuclear-weapon states. Since Brazil has made a bid for a permanent seat on the Council, it may feel the need to substantiate its claim by joining the nuclear club. To the extent possible, the world's multilateral bodies and the media must be utilized to reverse this status-awarding madness.

After global warming, the next most pressing challenge facing all of mankind is nuclear war; the Caribbean must continue to make its opposition to nuclear weapons central to its diplomacy.

Democracy's Place

In order to achieve success in sowing their message among the peoples of the world, the Caribbean island-states rely upon democracy among states and upon the work of the multilateral institutions where the world's peoples are represented. When democratic ideals drive states, their peoples' collective wisdom can be more perfectly exercised. There were diplomats and policy makers in the US Government who believed that dealing with a dictator is easier because policy choices need not go through the messy discussion and compromise that democracy requires. Prior to 1976, the USA operated under this assumption in its dealings with the states of Latin America. The end result was underdevelopment and cruelty of a sort that no civilized people can tolerate. Dictatorship is antiquated, barbaric and unacceptable, and the US Government now holds that view.

For decades, the US Government thought that the cruelty and deprivation that characterize un-democratic states did not matter, provided the leaders opposed communism. Americans were insulated from the harm which unelected governments imposed on their peoples. Wisdom has proven that approach to be faulty and harmful to US interests. Democracy is better for all of the world's peoples, including Americans and Europeans, and for the health of the earth's environment, upon which all living creatures depend.

In its dealings with the oil producers of the Middle East, the USA has not abandoned coddling dictators and brutal regimes, except for those whose regimes are hostile to the USA. The USA believed that it could turn Iraq into a modern democracy by defeating Iraq militarily and ousting its dictator, Saddam Hussein. It has since discovered that ethnic and religious hatreds have dealt any hope of a unified Iraq a terrible blow. The planting of democracy, by the USA, in that part of the world will have to wait for another time. The Caribbean states are free to be critical of those antiquated regimes but they have chosen to remain silent. Again, it is because those states do not profess democratic ideals and can thus not be held to a standard by which they judge others.

Democracy is sometimes narrowly determined to mean regular, periodic elections and the voluntary demitting of governments from office when the electorate so decides. That test is a necessary but insufficient expression of democracy. There is a far more complex set of circumstances that define democracy within states. They include a functioning independent judiciary, an effective police force, legal acknowledgement of workers' rights, a system of fair tax imposition and collection, accessibility to capital and finance, sharing of the nation's resources equitably, the end of racism, sexism, of ethnic and religious persecution. There are many other features that are articulated in the Inter-American Democratic Charter (as pointed out several chapters ago). The periodic holding of elections serves as a litmus test or framework without which democracy cannot be said to exist.

Caribbean island-states wish to ensure that, at the very least, elections take place regularly. The US Agency for International Development (USAID) also adopts this policy, spending millions of dollars each year to meet the cost of general elections and to plant democracy in states that are tottering on the brink of, or are recovering from, political disasters that threatened to make them failed states. The OAS created its own Unit for the Promotion of Democracy which monitors elections, provides support of varying forms to the electoral commissions that manage elections, and lends legitimacy to elected governments that help to plant democratic ideals in the states of the hemisphere. The export of democracy has fallen to the primary inter-American institution that possesses the required legitimacy, and though many Caribbean citizens are not employed within it, the states of the Caribbean are instrumental in making democracy the accepted model by their diplomats' contributions to the debates and the resolutions that serve as the basis of the work of the multilateral institutions.

Democracy will not survive the cataclysm of global warming.

Illicit Drugs

The third most significant challenge facing the Caribbean is the continued global demand for and unlawful trade in illicit drugs. Except for small amounts of grown marijuana, the Caribbean is a trans-shipment point for cocaine leaving South America for the US, Canada and Europe. The demand for the illicit drug will not decrease in the decades ahead and so the dangers will not disappear. Employment among young males and the availability of universal primary and secondary education are the most important anti-drug tools which Caribbean states can rely upon to fight the trade.

A stronger police and Coast Guard force are also required to deter criminals. Since police and military personnel are deployed in an effort primarily to prevent cocaine from reaching the developed countries, the USA has an abiding interest in the region's success.

II

CHINA AND THE FUTURE

Prior to his death in 1965, Malcolm X predicted that China would become a very powerful nation with which the US would have to reckon. He even proposed to many African-Americans that they learn to speak Chinese so that the two peoples could easily communicate. In the period after World War II and up until US President Nixon's overtures to China, the US acted as though China did not exist. The US refused to recognize China and instead engineered to have Taiwan seated on the UN Security Council until 1971. When China exploded its nuclear weapon, flexed its muscle among its Asian neighbors, and indicated by signals that its interests in Asia could relegate the US to a more lowly status, China was accorded a different role. The USA also regarded China as a possible counterweight to the USSR, given the friends won by the USSR in the emerging Third-World.

No CARICOM states existed at the time of the 1950 Korean War when China and the USSR provided the resources to help the North Koreans to mount attacks against their South Korean neighbor. That was a defining moment in China/America relations from which neither nation could easily recoil. By their very absence from the UN during that 1950s conflict, the CARICOM could not play any meaningful role in the events unfurling at the UN at the time. The Korean conflict marked an intensification of the Cold War, the commencement of one of the first proxy wars between the USA and the USSR, and the dividing of the world into two conflicting camps. It was a period of great uncertainty about the future and the looming threat of violent conflict fuelled by competing economic and social systems.

It is not difficult to speculate about the position that the states of the CARICOM would have taken did they exist in 1952. Dwelling in the shadow of the giant, they would have been compelled to abide by the dictates of the Monroe Doctrine. Haiti, the Dominican Republic and Cuba in 1952 towed the line at the UN. Even the Cuban Missile Crisis of 1962, ten years following the 1952 Armistice that ended the Korean conflict, would not be a defining moment for the Caribbean. There was no China as a countervailing power; Japan and Western Europe were just recovering from the after-effects of World War II, and the USA was clearly supreme. Only the USSR could challenge the mighty USA. Thirty years later, the world has been reshaped.

Jamaica has, in this century, sat on the UN Security Council, as has Guyana and Trinidad and Tobago. Given an opportunity to shape decisions in international arenas, the smallest of states have brought their own peculiar thinking and set of interests that help to define their character and personality. Though the smallest of the CARICOM states have weighed the costs of Security Council membership and have decided that their taxpayers' resources are better spent on other investments, the states still exercise enormous leverage when measured against their size and resource base. But China takes note of the presence of the 14 CARICOM states within the UN and responds to the bloc with deference.

China's return to the UN has allowed the body to reflect more closely the make-up of the world's peoples and the competing systems which it represented. Not long following Chairman Mao Tse Tung's death, in 1976, came another revolution within China that allowed it to find a place within the capitalist trading system. China has mastered the intricacies of capitalism in a very short time and now holds billions of US treasury bills in its own coffers. The future for China is certainly brighter than its past, and the countries of the Caribbean have done their best to befriend this giant. A few CARICOM states preferred to recognize Taiwan; they have done so for purely economic reasons. Taiwan promised more development assistance than China.

Antigua and Barbuda, Barbados, Guyana, Jamaica and Trinidad and Tobago from the very beginning of their sovereignty, chose to recognize the Peoples Republic of China. Foreign Minister Lester Bird of Antigua and Barbuda was responsible for his country's decision; acting on principle and with the foreknowledge that China would become the economic powerhouse that it has become in the 25 years since. Mr. Bird did not incline to Taiwan.

China has indeed been very generous to the countries of the Caribbean, providing several with a number of projects that have helped to cement the close relationship between the states. In 1994, when the UN held its Global Conference on The Sustainable Development of Islands, in Barbados, the conference facilities were brand new, built by China. When Cricket World Cup commenced in the Caribbean in March 2007, many of the new stadiums which played host to the games in Caribbean islands were also built by China. There is strong trade between China and many Caribbean countries with export credit being extended to the island-states for the construction of hospitals, government buildings, schools, conference facilities, hotels and other infrastructural projects. Like the Japanese, the Chinese do not consider small numbers to be a disincentive. Many US firms are not attracted to small markets or small projects. The Chinese seem to think that there is potential for growth in small places, or that many small markets constitute the equivalent of one large market. The Chinese construction firms, suppliers and bankers are unrelenting in their effort to sell their goods and services to Caribbean countries; and the island-states are most welcoming of the overtures.

The future of China in the Caribbean is good and will get better during the first half of the new century. Yet, the Caribbean states do not speak to China about democracy and democratic ideals. It could be that since China and the Caribbean do not share regional membership in any organization of states, there is little opportunity to challenge China's leadership on values dear to the Caribbean countries. It could also be that the Asian giant is so large that it is immune to the voices of states from the Caribbean, whose leaders are doing their best to squeeze benefits from China and dare not imperil the relations between both. China has extended loans and other benefits to states with which the USA refuses to deal. Zimbabwe, under President Mugabe, draws the ire of the USA and cannot hope to access assistance from the USA or any of the Bretton Woods institutions that the USA controls. But that is not the approach which China takes with states regarded by the West as renegade.

In 1989, when the Tiananmen Square demonstration was quashed, not one Caribbean state summoned the Chinese Ambassador to express their displeasure at the turn of events. One could argue that unlike the USA, which gives the promotion of democracy a prominent place in its foreign policy, the Republic of China makes clear through its foreign policy that it could not care less what the domestic policy of a state might be for it to treat with it. Hence, to speak to the Chinese about democracy would not place them in the same frame of mind as speaking to the American Ambassador.

III

MODEL OF DEVELOPMENT:
Looking To Africa

English-speaking countries of the Caribbean have a singular –not passive- role to play in a world where African nations are at the bottom of the development ladder. The Anglo-Caribbean nations serve as models of achievement in democracy, development and competence by people of majority African descent. The Caribbean states demonstrate (without actively trying but) by their very successes that the colonial subjugation of the world's non-white peoples by the states of Europe bears no relation to the intelligence or the inherent superiority of Europeans. Many whites secretly tend to think, according to Jared Diamond, the white author of *Guns Germs and Steel*, that their whiteness is a mark of intellectual and other superiority.

The poor performance by African states is in part the result of geographic conditions, the historic unavailability of useful plants and draft animals, the prevalence of deadly microbes, and disruptive wars. Poor management by the leaders of these countries, violent conflict by the tribalism that locks many groups into deadly competition within states, and the support for dictators by developed countries that destroyed democratic yearnings in the post-colonial era, have also contributed to the African states' under-development.

Caribbean states are far less complex, more easily manageable, and because of their use of English have countless traditions and storehouses of knowledge available to them. They have made the best use of these circumstances, to the benefit of their peoples.

Conditionalities

The continuing poverty of the African peoples is the result of the conditionalities imposed by those developed states whose administrations make harmful decisions relating to agricultural trade and trade in commodities, and by the inability of weak states to ensure adherence to fair trade rules. The attempt through the Doha Round of Negotiations to remove many of the obstacles that prevent African states from getting their goods to the markets of the wealthy states is a welcome sign. The same is true of the ACP trade negotiations, where the former colonies and the former colonial empires have tried to work out a system that will benefit both groups equally. In colonial times, the benefit flowed in one direction. Today, the hope is that "fair trade" will become the standard by which the trade relations between the wealthy and the poor will be conducted.

The poverty of the African states is equally the fault of their rulers' inabilities to engineer adherence to democratic ideals within their borders. Cynics may argue that the leaders did not wish for democracy to emerge. Certainly, there was an irresistible magnetism in the system employed by the USSR, transforming it from a backward nation to a first-world power in one generation. The deficiencies in the Marxist-Leninist control system would not be made manifest in the immediate post-colonial era, and those African states whose leaders relied upon it were doomed to failure. In the English-speaking Caribbean states, pragmatism not ideology determined their approach to development.

In Africa, militaries and coup plotters relied upon brute force to retain power and were disinclined to yield. But after being left so far behind in development, and the USSR having collapsed to the delight of the USA, different considerations have informed the choices of the African leaders and their peoples. The export of petroleum, which has begun to impact many West African producers, will clearly place them in a better position to provide resources to their impoverished peoples. However, the resulting challenges posed by petroleum windfalls have not been as expected. Nigeria remains a very poor stated despite the fact that it is the eighth largest oil exporter in the world. Merely having a source of wealth does not guarantee an accumulation of useful capital.

The revolution in telecommunications systems, including television and the computer, has fuelled a determination to reach the highest development level in the shortest period of time. These considerations have helped to inform the choices which African leaders and their peoples have embarked upon, and it is the responsibility of the English-speaking Caribbean states to join with them in their struggle. The adherence to rules in any society is preferable to chaos, violence and want.

While democratic ideals can be nurtured from abroad, complimentary domestic efforts are absolutely required. In the case of the developing African states, the necessary institutions that have been created are not yet very strong. The poorest states are hampered by the lack of resources to enforce respect for human rights, especially by those who have access to the tools of violence -including non-state actors. One obstacle to planting democratic ideals is the spread of weapons and small arms within poor states. There cannot be an escape from grinding poverty in the new century if violent criminals stalk the land and businesses' efforts are stymied by the terms of trade, by lack of access to capital, and by violent thugs who terrorize their populations.

The African Growth and Opportunity Act (AGOA) adopted by the US Congress at the urging of the US Congressional Black Caucus is a step in the right direction. France, Holland, Britain, Portugal and other European colonialists need to provide similar incentives and are attempting to alter the relationship of the past through their own trading regimes, including the Lome Agreements.

In December 2006, just prior to retiring, the 109th US Congress extended provisions of the AGOA and the Caribbean Basin Initiative which will indeed help the poorest states in Africa and the Americas. The creation of the Millennium Challenge Account, and the establishment of the UNAIDS agency are all very helpful steps in the right direction.

Mediation and Pensions

The English-speaking Caribbean leadership can help to alleviate many of these adverse conditions by their very successes and their willingness to intervene when there is a need for mediators. A Sudanese billionaire recently announced a retirement fund for African leaders who demit office peacefully, and whose period of leadership was free of corruption and wealth-grabbing. One of the difficulties which leaders in very small islands and in African states face is the lack of alternatives once they have demitted office. In wealthy European countries and the US, the opportunity for former leaders to sit on the boards of corporations, to lecture at prestigious universities, to write books and cruise the lecture circuit making a decent living, are not available to erstwhile political leaders in African and Caribbean states. That has not yet become a norm.

In the Antigua and Barbuda of the author's youth, elected representatives were not even entitled to a pension. After VC Bird lost the election of 1971, he and his Ministerial colleagues found themselves without resources and without an income; one parliamentarian reverted to driving a taxicab to make a living. Today, those who serve at least two terms in the Parliament of Antigua and Barbuda are entitled to a reasonable pension.

On the African continent, the situation is equally dangerous for former heads of state. The treatment meted out to former President Kenneth Kaunda of Zambia, just a decade ago, served as a disincentive to incumbent presidents to demit office peacefully. He was honest and competent, an adherent of democracy during his tenure. Yet, he lost an election and peacefully demitted office. His nemesis then sought to deny him Zambian citizenship, to violate his freedom and his right to the small pension to which he was legally entitled, and even threatened to deport him. It was the judiciary that saved him. Under those kinds of circumstances, it is understandable why Zimbabwe's President will do all that he can to remain in office, and to ensure that he cannot be removed.

If the UK and the USA wish to help African states to escape their poverty and leadership excesses, they must also quietly contribute to funding adequate pensions and providing means of survival to former African heads of state upon their demitting office. Lest anyone think that such a proposal smacks of neo-colonialism and a reward for being friendly to the US and the UK, the author would assert that it is a mild form of recompense for past sins and an investment that would surpass the return from paid consultants.

A former US president was paid US $1,000,000 dollars to make a speech in Japan following his demitting office. The editorials charged that such a whopping fee was a reward for having made decisions beneficial to several Japanese corporations while in office. There was no evidence forthcoming to support this claim. However, in the court of public opinion, the charge may have seemed reasonable. No-one would want to embarrass a former African head of state or Caribbean head of government with an obvious payoff, though the gift by the successful Sudanese entrepreneur, as mentioned above, is laudable. The author holds that discrete arrangements can be made to ensure that a leader lives comfortably after his time in office without the pledge of a handout. By guaranteeing the end of apprehension, which acts as an incentive by serving presidents to divert the resources of taxpayers while in office, governance would be greatly improved. USAID and DFID are very skilful at providing resources whose origins are not known.

In several Latin American countries, where presidents are limited to one term, the effect has also been to seek to enable the holder to safeguard his future by enriching himself during his single tenure. This incentive to enrich oneself whether lawfully or unlawfully has been addressed by adequate pension plans and several of the same incentives relied upon by US heads of state and former UK prime ministers. It thus appears that development brings unanticipated rewards which inure to the benefit of retired leaders. The US and the UK's generous assistance to former African and Caribbean heads would thus only be for a short period of time and only in those instances where a need is identified; the arrangement would not last forever.

Disasters

It seems, however, that no matter how well man plans, natural disasters can undo the most well-thought-out strategies. Nature sometimes seems to conspire against the African states, as in the case of drought and creeping desertification which imperil food production among many West African states. CARICOM support for the Convention on Desertification was remarkable. In the lead-up to the 1992 Global Conference on Sustainable Development, a CARICOM national chaired several of the preparatory sessions and brought to near the weight of the CARICOM states.

Natural disasters continue to plague the countries of the Caribbean. Some have suggested that we plan for those disasters in the same way that northern hemisphere states plan for winters. However, the increased number of hurricanes in the decade of the 1990s have been as destructive as the tsunamis that the world witnessed along the coast of Malaysia, Indonesia and elsewhere. It is not possible, given their narrow resource base, to respond adequately each year to the level of destruction which the hurricanes inflict. Seasonal crops are destroyed, hurricanes disable the tourism infrastructure, and the news of the disasters have dampened investments, increased the cost of insurance, and discouraged travel to the region. These exogenous responses are outside of the control of the Caribbean governments and their people. Disasters are not good for business.

In agricultural societies, whenever populations are unable to rely on their own agricultural production, their people tend to move. This movement of people tends to create conflict which ultimately leads to civil wars.

Civil Wars

The crises spawned by violent ethnic rivalry, as in Sudan, Somalia, Burundi and Rwanda, make development less likely or impossible. The rich deposits of minerals, diamonds and other natural resources that give groups reasons to fight, as in Angola, the Congo, Sierra Leone, Liberia and other West African states, also imperil development. There is little or nothing that Caribbean states can do to prevent or to end violent conflicts that are spawned by hatreds. However, there is a need for the United Nations to act to prevent conflicts from worsening and taking lives, for years on end. The CARICOM states can voice displeasure at those events with such frequency that the membership must listen. The states did play a meaningful role in ending apartheid and can play a continuing role in ending violent conflicts.

IV

The Early 21ˢᵗ Century

Before 2050, more states will be born from fragmenting large states, though a precise number is hard to predict. The number of states within the CARICOM will remain unchanged until the earth's weather system collapses. Until such time, the Caribbean frame of mind is built on optimism and high expectations, leaving no doubt in the minds of their leaders that the immediate future will witness continued improvement in the lives of their own people during their lifetimes; and that the institutions that enable development will be further strengthened.

By all accounts, the island-states will need to continue to support the growth of democracy and respect for human rights in those countries in

Latin America and Africa where the challenges still exist. What seems clear is that the spread of information technology will continue, and accessibility by people in places where the World Wide Web may not now be available is likely to change. As more people gain access to the world's storehouse of knowledge, the demand for freedom to choose will inexorably encompass and engulf generations of people whose fathers and mothers are today mired in poverty, underdevelopment and chaos. Nigeria, for example, can overcome many of the challenges it now faces within a generation. Given its large population and resource base, Nigeria's influence is likely to grow, becoming a greater influential power in Africa sufficiently so to challenge South Africa's leadership. Angola and Mozambique may also become better organized within the early years of this century. They will all produce and consume more energy, since development and increased energy consumption correlate.

One Caribbean country whose immediate future is greatly uncertain is Cuba. It is impossible to forecast whether the Cuban experiment led by Fidel Castro will last for a long time after his death; revolutions tend to have lives also, and conditions that spurned them are sometimes long forgotten by generations who come after. Many US citizens have no idea how significant religious persecution was in their own country's founding. Modern China, in the post Mao era, hardly fits the image which its 1949 founder had in mind for it. If the USA persists with sanctions then the Cubans will have good reasons to continue their revolution.

At any rate, the small Caribbean island-states have a responsibility, conferred by their history, to help prevent misery, war and environmental degradation from engulfing humanity. The small states can exercise that responsibility by continuing to make their voices heard in multilateral institutions as they have been doing for more than twenty-five years.

Books Cited or Recommended:

Anderson, C. (2003). *Eyes Off The Prize*, New York, Cambridge University Press.

Beckles, H. & Stoddart, B. (1995). *Liberation Cricket*, Kingston, Ian Randle Publishers.

Chomsky, N. (2006). *Failed States*, New York, Metropolitan Books.

Coram, R. (1993). *The Caribbean Time Bomb*, New York, William Morrow & Co.

Dawkins, R. (2006). *The God Delusion*, New York, Houghton Mifflin Company.

Diamond, J.(1997). *Guns Germs and Steel*, Norton Press, New York.

Dubois, W. (1961). *The Souls of Black Folk*, Greenwich, Fawcett Publications.

Fanon, F. (1963). *The Wretched of the Earth*, New York, Grove Press..

Friedman, T. (2006). *The World Is Flat*, New York, Farrar, Straus and Giroux.

Garvey, M. (1986). *The Philosophies and Opinions*, New York, Continental Press.

Gaspar, B. (1976). *Bondsmen and Rebels*, New York, John Hopkins University Press.

Henry, P. (1985). *Peripheral Capitalism and Underdevelopment in Antigua*, Transaction   Books, New Brunswick.

James, C. (1963). *The Black Jacobins*, New York, Vintage Press.

James, C. (1963). *Beyond the Boundary*, London, Hutchinson.

Kincaid, J. (1988). *A Small Place*, New York, Farrar Straus Giroux.

King, M.L. (1967). *Where Do We Go From Here*, New York, Harper & Row.

Kissinger, H. (1994). *Diplomacy*, New York, Simon & Schuster.

Langham, M. (1844). *Antigua and the Antiguans*. London, Saunders and Otley.

Lewis, G.K. (1968). *Growth of the Modern West Indies,* London, Monthly Review Press.

MacIntyre, A. (1968) *Marxism and Christianity,* New York, Schocken Books.

Malcolm, X. (1965). *The Autobiography of Malcolm X,* New York, Grove Press.

Mandela, N. (1994). *Long Walk To Freedom,* New York, Little Brown and Company

Nkrumah, K. (1961). *Ghana: An Autobiography,* New York, International Publishers.

Padmore, G. (1961). *Pan Africanism or Communism,* London, D. Dobson Publishers.

Powell, C. (1995). *My American Journey,* New York, Random House.

Richards, N. (1967). *The Struggle and the Conquest,* Portsmouth, Eyre and Potiswood.

Robeson, P. (1958). *Here I Stand,* Boston, Beacon Press.

Rodney, W. (1973). *How Europe Underdeveloped Africa,* London, Bogle-L'Ouveture.

Sanders, R. (2005) *Crumbled Small,* London, Hanif Publications.

Smith, K. (1994). *No Easy Pushover,* Scarborough, Edan Press.

Smith,K & Smith, F. (1986). *To Shoot Hard Labour,* Scarborough, Edan Press.

Sowell, T. (1985). *The Economics and Politics of Race,* New York, Harper Perennial.

Styron, W. (1966). *The Confessions of Nat Turner,* New York, Signet Books.

Williams, E. (1944). *Capitalism and Slavery,* Chapel Hill, Univ. of N. Carolina Press.

Williams, E. (1984). *From Columbus to Castro.* New York, Vintage Books.

ENDNOTES

[1] The New York Times, January 16, 2007.

* In the case of Jamaica, the year of adult suffrage was 1948.

[2] BEST, L. (1965) From Chaguaramas to Slavery. *New World Quarterly*, **2**, 10.

[3] I have intentionally retained the "u" in labor in these paragraphs so that they accurately reflect the names.

[4] The Mighty Sparrow is the author of this song.

[5] Another of the Mighty Sparrow's social/political commentaries in song.

[6] The New York Times, page A 20, March 10, 2007.

[7] Sunday New York Times, May 7, 2007, page A4.

[8] http://www.caricom.org/jsp/projects/personalities/lucille_mair.jsp?menu=projects

[9] This and subsequent quotations of the IADC are drawn from the OAS website, www.oas.org.

[10] USAID web page *http://www.usaid.gov/policy/budget/cbj2004/latin_america_caribbean/*

[11] Same as footnote #12 below.

[12] The New York Times, Editorial, Saturday, November 25, 2006, page A25

[13] See the New York Times of December 30, 2006, Crowds of Pupils but Little Else in African Schools by Sharon LaFraniere, p A 3.

[14] See http://www.barbados.gov.bb/panafrican/index.htm#

www.ingramcontent.com/pod-product-compliance
Lightning Source LLC
Chambersburg PA
CBHW061343280526
45784CB00001B/111

* 9 7 8 1 4 3 4 3 1 9 6 3 0 *